# Hierarchical Capitalism in Latin America

*Business, Labor, and the Challenges of Equitable Development*

This book argues that Latin America has a distinctive, enduring form of hierarchical capitalism characterized by multinational corporations, diversified business groups, low skills, and segmented labor markets. Over time, institutional complementarities knitted features of corporate governance and labor markets together and thus contributed to institutional resiliency. Political systems generally favored elites and insiders who further reinforced existing institutions and complementarities. Hierarchical capitalism has not promoted rising productivity, good jobs, or equitable development, and the efficacy of development strategies to promote these outcomes depends on tackling negative institutional complementarities. This book is intended to open a new debate on the nature of capitalism in Latin America and link that discussion to related research on comparative capitalism in other parts of the world.

Ben Ross Schneider is Ford International Professor of Political Science at the Massachusetts Institute of Technology. He taught previously at Princeton University and Northwestern University. His books include *Politics within the State: Elite Bureaucrats and Industrial Policy in Authoritarian Brazil* (1991), *Business and the State in Developing Countries* (1997), *Reinventing Leviathan: The Politics of Administrative Reform in Developing Countries* (2003), and *Business Politics and the State in Twentieth-Century Latin America* (2004). He has also published on economic reform, democratization, technocracy, education policy, the developmental state, business groups, and comparative bureaucracy in journals such as *Comparative Politics*, *Governance*, *Socio-Economic Review*, *Journal of Latin America Studies*, *Latin American Politics and Society*, and *World Politics*.

D1715705

*To Devon, Nick, and the memory of Mackay*

## Cambridge Studies in Comparative Politics

*General Editor*

Margaret Levi   *University of Washington, Seattle*

*Assistant General Editors*

Kathleen Thelen   *Massachusetts Institute of Technology*
Erik Wibbels   *Duke University*

*Associate Editors*

Robert H. Bates   *Harvard University*
Gary Cox   *Stanford University*
Stephen Hanson   *The College of William and Mary*
Torben Iversen   *Harvard University*
Stathis Kalyvas   *Yale University*
Peter Lange   *Duke University*
Helen Milner   *Princeton University*
Frances Rosenbluth   *Yale University*
Susan Stokes   *Yale University*

## Other Books in the Series

(*continued after the Index*)

# Hierarchical Capitalism in Latin America

## Business, Labor, and the Challenges of Equitable Development

BEN ROSS SCHNEIDER

*Massachusetts Institute of Technology*

# CAMBRIDGE
## UNIVERSITY PRESS

32 Avenue of the Americas, New York, NY 10013-2473, USA

Cambridge University Press is part of the University of Cambridge.

It furthers the University's mission by disseminating knowledge in the pursuit of education, learning, and research at the highest international levels of excellence.

www.cambridge.org
Information on this title: www.cambridge.org/9781107614291

First published 2013

Printed in the United States of America

*A catalog record for this publication is available from the British Library.*

*Library of Congress Cataloging in Publication Data*
Schneider, Ben Ross.
Hierarchical capitalism in Latin America : business, labor, and the challenges of equitable development / Ben Ross Schneider, Massachusetts Institute of Technology.
    pages cm. – (Cambridge studies in comparative politics)
ISBN 978-1-107-04163-9 (hardback)
1. Economic development – Political aspects – Latin America.   2. Capitalism – Latin America.   I. Title.
HC125.S3266   2013
330.98–dc23        2013007958

ISBN 978-1-107-04163-9 Hardback
ISBN 978-1-107-61429-1 Paperback

Cambridge University Press has no responsibility for the persistence or accuracy of URLs for external or third-party Internet Web sites referred to in this publication and does not guarantee that any content on such Web sites is, or will remain, accurate or appropriate.

# Contents

# List of Figures

# List of Tables

# Abbreviations

| | |
|---|---|
| Abrasca | Asociação Brasileira de Companhias Abertas (Brazilian Association of Listed Companies) |
| AEA | Asociación Empresaria Argentina (Argentine Business Association) |
| BNDES | Banco Nacional de Desenvolvimento Econômico e Social (National Bank for Economic and Social Development, Brazil) |
| BNDESpar | BNDES Participações (BNDES Shareholdings) |
| CCT | conditional cash transfer |
| CDES | Conselho de Desenvolvimento Econômico e Social (Council on Economic and Social Development, Brazil) |
| CEA | Consejo Empresario Argentino (Argentine Business Council) |
| CEO | chief executive officer |
| CEP | Centro de Estudios Públicos (Center for Public Studies, Chile) |
| CFC | Comisión Federal de Competencia (Federal Competition Commission, Mexico) |
| CGDC | Câmara de Políticas de Gestão, Desempenho e Competitividade (Chamber for Management Policies, Performance, and Competitiveness, Brazil) |
| Cieplan | Corporación de Estudios para Latinoamérica (Corporation for Research for Latin America, Chile) |
| CME | coordinated market economy |
| CMHN | Consejo Mexicano de Hombres de Negocios (Mexican Council of Businessmen) |
| CNIC | Consejo Nacional de Innovación para la Competitividad (National Council for Innovation for Competitiveness, Chile) |
| CPC | Confederación de la Producción y del Comercio (Confederation for Production and Commerce, Chile) |
| CUT | Central Unitaria de Trabajadores (Workers' United Center, Chile) |

| | |
|---|---|
| DME | dependent market economy |
| Embrapa | Empresa Brasileira de Pesquisa Agropecuária (Brazilian Agricultural Research Corporation) |
| FGTS | Fundo de Garantia por Tempo de Serviço (Guarantee Fund for Time of Service, Brazil) |
| FIEL | Fundación de Investigaciones Económicas Latinoamericanas (Foundation for Economic Research on Latin America, Argentina) |
| Finep | Financiadora de Estudos e Projetos (Financing Agency for Studies and Projects, Brazil) |
| GDP | gross domestic product |
| HME | hierarchical market economy |
| IMCO | Instituto Mexicano para la Competitividad (Mexican Institute for Competitiveness) |
| IPEA | Instituto de Pesquisa Econômica Aplicada (Institute of Applied Economic Research, Brazil) |
| IPO | initial public offering |
| ISI | import substituting industrialization |
| IT | information technology |
| ITV | Instituto Tecnológico Vale (Vale Technological Institute, Brazil) |
| LME | liberal market economy |
| MNC | multinational corporation |
| MP/PRL | majoritarian presidency/proportional representation legislature |
| NAFTA | North American Free Trade Agreement |
| NME | network market economy |
| OECD | Organisation for Economic Co-operation and Development |
| PAN | Partido Acción Nacional (National Action Party, Mexico) |
| PISA | Program for International Student Assessment |
| PR | proportional representation |
| PRI | Partido Revolucionario Institucional (Institutional Revolutionary Party, Mexico) |
| PSDB | Partido da Social Democracia Brasileira (Brazilian Social Democracy Party) |
| PT | Partido dos Trabalhadores (Workers' Party, Brazil) |
| SOE | state-owned enterprise |
| Sofofa | Sociedad de Fomento Fabril (Society for Manufacturing Promotion, Chile) |
| VNN | Votorantim Novos Negocios (Votorantim New Businesses, Brazil) |
| VSE | Vale Soluções em Energia (Vale Solutions in Energy, Brazil) |

# Preface

Some years ago I thought it would be interesting to write a paper mapping the "varieties of capitalism" framework onto contemporary Latin America to see what might be gained. Quite a bit, it turned out, which started me on a much longer engagement, initially with the pathbreaking work by Peter Hall and David Soskice, and then beyond with the broader and growing field of comparative capitalism.

Nearly all of this field is preoccupied with distinctions among developed countries, especially liberal and coordinated economies, with occasional reference to Asia but little or nothing to the rest of the world, including Latin America. At a minimum, I thought, here was a golden opportunity to connect Latin America back to these innovative debates on comparative capitalism. The lingua franca in this field includes terms like "institutional complementarities," "patient capital," "firm-specific skills," and "interfirm coordination," as well as a host of other concepts that can illuminate analyses of the political economy of Latin America and then link these analyses back to comparisons with the wider world.

To take the private sector – corporate governance, business strategies, private labor markets, employee training, and so forth – as the point of departure was novel and refreshing. It also took some practice before I could do it myself – my prior reflex had always been to start with the state. Keeping the light on business is still, I think, crucial to advance the field of Latin American political economy. We know far more about states than even the basics of how big firms operate, strategize, hire, innovate, and train. Little did I suspect at the start how many years I would spend trying to get at those basics, especially for business groups. Notwithstanding this new fascination with business groups and MNCs, the state is rarely absent for long in the pages that follow. With the state and business in Latin America, it is never an either/or decision but rather one of relative balance, and a goal here is to shift that balance to the less understood business side.

Students of comparative capitalism – economists, political scientists, and others – have long used the concept of institutional complementarities to insightful analytic effect. Yet, in research on development in Latin America, the term is very new, and there is ample room for extending it to numerous realms to ask whether particular sets of institutions fit together, how they complement one another, and what consequences follow. To those of us (and I include myself) accustomed to working mostly in various "silos" with fairly exclusive attention to research areas like skills and education, labor markets, or corporate governance, thinking about the institutional connections across these realms can be pretty mind-expanding. Even for those skeptical of taking on the full varieties-of-capitalism package, much can be gained by trying out institutional complementarities.

The apparent catch, which deters many, is that institutional complementarities – where one institution increases the returns to another – are best deployed to explain continuities and can consequently lead an argument into an uncomfortable, constraining equilibrium that makes possibilities for change and evolution seem unrealistically small. For some, the solution, which I attempt to develop further, is to think of complementarities as more contingent, coincidental, politicized, and subject to contestation. This is especially the case in Latin America where complementarities are often dysfunctional with negative consequences. The result is more a sense of path dependence, with incremental shifts within evolving parameters, than fixed equilibrium.

A last benefit I see from engaging the comparative capitalism field is, perhaps more by my own extrapolation, a normative concern with the quality of jobs. This, I argue, needs to be at the core of any theory or long-term strategy of equitable development or movement to a knowledge economy. For the past several decades, creating plentiful, high-skill, well-paying jobs has rarely been an explicit target of development policy. At most, good jobs have been assumed to follow other policies like trade liberalization, FDI promotion, or education. Social policy too has concentrated mostly on cash transfers and extending education and health care without much consideration of employment solutions for social welfare and redistribution.

The book presents a single ideal type of hierarchical capitalism for the region. My goal is not to shoehorn every country in Latin America into some conceptual category. Rather, the ideal type of hierarchical capitalism is meant to help start a discussion about the institutional foundations of capitalism in the region, and especially the complementary relations among them. Covering the whole region, even if focusing mostly on the larger countries, means that many aspects in many countries will necessarily lack the nuance and depth of a more narrowly focused book. Moreover, the available data for most indicators are uneven, partial, indirect, and often not comparable across countries or periods (certainly compared to plentiful, standardized OECD data), so this book is necessarily a first rough cut.

Although the project was conceived from the beginning as an integrated whole, many chapters include some material that has already appeared elsewhere. Initially, I thought I would be able to rely mostly on secondary sources, but each core empirical chapter – business groups, MNCs, labor markets, and skills – required more extensive original field research, and along the way I published several articles on partial and preliminary results. I am grateful to Oxford University Press and the *Socio Economic Review* for permission to reprint portions of some articles.

My list of benefactors is long, and it is a great pleasure finally to have a chance to acknowledge their contributions. I consider myself very fortunate to have received feedback and suggestions from many of the sharpest minds in comparative political economy, including Bruno Amable, Janine Berg, Suzanne Berger, Renato Boschi, Luiz Carlos Bresser-Pereira, Ernesto Calvo, Eli Diniz, Richard Doner, Patrick Egan, Sebastian Etchemendy, Marco Fernandez, Edward Gibson, Frances Hagopian, Peter Hall, Thomas Kenyon, Richard Locke, Scott Mainwaring, Leonardo Martinez-Diaz, Juliana Martínez Franzoni, Gerald McDermott, Naércio Menezes-Filho, Rory Miller, Edson Nunes, Margaret Pearson, Michael Piore, Andrew Schrank, Kenneth Shadlen, David Steinberg, Kathleen Thelen, and Laurence Whitehead.

For going well beyond the call of collegiality, I am deeply indebted to Stephan Haggard, Robert Kaufman, Aldo Musacchio, and Andrew Schrank, who sacrificed a day to come out to Cambridge to discuss an early draft of the manuscript. Their collective wisdom and commentary guided a year of revisions and decisively shaped the final manuscript. I hope I can think of further pretexts to bring this great group together again. Long, deep, and wide-ranging conversations with David Soskice were among the most enjoyable and enlightening parts of working on this book. David's infectious engagement with comparative capitalism and insatiable curiosity over intricacies and anomalies of Latin American political economy made each meeting a delight and total boost to the progress of the project, while setting new standards for intellectual generosity.

I am also grateful for feedback from seminar participants at Brown University, the Danish Institute for International Studies, Duke University, European University Institute, Georgetown University, Georgia Tech, Harvard University, Hebrew University, the Inter-American Development Bank, MIT, Northwestern University, Oxford University, Princeton University, Sciences Po, Tulane University, Universidad Torcuato di Tella, Universidade Federal do Rio de Janeiro, University of London, and the World Bank, and at conferences of the American Political Science Association, Latin American Personnel Association, and Latin American Studies Association. I also thank the Tinker Foundation for support for research on education. I benefited greatly from discussions with my students in graduate seminars on comparative capitalism at Northwestern, the

Fundação Getúlio Vargas, Universidad di Tella, and MIT. A number of them provided able and innovative research assistance, and I thank Pedro Ariera, Diego Finchelstein, Carlos Freytes, Joyce Lawrence, Renato Lima-de-Oliveira, and Bruno Verdini Trejo. I am indebted to my coauthors on three papers: on skills with David Soskice, on labor markets with Sebastian Karcher, and on commodity dependence with David Steinberg. These collaborations were eye-opening and helped me venture into and navigate what for me were completely new areas of research. It was wonderful to have such congenial and adept guides.

As I was going into the final writing of the manuscript, my extended family suffered several tragic losses. After many years with little contact, my far-flung siblings coalesced into a remarkable support network with near daily communications that kept our mourning families going. If there are liberal, coordinated, and hierarchical families, I count my lucky stars that I ended up in one of the more coordinated ones. I dedicate this book to my brother and sisters.

As always, my deepest gratitude is to my life partner and intellectual companion, Kathleen Thelen, for her unflagging support, incisive critiques, and restorative family diversions. Without them, the end product and the lengthy process would have been immeasurably diminished.

PART I

THEORY AND FRAMES

1

# Hierarchical Capitalism in Latin America

## I. Introduction: Perspectives and Arguments

In the many intense debates over development in Latin America in recent decades, the question rarely arose, as it had in previous decades, as to what kind of capitalism existed or whether capitalism in Latin America was somehow different. If anything, the homogenizing Washington Consensus of the 1990 sidelined such queries with expectations that market reforms would soon make the economies of Latin America resemble liberal economies elsewhere. Market reforms and globalization have transformed many aspects of capitalism in Latin America, but areas of convergence are often, as elsewhere, less interesting and less consequential for development than are the areas of continued divergence. So, it is worthwhile to raise again the question of what sort of capitalism exists in Latin America.

Most attempts to characterize the political economies of Latin America as somehow distinctive can be roughly classified as internationalist or statist.[1] The former was famously staked out in various dependency arguments of the 1960s and 1970s that claimed that international economic ties created a stunted form of capitalism with limited possibilities for autonomous development. The internationalist perspective later resurfaced in several guises including global production networks (Gereffi, Humphrey, and Sturgeon 2005), natural resource curses (Karl 1997), and other macro perspectives on debt and international capital flows (Maxfield 1997). Internationalist perspectives are indispensable in some places (such as oil exporters or export zones) or some periods (such as the debt crisis of the 1980s), but these are only partial views because they miss most of the domestic political economies of the rest of the region in more normal times.

[1] Many narrower political economic studies of particular areas or policies do not necessarily fit this binary classification, but I am thinking here of broader studies of the whole political economy.

By the 1980s, the mainstream focus shifted to the domestic economy and emphasized comparisons across development strategies (import substitution vs. export promotion) and the variable role of the state, often invoking revealing comparisons between Latin America and East Asia (Haggard 1990; Gereffi and Wyman 1990; Amsden 2001). After 1990, research on the political economy of Latin America mostly concentrated on the changing role of the state, especially during market reforms of the 1990s, but then on into the 2000s with attention to social welfare, the new left, and various forms of renewed state intervention.[2] Of course, not all past work in political economy fits the division between internationalist and statist, but little research, save specialized publications, asked whether there was something distinctive about the domestic private sector.

Much of the recent statist bias is fully warranted as shifts in the role of the state in Latin America have been epochal. However, the statist perspective tends to overstate the extent of change and to obscure the pivotal economic agents – firms and workers – that are driving development in the wake of state retrenchment in the 1990s. Key questions – such as Why is education so low? Why has productivity not increased? Why have good jobs been so scarce? and Why do firms not invest more in research and development? – cannot be answered in a statist framework and require instead an analysis of the types of firms, labor markets, corporate strategies, and skill regimes that constitute the institutional foundations of capitalism in Latin America. Moreover, recent scholarship on change, in policies and development models, has missed significant continuities in patterns of organization and behavior by business and labor.

This book starts with business and labor and develops four main hypotheses: (1) that Latin America has a distinctive, enduring form of hierarchical capitalism characterized by multinational corporations (MNCs), diversified business groups, low skills, and segmented labor markets; (2) that institutional complementarities knit together features of corporate governance and labor markets and thus contributed to the resiliency of hierarchical capitalism; (3) that elements of the broader political system favor incumbents and insiders who pressed governments to sustain core economic institutions; and (4) that hierarchical capitalism has not generated enough good jobs and equitable development nor is it, on its own, likely to.

Developing these arguments requires a new approach to the study of Latin American political economy. Theoretically, drawing on the literature on comparative capitalism and especially varieties of capitalism (Hall and Soskice 2001), the analysis brings three main innovations. First, it uses a "firm's-eye"

---

[2] For example, on social welfare, see Haggard and Kaufman (2008) and Huber and Stephens (2012); on the new left, Levitsky and Roberts (2011) and Weyland, Madrid, and Hunter (2010); and on state intervention, see Musacchio and Lazzarini (forthcoming).

focus on the structure of corporate governance and labor markets and on the predominant economic strategies of firms and workers. Second, it examines interactions across realms of the economy. The separate literatures on business groups, MNCs, labor markets, and skills are large, but they rarely overlap or speak to one another. This book tries to link them. Third, I use the economic strategies of firms and workers, and the institutional complementarities that animate them, to reinterpret the sources of policy preferences and political strategies of business and labor. Again, existing research on business and labor politics is extensive, yet it rarely connects political activity back to firm strategies and institutional complementarities.

The best way to answer the question of what kind of capitalism Latin America has is to compare it to other varieties, especially liberal market economies (LMEs) in the United States, Britain, and other Anglo economies; coordinated market economies (CMEs) in Northern Europe and Japan; and to other developing economies. These broad comparisons, elaborated in Chapter 2, help pinpoint the distinctive configuration of hierarchical capitalism. Within this comparative framework, my focus is primarily on Latin America, especially the larger countries of the region, but hierarchical capitalism is not just Latin capitalism. The model should also apply, with modifications, to other middle-income countries outside the region, such as Turkey, Thailand, or South Africa. Moreover, within Latin America, not all countries are equally close to the ideal type of a hierarchical market economy (HME).

This book draws on a long tradition of comparative institutional and historical institutional analysis, but with a crucial shift in analytic focus to incorporate firms and organizations. Following Douglass North, many institutional approaches have assumed organizations such as firms and paid them little heed. North (1990, 4) insisted on a "crucial distinction" between institutions and organizations: "institutions are rules" of the game and firms and other organizations are merely the "players." The implication, followed in most institutional analysis in political economy, was to concentrate primarily on the rules and neglect organizations that were assumed to adapt more or less automatically to the rules.[3] My focus instead problematizes firms and makes them core components of an institutional approach to Latin American political economy (Evans 1979; Guillén 2001). Organizations in Latin America – from the Church, to state-owned enterprises, to business groups – have always been hybrid, syncretic, complex, interrelated, and politicized, and understanding them requires the full analytic toolkit from comparative institutional analysis.

---

[3] Ronald Coase (1937) and later Oliver Williamson (Williamson and Winter 1993), of course, focused on organizations and firms, though in the end firms were rational responses to their environments and transactions costs that derive largely from overall rules. Thus, ultimately, rules still largely determined firm behavior. For a discussion of various definitions of institutions, some that include organizations, see Aoki (2001, chap. 1).

Thus, beyond the macro Northian rules of the game, the analysis needs always to have in mind the incentive structures that variable organizations create for politicians, managers, workers, and outsiders. Organizations often are not mere reflections of the rules-as-incentives structure and vary independently from rules, and thus have direct, independent impacts on political economic outcomes such as equity, innovation, skills, and political representation. For instance, despite operating under the same rules in any given country, the core corporate organizations of MNCs and business groups differ greatly from each other in terms of their corporate structure, skill strategies, and political behavior. Conversely, rules can vary independently from organizations; despite variation across Latin America in basic rules of corporate governance (competition, stock market, financial, and other regulations), similar sorts of business groups – the dominant organizations of the domestic private sector – exist throughout the region. In sum, rules and organizations require equal treatment in institutional analysis.

This neglect of organizations feeds into policy as well. Policy makers in Latin America rarely ask what kinds of firms they want to have.[4] Instead, the primary focus of institutional reform is on the preferred kinds of markets needed to promote development: competitive, regulated, protected, and so on. The firms that are likely to result either are presumed to be outside the range of policy targets or are assumed in Northian fashion to form naturally, and optimally, in response to market signals. In contrast, in the 1960s and 1970s, policy makers were more concerned with promoting specific kinds of domestic firms, mostly because states were already actively managing both MNCs and state-owned enterprises (SOEs). By default, they were thus also making decisions on where domestic firms would operate. However, with market reform, states mostly relinquished both SOEs and regulations on MNCs and stopped worrying about policies to shape domestic business. One of the policy implications of this book is that it behooves policy makers to think again more actively about the kinds of firms they want to lead development (as they have been recently in Brazil).

## II. Core Institutions of Hierarchical Capitalism

What are the institutions in Latin America that organize investment, labor, technology, and skills into an overall production regime?[5] The comparative capitalism framework for developed countries gives a guide on where to look, but that framework cannot be imported wholesale. On the side of capital and investment, scholars of developed countries start with capital markets – banking systems and stock markets – and the myriad rules and practices that

---

[4] The policy community in multilateral development agencies in Washington, D.C., has published almost nothing on business groups and little on MNCs.

[5] My point of departure here is inductive. Chapter 2 provides a more deductive and abstract formulation of an ideal type of hierarchical capitalism.

regulate them (Zysman 1983). However, in Latin America, equity markets and banks were not the sources of long-term productive investment (nor markets for corporate control). Instead, the private institutions (as organizations) that mobilized capital for investment were business groups and MNCs. In terms of strategic interactions, CEOs in developed countries are usually preoccupied with managing relations with stock markets (quarterly earnings and guidance, institutional investors, etc.) in equity-based financial systems or with bankers in bank-based systems. In contrast, managers in hierarchical capitalism are most keenly attentive to relations with family owners in business groups or with headquarters in MNC subsidiaries. Most research on corporate governance, narrowly conceived, examines relations between financial principals (shareholders or creditors) and their managerial agents; in hierarchical capitalism, these external financial principals have little leverage over managers.

Similarly, scholars of labor in developed countries focus on overall regulations, collective bargaining, and employment practices. Such a focus in Latin America would underscore the high levels of regulation, but it gets only part way because almost half of jobs are informal and not subject to formal regulation. Moreover, employment practices point less to long-term relations (save for a few) as in Japan and Germany but rather very short-term employment. For lack of a better term, I use the shorthand of atomized labor relations and segmented labor markets to characterize the result of this complex institutionalized mix of formal regulations and informal practices. On skills, the institutions in Latin America resemble those in developed countries, and the overall skill regime comprises basic education, technical education, universities, public training programs, unemployment insurance, regulations on company spending on training (compulsory in-house training, tax incentives, etc.), and general private practices on training.[6]

Capitalism in Latin America might first be characterized simply by weak or missing formal institutions: undeveloped financial markets, unenforced labor regulations, and shallow and partial coverage by the skills regime. One could then write, as others have (Levitsky and Murillo 2009), about how and why these institutions are weak and develop a comparison of weakly versus strongly institutionalized varieties of capitalism. My approach is less concerned with standard formal institutions – and how and why they lack force – and focuses instead on the organizational and behavioral responses to weak or absent institutions, namely, diversified business groups, MNCs, segmented labor markets, and a low-skill regime. Thus, business groups and MNCs mobilized capital without stock markets or banks. Unlike firms in other varieties of capitalism

---

[6] As should be clear, my understanding of institutions is expansive, along the lines of Peter Hall (2010, 204) who defines institutions "as sets of regularized practices with a rule-like quality [that] structure the behavior of political and economic actors," or earlier of Samuel Huntington (1968, 12) as "stable, valued, recurring patterns of behavior."

whose strategies were conditioned by bank-centered or equity-centered financial systems, business groups and MNCs are freer from these constraints, and
thus, their internally generated strategies and behaviors are more consequential
for development outcomes (hence the importance of organizations or institutions in corporate governance).

In labor markets, the responses to unevenly enforced regulations and limited training and education were segmented labor markets, atomized labor
relations, and low skills. These responses are not recognizable organizations
such as business groups, but rather are dispersed, though regular, patterns of
behavior. However, these patterns of behavior in informality, in school leaving, and in high job rotation are enduring, and shape long-term expectations of
workers and managers and, as such, constitute themselves informal institutions
that regulate labor markets in the absence of formal rules. By analogy, albeit
imperfect, much of the comparative institutional literature looks at the mold
(the formal institutions and rules that shape behavior) whereas I focus more on
the object that emerges with only a partial mold (behaviors and organizations
in the absence of constraining formal institutions). However, the end goal of
each approach is the same – to explain the strategic interactions and behaviors
of owners, managers, and workers.

In HMEs, hierarchy often replaces or attenuates the coordinated or market
relations found elsewhere. For example, whereas postsecondary or on-the-job
training is more market based in LMEs and more negotiated in CMEs, it is
often unilaterally decided by firms or business associations in Latin America.
Hierarchical relations also characterize more general employment relations
where employees lack formal grievance procedures and representation and
informally lack voice because workers rotate quickly through firms. Unions
have little influence on hierarchies within the firm because so few workers are
unionized and because where unions do exist they are often distant from the
shop floor. Industrial relations are further structured by top-down regulations
issued by national governments and are enforced by labor courts.[7] On the
dimension of corporate governance, relations are even more clearly hierarchical
because most firms are directly controlled and managed by their owners, either
wealthy families or foreign firms. In sum, hierarchy, in simple descriptive terms,
is apt for characterizing the economic institutions and organizations in Latin
America.[8]

Some might object to comparisons between Latin America and developed
countries on the grounds that large income disparities explain differences in

---

[7] At first glance, labor markets in hierarchical capitalism resemble liberal economies. However,
as will become clearer, workers in hierarchical economies lack the legal protections and market
leverage of workers in LMEs. Moreover, a minority of workers in Latin America are subject to
some of the strictest regulations in the world, quite different from the minimal regulations in
liberal economies.

[8] See Nölke and Vliegenthart (2009), who also emphasize hierarchy as the core mechanism of
allocation in the "dependent" variety of capitalism they identify in East Europe.

the core institutions of capitalism. However, most of the differences would remain if we adjusted the comparison for levels of GDP per capita by comparing Latin America in recent decades with liberal and coordinated economies in the mid-twentieth century when levels of GDP per capita in now developed countries were around what they are today in Latin America (Maddison 1983). CMEs and LMEs took distinctive shape in the early postwar period (Hall 2007; though historical roots go back further; Iversen and Soskice 2009). By then levels of union density were high in both liberal and coordinated economies, shop-floor coordination existed in CMEs, basic patterns of labor market regulation were established, financial markets were consolidated, and the informal economies were not large. Moreover, by the end of the twentieth century, the larger, richer countries of Latin America had completed the major modernizing transition from rural to urban societies and much of the postindustrial transition to service-based economies. So there is less reason to expect that ongoing economic growth will automatically push corporate governance and labor market indicators for Latin America closer to patterns in developed countries. The adjectives of "emerging" or "developing" continue to give the false impression that middle-income countries are in flux and unformed and have not already consolidated enduring economic institutions.

On most dimensions, hierarchical capitalism was in fact reasonably consolidated by the last quarter of the twentieth century. By the 1970s, MNCs were well ensconced, and major, diversified business groups had emerged in most countries. Labor unions were bigger then, but were more politically constrained or repressed. Education had progressed but attainment was still low. As in coordinated and liberal economies, many components of hierarchical capitalism have deep historical roots (some considered in Chapter 9). Overall, however, this book has less to say about the origins and consolidation of hierarchical capitalism in order to delve deeper into the evolution and consequences from the 1980s to the 2000s.

Much of the book analyzes a single variety of capitalism in Latin America. And, in fact, in comparison to variations within other regions such as West Europe, East Europe, or Asia, these core aspects of capitalism in Latin America manifest greater homogeneity across the region. Of course, countries of Latin America differ greatly in terms of size, level of development, commodity rents, degree of integration with the U.S. economy, and ability of governments to mitigate the effects of negative complementarities in hierarchical capitalism (variations that are explored in Chapter 8). Yet, what is remarkable is that despite these variations, similarities on the four core features remain, especially across the larger and richer countries of Latin America: Argentina, Brazil, Chile, Colombia, and Mexico.[9]

---

[9] The field research for this book is drawn from these countries, but much of the quantitative data and the secondary literature cover more or all countries of the region.

## 1. Diversified Business Groups

One of the most comprehensive studies of big business in Latin America begins by noting that the universe of big stand-alone firms "is very small in the region. Big firms are, by a large majority, part of formal or informal groups" (Garrido and Peres 1998, 13). There are four things to emphasize about large business groups in Latin America.[10] First, most are widely diversified into subsidiaries that often have little or no market or technological relation to one another. Second, a typical large business group maintains direct hierarchical control over dozens of separate firms. Third, small numbers of huge business groups account for large shares of economic activity, estimated sometimes as high as a fifth or more of GDP. And, fourth, business groups are mostly owned and managed by families, often spanning several generations.

Contrary to expectations of convergence toward U.S.-style corporate governance, diversified business groups survived and prospered through the liberalization and globalization of the 1990s and 2000s. Competitive pressures of liberalization did lead some business groups to spin off unrelated holdings, but at the same time, privatization and regulation opened up other new opportunities for greater diversification. By the 2000s, most business groups had significant holdings in regulated and nontradable sectors. Even in Chile, the regional leader in liberalization, diversified business groups flourished, especially those based in commodities and services (Lefort 2005). As a top financial executive at the Grupo Matte (electricity, finance, forestry, construction, and other sectors) explained it, the group strategy was to be big in four or five "sectors with high profitability, regulated, but also, as a consequence [por lo mismo], low risk and capital intensive" (*Qué Pasa*, 5 November 2005, p. 22). Family ownership and management also survived and thrived, adding another layer of hierarchy (see IDE 2004). In the 2000s, more than 90 percent of 33 of the largest groups in Latin America were family owned and managed (F. Schneider 2008).

## 2. Multinational Corporations

Whereas most varieties of capitalism are characterized by a single dominant form of corporate governance, large companies in Latin America are divided between domestic business groups and MNCs. Foreign firms, mostly from the United States, made massive direct investments in Latin America throughout the twentieth century: first, in raw materials and railroads in the early twentieth century, then in other infrastructure and public utilities through the decades up to World War II, then into Fordist manufacturing (especially consumer durables), and after market reforms in recent decades back into infrastructure and services and expanding into finance. By 1995, the stock of FDI as a percentage of GDP was, on average, 16 percent for the four largest countries of Latin America (compared to 2 percent for Korea and 10 percent for Thailand;

---

[10] See Colpan, Hikino, and Lincoln (2010) for a full comparative analysis of business groups.

Guillén 2001, 126). MNC presence was especially visible among the largest firms. The share of MNCs in the sales of the 500 largest companies in the region ranged from 30 to 40 percent for most of the 1990s and 2000s, and the MNC share of the top 200 exporters grew to nearly half in 2000 before dropping back to a third in 2004 (ECLAC 2006, 11). In terms of coordinating functions, MNCs administered in hierarchical fashion technology transfer, capital for investment, some relations with suppliers and customers, and especially trade.[11] In addition, though not formally owned by MNCs, many export firms in Latin America are dependent on one or two international buyers in closely linked global commodity chains in which the interfirm relationship is more vertical than horizontal (Gereffi et al. 2005).

In sum, on the side of corporate governance, diversified business groups and MNCs were the key conduits for organizing access to capital, technology, and markets through Coasian internalization and hierarchy. The 1990s and 2000s brought a flurry of changes to big business in Latin America with privatization, concentration, and increased FDI, both inward and outward. What emerges from a composite picture of these changes is an unmistakable Coasian onslaught: a pervasive strategy by large private businesses to extend corporate hierarchies through mergers and acquisitions. In an oversimplified sense, economic activity in Latin America is still largely subject to planning, rather than to the spontaneous free play of market forces, but the planning shifted after the 1990s from ministry offices to corporate boardrooms.

### 3. Segmented Labor Markets

Labor relations in Latin America are atomistic and often anomic because most workers have fluid, short-term links to firms, and ephemeral or no horizontal links to other workers through labor unions. Table 1.1 summarizes key differences in labor markets among different varieties of capitalism. Very high turnover (half of workers have held their jobs for fewer than 3 years) in Latin America is a first major factor contributing to atomized employment relations because workers enter firms with few expectations of staying long. Once in the firm, most workers are unlikely to have plant-level union representation, both because union density is so low and because even where unions do exist, they often do not have much of a formal presence on the shopfloor, and overall "organized labor . . . is extremely weak" (Huber 2002a, 458–59).[12] In addition, there are few other well-functioning mechanisms (like German-style codetermination) for mediating relations between workers and employers.

---

[11] Although difficult to measure precisely, estimates of intrafirm trade between Latin America and the United States vary between one-third and two-thirds (Petras and Veltmeyer 1999; Zeile 1997). Although the patterns are similar for other regions, it is important to note that this trade is not a market exchange between independent buyers and sellers, but more a shipping order between members of the same corporate organization.

[12] Chapter 8 considers the exceptional strength in the 2000s of organized labor in Argentina.

TABLE 1.1. *Labor Markets in LMEs, Latin America, and CMEs*

|                                  | LME | Latin America | CME |
|----------------------------------|-----|---------------|-----|
| Union density (percent)          | 28  | 15            | 45  |
| Job tenure (median years)        | 5.0 | 3.0           | 7.4 |
| Index of labor market regulation | 1.0 | 1.8           | 1.4 |
| Informal economy (percent)       | 13  | 40            | 17  |

*Source*: Schneider and Karcher (2010).

Labor market regulations, on the books, are surprisingly more extensive on average in Latin America than in LMEs or even CMEs. However, the de facto reach of these regulations is limited because they do not cover the large informal sector and compliance in the formal sector is uneven (Perry et al. 2007).

Labor markets in Latin America also differ in patterns of segmentation that are obscured by these averages. In simple terms, the three main segments are (1) a large informal sector, (2) a large group of workers in formal jobs but with low skills and short tenure, and (3) a small segment, a labor elite, that has long tenure, high skills, union representation, and significant benefits from high labor regulation. Few precise measures exist for the size of these segments, but my estimates (see Chapter 5) put the labor elite at less than a fifth with the other four-fifths divided between formal, low-tenure workers and the informal segment.

### 4. Low Levels of Education and Vocational Skills

Educational levels in Latin America remain lower than those in developed countries and East Asia. From 1960 to 2000, the average educational attainment in the adult population in Latin America almost doubled from 3.3 to 6.1 years of school (Barro and Lee 2000, 29–30). Yet, by 2000, educational attainment in Latin America lagged behind East Asia (6.7 years) and developed countries (9.8 years), and especially for secondary education, the level most relevant for technical education and vocational training, and these regional disparities were similar in 2010 (Barro and Lee 2010). In cross-national regressions, education levels in Latin America fall far short of what would be expected for their income levels (de Ferranti et al. 2003, 3). On achievement tests like PISA, most countries of Latin America scored well below averages for the OECD and below what would be expected for their income levels (OECD 2010c). Lastly, governments in Latin America spent little on training unemployed workers (IDB 2003, 282).

Overall, problems in labor relations and skills explain a large portion of lagging productivity in Latin America (Pagés 2010). The Inter-American Development Bank reported that,

in a study of 47 countries including most developed countries, six Latin American countries and a sampling of countries in Asia and Africa, Argentina was ranked 29th in productivity per worker, Mexico 34th, Chile 36th, Brazil 38th, Colombia 40th, and Venezuela 42nd. The reasons for these low productivity levels include slow progress in education, the failure of training systems, poor labor relations, and the absence of compensation mechanisms for workers who stand to lose their jobs or job standing due to innovations. (IDB 2001, 105)

What explains the low levels of investment in skills? Why are incentives for public provision and individual investment in education and training so weak? For fuller answers to these questions, as well as a deeper understanding of why other institutions and organizations persist, it is essential to examine complementarities among them.

## III. Institutional Complementarities

The core features, as well as other background factors, were complementary and reinforced one another in ways that sustained key institutions of hierarchical capitalism in Latin America and impeded convergence toward either liberal or coordinated capitalism. For Hall and Soskice, "two institutions can be said to be complementary if the presence (or efficiency) of one increases returns from (or efficiency of) the other" (2001, 17). Complementarities are fundamental because they connect the four sets of institutions in hierarchical capitalism and make the whole (the Gestalt or configuration) greater than the sum of the parts (Crouch 2010). At first glance, the four components – business groups, MNCs, atomized and segmented labor, and low skills – seem incommensurate. This is the result of using a descriptive shorthand in which atomized and segmented labor is a composite of formal and informal institutions (including labor unions, collective bargaining, rapid turnover, and labor market regulations), and the label of low skills comprises educational institutions and corporate training practices. When the discussion turns to complementarities among these composite shorthand terms, it is focused on the institutional subcomponents, as, for example, between rapid turnover and on the job training.

Complementarities have a positive connotation in the varieties of capitalism lexicon, as in raising incentives for investing in skills. However, strictly speaking, complementarities are just neutral relationships; it is their consequences that are positive or, as is often the case in hierarchical capitalism, negative. References in later chapters to negative and positive complementarities refer to these consequences, not any fundamental differences in the logic of complementarity. This section summarizes a few crucial connections, especially those related to skills. Chapter 2 examines complementarities in greater detail.

*MNCs and business groups.* Over the course of the second half of the twentieth century, the existence of MNCs in higher technology manufacturing reduced the returns for domestic groups to investing in these sectors and increased the returns to business groups that invested in other areas such as natural resources, commodities, and services that used lower skills and technologies.[13] The few domestic firms that did invest in developing technologies were often in the end bought out by MNCs entering the market, thereby reinforcing the division between MNCs and domestic groups.

*MNCs, business groups, and low skills.* Both MNCs and business groups had relatively low demand for skilled labor and weak incentives to press for widespread investment in education and training. MNCs and business groups were divided between capital-intensive firms that did rely on skilled workers, but only small numbers of them, and labor-intensive activities that employed lots of unskilled workers. Neither MNCs nor business groups invested much in R&D and related innovation that would have generated abundant jobs for very skilled workers.

*Short tenure and low skills.* When turnover is high, then employers have few incentives to invest in workers' skills because they expect them not to stay long. For workers, short tenure limits their time horizons and lowers their interest in investing in firm, specific skills, or even in sector specific skills if they move regularly among different sectors.

*Low skills and business groups.* The absence of a large pool of skilled workers discouraged domestic firms from investing in upgrading their production or in other higher technology sectors, and instead encouraged domestic firms to target lower technology investments where appropriate skills were abundant in the labor market.

The overall skill regime is the central nexus linking business and labor markets. Firm and worker strategies are in aggregate closely related and codependent and, in individual firms, may be deliberately coordinated or imposed. In the short run, firm strategies depend on the stock of available skills, and workers' skill strategies depend on the jobs firms offer. Skill regimes are also a core dimension for distinguishing varieties of capitalism. The prevalence of general skills, and firm strategies based on them, differentiates liberal economies from coordinated economies in which firms and workers invest in, and rely on, more specific skills (Estevez-Abe, Iversen, and Soskice 2001). The low-skill equilibrium distinguishes hierarchical capitalism from both coordinated and liberal models.[14] Skills are also fundamental to rethinking development strategies. Overall, education has not been contributing much to growth in Latin America:

in contrast to Asia, Latin America shows a distinctive growth pattern, primarily supported by the accumulation of labor, combined with a remarkably minor contribution of human capital and technological knowledge, usually included as the main component of total factor productivity. (Lora, 2008, 124)

---

[13] I use commodity in the broadest sense of mass produced, unspecialized goods including agricultural and agro-industrial products, minerals, metals, pulp and paper, and simple manufactures like basic foods, beverages, and textiles.

[14] In earlier work, Finegold and Soskice (1988) refer to a low-skill equilibrium in British industry; however, they did not develop the concept. Although this suggests some similarities between liberal and hierarchical capitalism. In general, skills in service sectors LMEs have a much higher skill equilibrium.

Complementarities reveal the use-value of the concept of hierarchical capitalism beyond typological extensions by showing, among other things, why business groups do not converge on the types of corporate governance found in developed countries, why the strategies of business groups and MNCs are not geared toward upgrading and innovation, and why these firms do not in turn help break out of the low-skill equilibrium.

These core complementarities, analyzed in detail in later chapters, are also embedded in, and sustained by, their institutional environment. The state is the main external institution that historically reinforced the core features of hierarchical capitalism as it regulated markets for capital, labor, and technology. States invited MNCs in and regulated the terms of their entry. States encouraged and shaped – directly or indirectly – patterns of diversification in business groups (Schneider 2009b). States, especially after the 1930s, intervened deeply in labor markets and initial worker training; at the same time, they decided how much (or little) public education to provide and to whom. Moreover, the long history of deep state intervention in the economy may have "crowded out," or inhibited the emergence of, other kinds of nonstate, nonmarket institutions common in coordinated capitalism. Some typologies of capitalism include the state as an integral part of a statist variety (Schmidt 2003). Yet, except in extreme cases of where the state controls much of the economy, more can be gained by keeping the state analytically separate to better understand its role in shaping a country's type of capitalism (see Chapter 2).

Latin America has long been a world leader in socioeconomic inequality that worked in recent decades to reinforce hierarchies as well as stymie efforts to promote education and investment in human capital. Vast differences in education, norms, ethnicity, and sometimes gender and language create a gulf between workers and managers that makes both sides less disposed to engage in coordination and negotiation. And, inequality reduces incentives on both sides for incremental investment in education and training, because the gap between actual and desired skills is so great. Perversely, in Latin America, the returns to education were lower for poor households (Perry et al. 2005). Yawning sociocultural inequality, both partial cause and consequence of hierarchical capitalism, impeded movement toward either market or coordinated capitalism.

Political systems in Latin America worked to reinforce hierarchical capitalism in ways that resemble the political underpinnings of liberal and coordinated capitalisms in particular electoral systems, majoritarian, and PR (proportional representation), respectively (Hall and Soskice 2001). In Latin America, these political influences were both formal and informal (and covered in greater depth in Chapter 7). On the informal side, insiders like business groups and labor unions had easy access to policy makers in large part because the bureaucracy was generally porous and because most top positions were appointive and usually filled with appointees who were open to talking to labor leaders and owners of business groups. On the formal side, electoral systems for legislatures based on proportional representation, common across

Latin America, fragmented party systems and facilitated access and influence by business groups and labor unions.

In the 2000s, renewed commodity-led development played to the relative strengths of hierarchical capitalism. MNCs and business groups were well positioned to expand commodity production. Many of the largest business groups such as Votorantim (aluminum and pulp and paper) in Brazil, Grupo México (mining), and Luksic (mining) in Chile were concentrated in commodities prior to 2000 and expanded production thereafter. The lack of a pool of skilled workers was not a major obstacle as firms, reaping bonanza prices, could absorb the cost of training. At the same time, the commodity boom reduced pressures, as growth rates stabilized and currencies appreciated, to find higher-skill niches in the global economy that could generate more and better employment. To the extent that hierarchical capitalism has a competitive advantage, it is in commodities. In contrast, liberal economies have advantages in radical innovation and high-end services, and coordinated economies excel in incremental innovation and manufacturing (Hall and Soskice 2001). In the case of commodities, competitive advantage derives first from geography, but the institutions of hierarchical capitalism are well suited to exploiting that advantage.

In sum, complementarities were mutually reinforcing, and other contextual factors like state intervention and inequality tended to shore up hierarchical capitalism. Institutional complementarities help explain past resilience in hierarchical capitalism, especially through the profound transformations of industrialization under ISI and the political and economic liberalization of the late twentieth century. Yet, in all, hierarchical capitalism is not in immutable equilibrium, nor is it impervious to change and reform. In fact, the negative consequences of some complementarities generate political pressures for change, pressures that are analyzed further in Part III.

By the 2000s, the governments of Latin America managed to overcome the main economic scourges of the twentieth century by vanquishing inflation and balance of payments crises and then restoring growth and lowering unemployment. By the 2010s, two of the most important remaining barriers to sustained, shared development were lagging productivity and entrenched inequality. Although most countries reduced inequality in the 2000s, levels remained among the highest in the world (López-Calva and Lustig 2010). Less noted, but highly problematic, was the comparatively very low rate of increase in productivity. From 1961 to 2008, total factor productivity in the seven largest countries of Latin America grew by 0.3 percent per year compared to 2.2 percent in East Asia. The rate of increase picked up in Latin America in the 2000s to 1 percent, but that was still half the rate in East Asia (World Bank 2011, 30). Lasting solutions to both inequality and lagging productivity require more skilled, productive, and well-paid jobs. Understanding the causes of low productivity and the potential sources of more and better jobs in turn requires an in-depth analysis of institutions and institutional complementarities in hierarchical capitalism.

## IV. Plan of the Book

Chapter 2 explores types of capitalism at greater conceptual and comparative length in order to highlight the distinctive elements of hierarchical capitalism in comparison with liberal, coordinated, and network economies. Chapter 2 also elaborates more on the complementarities in hierarchical capitalism among business groups, MNCs, low skills, and segmented labor. Readers more interested in empirical material on Latin America can skip ahead to Part II.

Part II has chapters on each of the four main components of hierarchical capitalism. Due to the neglect of business groups in most scholarship on Latin America political economy, Chapter 3 provides extensive empirical coverage and examines their resilience over time, and contrasts business groups in Asia and Latin America. Chapter 4 turns to MNCs to highlight their renewed influx into Latin America to analyze the consequences, often negative, for the growth of local firms and high-skill employment and to examine their political exclusion. Chapter 5 covers segmented labor markets and atomized labor relations, focusing especially on informality, weak unions, rapid turnover, and extensive regulation. Chapter 6 delves into the low-skill trap, in which employers do not invest in activities requiring skilled workers because so few are available and workers do not invest in their human capital because of the lack of skilled jobs on offer.

In Part III, Chapter 7 enters into the political dynamics in hierarchical capitalism, concentrating on the formal institutions and informal practices that favor business groups and analyzing how firm strategies and general institutional complementarities inform their policy preferences. Chapter 8 examines some contemporary variations on hierarchical capitalism in Mexico, Argentina, Chile, and Brazil, highlighting the potential in the latter two countries for breaking out of the low-skill trap. Chapter 9 concludes with some reflections on further theorizing in the study of comparative capitalism and on institutional origins and change.

The core arguments of the book revolve around an interlocking set of complementarities. The analysis of institutional complementarities has a long tradition in economics and has been ubiquitous in research in the past decade on Europe and other developed countries, but almost never comes up in Latin America.[15] Examining complementarities is a different analytic enterprise from traditional causal approaches that take an outcome and attempt to single out the main cause. With complementarities, the goal is to find out how the existence or strength of an institution in one realm of the economy affects incentives and institutions in another realm, without intending to establish that the complementarities are the main or single cause. In fact, some complementarities do have the force of sufficient causes, such as in the way the dominance of

---

[15] See, for example, Milgrom and Roberts (1994), Amable (2000), and Aoki (2001) and other works by these authors. For reviews of institutional complementarities in developed countries, see Höpner (2005), Crouch et al. (2005), Deeg (2007), and Deeg and Jackson (2007).

MNCs in higher technology manufacturing increased incentives for, or caused, business groups to invest in other sectors. In other complementarities, the relationship is more probabilistic – one of a range of likely causes. So, for example, the lack of skilled jobs in business groups lowers incentives for students to invest in education, but it is only one of several factors constraining school achievement.

The analysis of complementarities opens a novel window on Latin American political economy, and this book works to develop the concept in several directions. The book first extends the concept of complementarities to explain negative as well as positive outcomes. And, while the central complementarities are among the four core components – MNCs, business groups, atomized labor markets, and low skills – later chapters uncover crucial additional complementarities within the corporate governance of business groups (Chapter 3) and within labor markets (Chapter 5). These "within realm" complementarities go beyond the basic interactions in most studies in comparative capitalism and are instrumental in explaining the workings of hierarchical capitalism. Overall, complementarities are indispensable to understanding many of the anomalies of Latin American political economy such as Why is labor regulation higher than anywhere else? Why did big business not oppose trade liberalization? Why did so many business groups start in cement? and Why is family capitalism thriving?

The book provides original research from archives, government documents, periodicals, firm histories and annual reports, and scores of interviews (see the Appendix), much of it collected through field research in six countries: Argentina, Mexico, Colombia, Peru, Brazil, and Chile (with special emphasis on the last two). Additional evidence and insights come from synthesizing existing research and integrating extensive but dispersed scholarship on corporate governance, business groups, MNCs, global production networks, R&D, labor markets, education, and worker training.

In focus, this book runs counter to – but in the end complements – a recent wave of research focused on the poor, the bottom of the pyramid. The analysis of hierarchical capitalism concentrates attention instead on the top of the pyramid in terms of both corporate governance and the higher-skilled labor elite. Much groundbreaking research, and innovative policies following from it, tackles the question of how to bring the bottom of the pyramid out of poverty. The boom in experimental research, which revived development studies in economics, looks almost exclusively at the very poor (Banerjee and Duflo 2011). Without doubt, it is essential to find ways to provide basic subsistence needs, education, and health care, but longer term, it is equally pressing to provide more good jobs and increase productivity (Amsden 2010). For a concrete example, the popular and ubiquitous conditional cash transfer (CCT) programs are succeeding in keeping more children in school longer. But, these successes will not mean much over the longer run if these students cannot find jobs that let them use their new skills. Understanding whether those jobs will materialize and where they might come from requires closer attention to the top of the pyramid where decisions are made on what jobs to create.

This book, and the varieties of capitalism framework generally, focuses attention centrally on the quality of jobs. The skill regime is the crucial analytic nexus between business and labor through several of the main complementarities. The central policy and normative implication is that the quality of jobs, not just the quality of labor markets, should be central concerns in devising development strategies and policy packages. The quality of jobs can be a guiding issue, of course, in various direct kinds of labor reforms and active labor market policy (unemployment insurance, training programs, skill certification, etc.), but an abiding concern with jobs can also be built into broader policies in science and technology, trade, and education, as well as the industrial policies that came back in fashion in the 2000s.

**2**

# Comparing Capitalisms

## *Liberal, Coordinated, Network, and Hierarchical*

## I. Introduction[1]

For a number of years now, scholars of comparative political economy have been asking how many types of capitalism exist in contemporary societies. To date the most common answers – based almost exclusively on comparisons among developed countries – are one, two, three, four, five, or many. The answer offered here is four, based primarily on ideal types constructed around four basic mechanisms of allocation that are compatible with various ways of organizing capitalism: markets, negotiation, networks, and hierarchy.

For those seeking a more inclusive and exhaustive taxonomy of capitalisms, the lament over Hall and Soskice's (2001) original dichotomous formulation was that it was too inductive, empirically complex, and geographically narrow (only developed countries).[2] However, even their original formulation contained hints for possible extensions. For one, their category of coordinated capitalism lumped together two different subtypes, Japanese and European CMEs, that operated on distinctive principles: group-based versus industry-based coordination, respectively (p. 34). Moreover, they speculated that some countries of southern Europe might be hybrid "Mediterranean" varieties, with more coordination on the capital side and more markets for labor. However, these possible subtypes remained undeveloped.

Without going into a full review of other attempts to differentiate types of capitalist systems, it is still worth noting that most offerings continue to focus on inductive clusterings that usually exclude developing economies.[3]

---

[1] This chapter draws on Schneider (2012).

[2] Hancke et al. (2007a) review these and other critiques.

[3] Coates (2000, 9–10) distinguishes three "ideal types of capitalist organization:" market-led, state-led, and negotiated or consensual. Representative cases of each include, respectively, the United States and the United Kingdom, Japan and South Korea, and Germany and Sweden.

For example, Bruno Amable (2003) provides finer distinctions among European capitalisms and attempts some broader geographic comparisons. Amable's distinction among five types of capitalism – market-based, social-democratic, Continental European, Mediterranean, and Asian – steps further south and ventures a bit out of the developed world. But his approach is heavily inductive, more multifaceted as he folds in social welfare and educational systems as well as other features of the productive system, and not designed to extend to developing countries.

My more deductive point of departure is that capitalist systems – defined by the predominance of mostly free markets and private property – accommodate a limited number of alternative mechanisms for allocating resources, especially the gains from investment, production, and exchange. These mechanisms are markets, negotiation, trust, and hierarchy, and correspond in systemic terms to, respectively, liberal market economies (LMEs), coordinated market economies (CMEs), network market economies (NMEs), and hierarchical market economies (HMEs).

My typology takes a firm's eye view on comparative political economy and focuses primarily on the internal organization of large private firms and their relations with their political and economic environments. Alternative typologies that focus instead on state activities like social spending or development promotion are useful for other purposes, but are less helpful in identifying distinctive features of business and the kinds of development, jobs, innovation, and competitive advantages large firms are likely to generate. In some instances, to which I return, states and politics overwhelm the private sector, making a "state's eye" perspective more appropriate.

This fourfold typology offers several advantages over previous formulations. First, it provides additional conceptual tools for analyzing capitalism outside the developed world. To date, most discussions view capitalism in poor countries as transitory, dependent, premodern, developing, emerging, or some other gerund, with the implicit presumption that the trajectory is toward some already recognizable form of capitalism in rich countries. The conceptual addition of the new hierarchical variety (HME) allows us to conceive of a distinct, rather than derivative, kind of production regime that has its own reinforcing dynamics and institutional advantages and disadvantages. Middle-income regions such as Latin America may still lag as far behind developed

Schmidt (2002, 112–18) uses a similar three way typology of market capitalism, managed capitalism, and state capitalism with France and Italy in the last category. Kitschelt et al. (1999) distinguish four main types: uncoordinated liberal market capitalism (same countries as LMEs), national coordinated market economies (labor corporatist) in Scandinavia, sector-coordinated market economies (Rhine capitalism) in much of Continental Europe, and "group-coordinated Pacific Basin market economies" in Japan and Korea. For Boyer (2005, 509), regulation theory "recurrently finds at least four brands of capitalism: market-led, meso-corporatist, social democratic and State-led." See Crouch (2005) and Jackson and Deeg (2008) for extended reviews of typologies, and Boschi (2011) for a recent extension to Latin America.

countries in terms of GDP per capita as they did decades ago, but on many social and economic indicators, contemporary middle-income countries are as "modern" as developed countries were by the middle of the twentieth century when varieties of capitalism there became institutionalized and consolidated (Hall 2007). Thus, there are good reasons to think that capitalism in many middle-income countries may have settled into institutional foundations of its own, and therefore requires analysis on its own terms rather than as some form of capitalism manqué or in formation. In short, it may be that capitalism in many developing countries is what it is, rather than on its way to becoming something else.[4]

Second, a typology based on core allocative principles offers an option for theoretical closure on the question of how many varieties there are. This closure is conceptual and does not imply that all countries are, or are transitioning toward, one of the four varieties. The point is that the number of alternative principles for allocating resources in a capitalist economy is limited. Third, the proposed typology helps distinguish different forms of capitalism within particular countries.[5] Even if comparison of national models is the primary purpose, it need not require us to ignore intracountry variation. So, for example, the expanding service sectors in most CMEs look more liberal than coordinated. Although the analysis here is based primarily on cross-national variation, for some purposes, it may be more useful to think of all national economies as evolving mixtures of various sorts (Boyer 2005; Crouch 2005: 26, 41). Assessing patterns in these mixtures, however, requires prior delineation of clear conceptual ideal types, rather than the often scumbled categories derived from empirical clusters of national-level indicators.

Section II explores in greater detail the main differences across the four varieties in the basic allocative and commitment mechanisms, corporate governance, labor relations, and skills. This section also briefly assesses the fit of various countries to these ideal types. Section III analyzes complementarities and other interactions that knit varieties together, focusing primarily on hierarchical capitalism. The conclusion considers some further regional comparisons.

## II. Allocative Mechanisms: Markets, Negotiation, Trust, and Hierarchy

Markets and coordination, the mechanisms in the original CME/LME dichotomy, do not exhaust all the primary logics or principles of allocation in capitalist economies. Hall and Soskice (2001) themselves note two quite

---

[4] Hancké et al. (2007b, 4) use the term "emerging market economy" (EME) to categorize countries "in transition with only partially formed institutional ecologies." This may apply to particularly fluid postcommunist political economies of Eastern and Central Europe but less so to other poor countries with longer trajectories of capitalist development.

[5] There is a long research tradition that compares within-country variation by sector or region. For example, see Piore and Sabel (1984) and Hollingsworth and Boyer (1997).

TABLE 2.1. *Basic Relations in Four Ideal Types of Capitalism*

|  | Liberal (LME) | Coordinated (CME) | Network (NME) | Hierarchical (HME) |
|---|---|---|---|---|
| Allocative principle | markets | negotiation | trust | hierarchy |
| Characteristic interaction among stakeholders | spot exchange | institutionalized meeting | reiterated exchange | order or directive |
| Length of relationships | short | long | long | variable |
| Representative case | United States | Germany | Japan | Chile |

different mechanisms for coordination in CMEs, negotiation in Europe and networks in Asia (hereafter, network market economies, NMEs). These three mechanisms resemble Hirschman's (1970) trichotomy of responses to decline – exit (LMEs), voice (CMEs in Europe), and loyalty (NMEs in Asia; though for Hirschman, loyalty was less a third principle and more a factor mitigating voice and exit). However, loyalty implies trust, which figures centrally in most analyses of Japanese networks, lifetime employment, and business-group coordination. Last, in terms of basic principles, hierarchy is a fourth crucial mechanism for nonmarket allocation. In post-Coasian economics, hierarchy is a feature of all modern firms and a universal response to higher transaction costs (Williamson and Winter 1993). However, transaction costs and hierarchy vary considerably across national institutional contexts, and hierarchy should also be considered an option adopted by economic agents in place of market, network, or negotiated alternatives.

Table 2.1 starts with abstract distinctions underlying each variety. Subsequent tables incorporate more empirical regularities associated with real-world manifestations. The issue of skills provides a useful illustration of the core principles of allocation. When workers and their employers invest in training, how are the gains from that investment divided? Following the possible mechanisms in Table 2.1, both parties can let the market decide the value of the new skills, and employees can sell them to the highest bidder. Or, workers and employers can negotiate a plan for sharing the gains from skills in the context of long-term employment relationships. Or, workers can invest in skills and trust that they will be compensated in some way in the future, such as seniority-based pay. Or, finally, employers can decide unilaterally who gets trained and how the gains are distributed. Of course, the power asymmetries between employees and employers are enormous in all types of capitalism, but shared expectations vary on how that power is wielded. Workers may expect employers, variously, to play the market, return regularly for negotiations, keep them on for lifetime employment, or just tell them what to do next.

The typical interactions in Table 2.1 characterize relations among different sets of stakeholders. So, for example, managers in LMEs would expect most relations with shareholders, creditors, suppliers, competing firms, and employees to be short term and market based. Managers in NMEs, in contrast, would expect these relations to be longer term, and each iterated exchange helps build trust for the next round. Managers in CMEs can count on many more meetings with formal, bargained commitments. In HMEs, relations among owners and managers tend to be hierarchical and longer term, whereas relations with other firms and with workers are shorter term and based on some combination of markets and hierarchy.

For a comprehensive and coherent set of ideal types, it is important to separate out the distinct network variety (NME). The conceptualization of NMEs draws on work on economic sociology, social capital, and sociological analyses of Asian capitalism (see Lincoln and Gerlach 2004; Granovetter 2005; Feenstra and Hamilton 2006, especially 44–45). The common thread in this work is the conviction that informal norms and nonmarket relations of trust and reciprocity are at least as relevant as strictly economic and formal relations in determining the performance of firms, regions, and countries. These informal relations are based on long-term, noncontractual, face-to-face interactions. In more complete NMEs, informal networks can permeate business groups (as in keiretsu), as well as relations with employees, banks, government agencies, and sectoral competitors (Witt 2006). In other cases, network capitalism may be confined to particular sectors or regions.

Hierarchy and the concept of a hierarchical market economy have not been considered in previous analyses of comparative capitalism.[6] In a Coasian perspective, hierarchy is of course the day-to-day result of firm decisions to "make rather than buy." In an HME, however, hierarchy regulates and orders much more than just internal relations of vertical integration. Hierarchy also informs relations between owners and managers (concentrated ownership) as well as employee relations (unmediated by labor unions) and decisions on investments in skills and training. Hierarchy is also evident in relations among firms, both within sectors where large firms dominate economically (oligopoly) and in associations as well as across sectors and borders in that business groups and MNCs buy and control firms that would be independent in other varieties. As such, hierarchies replace relations that in other varieties would be mediated by markets, networks, or coordination. Empirically, as discussed later, hierarchy is more common in developing countries, yet conceptually it is a distinctive mechanism of allocation that merits inclusion along with the other three better-known principles.

Conceptually, the four principles are mutually exclusive in the sense that they cannot be combined in equal measure. An allocation based on a hierarchical order, for example, cannot simultaneously be the result of negotiation. Of course, in everyday relations, elements of all four may come into play, and

---

[6] Hierarchy comes up occasionally (Hall and Soskice, 2001, 9; Crouch 2005, 33; Nölke and Vliegenthart 2009), but not as the basis for a distinct variety of capitalism.

TABLE 2.2. *Corporate Governance and Interfirm Relations*

| | Liberal (LME) | Coordinated (CME) | Network (NME) | Hierarchical (HME) |
|---|---|---|---|---|
| stock ownership | dispersed | blockholding | blockholding and cross ownership | family blockholding |
| predominant type of large firms | specialized managerial corporations, MNCs | bank controlled firms, business groups | informal business groups (keiretsu) | hierarchical business groups, MNCs |
| firm relations within sectors | competitive | sectoral associations | associations and informal ties | oligopolistic |
| firm relations across sectors | few | encompassing associations | informal connections | few (save acquisitions) |
| supplier relations | competitive bidding | long term, negotiated | long term, informal | vertical integration |

firms (all complex organizations, in fact) have at least some relations based on each of the four mechanisms. And, over time, particular economic relationships may evolve from, say, hierarchy to market, to network. However, for most major commitments of time and resources, the economic agents involved presumably have few doubts over which is the primary operative principle. The four core principles should also be collectively exhaustive in that other possible mechanisms of distribution such as theft, lotteries, or communalism are not compatible with capitalist systems based on free markets and private property. However, as multidimensional ideal types, these four varieties are not meant to be empirically exhaustive, and many countries may be hybrids that do not fit any of the four types.

How are these four abstract principles manifested in various spheres and relations of capitalist production? Tables 2.2, 2.3, and 2.4 turn to more specific distinctions and start to draw in more empirical examples. On the dimension of corporate governance, the first distinction is between dispersed ownership in LMEs like the United States and Great Britain and blockholding (concentrated ownership) in the other three varieties (Table 2.2) (La Porta, López-de-Silanes, and Shleifer 1999; Roe 2003; Gourevitch and Shinn 2005). Concentrated ownership and patient investment facilitated the longer-term relations in network and coordinated capitalisms as in Japan and Germany historically. Although ownership is concentrated in all three blockholding varieties, the type of control varies. In particular, large firms in Japan (NME) and Germany (CME) had more cross-shareholding by other firms and financial intermediaries that crowded out dispersed shareholding and shielded firms from outside takeovers

(Dore 2000, 34). In HMEs in many developing countries, ownership in business groups is more concentrated (without cross-shareholding, in part because of the relative underdevelopment of stock markets) and mostly held by families (which adds another element of hierarchy) (La Porta et al. 1999). Hostile takeovers, common in liberal capitalism, are rare or unknown in the other varieties.

Share ownership feeds into different types of corporate structure and authority in the large firms in each variety. Dispersed ownership in LMEs shifts power to managers, but also subjects them to short-term monitoring and performance pressures. Owners have greater control in the other nonliberal varieties where investors tend to be more "patient." Although business groups are common in nonliberal varieties, they tend to be different types, more informally connected in NMEs and more hierarchical in HMEs (see Granovetter 2005; Khanna and Yafeh 2007). As noted in Chapter 1, the relatively minor role of external finance – equity and credit – means that many of the traditional concerns of corporate governance and relations between external financiers (principals) and managers (agents) are less relevant in hierarchical capitalism. Business-group owners, mostly families, have full ownership and usually direct managerial control.

Direct hierarchical control is also the rule in MNCs that are common among the largest firms in both liberal and hierarchical capitalism but rarer in CMEs and especially NMEs. The debate about varieties of capitalism in developed countries pays little, if any, attention to MNCs, yet even among OECD countries the contrasts are large: the proportion of sales accounted for by MNCs was 21 percent in the United States, 31 percent in the United Kingdom, 11 percent in Germany, and just 2 percent in Japan (Barba Navaretti and Venables 2004, 5).[7] The presence of MNCs in most developing countries is even larger, especially in more complex manufacturing (such as autos and electronics), with the significant exceptions of Korea and Taiwan (Amsden 2001). MNCs are compatible with market and hierarchical varieties though not logically necessary.[8] MNCs though are logically inconsistent with coordination and networks, and in practice, when MNCs expand in CMEs and NMEs, they undermine interfirm coordination through business associations and informal networks.

---

[7] Soskice (1999, 118) devotes only a paragraph to MNCs, noting mostly that MNCs often seek out CMEs or LMEs to leverage their respective institutional advantages, as in German chemical companies with biotechnology investments in the United States. Other extensions to Hall and Soskice or contending perspectives on comparative capitalism also devote little attention to MNCs (Huber 2002b; Crouch 2005; Hancké et al. 2007a). See Morgan (2009) and Chapter 4 for more empirical details on MNCs across different varieties of capitalism.

[8] MNC subsidiaries are subject to hierarchical control, which adds a nonmarket element to liberal capitalism. However, LMEs are mostly large, open economies where MNCs are therefore subject to stronger market forces. In developing countries, MNCs often have greater market power or collective dominance of whole sectors, so the hierarchical element is more evident and consequential (see Shapiro 2003).

Comparisons across three dimensions of interfirm relations – within sectors, across sectors, and with suppliers – reveal differences that are closely related to the guiding principles of each variety.[9] In LMEs, relations are competitive within sectors, largely absent across sectors (encompassing associations are weaker or non-existent), and competitive among suppliers. At first glance, HMEs seem to resemble LMEs in their shared absence of interfirm coordinating mechanisms. However, firms in HMEs tend to encounter many more hierarchies than market relations. High concentration ratios in many sectors structure markets as oligopolies with a few dominant firms (that are likely to exercise control over industry associations; see Chapter 3).[10] Moreover, across sectors and across borders, firms in hierarchical capitalism are more likely to be owned and controlled by either large business groups or MNCs, and relations with suppliers are typically hierarchical, either through direct vertical integration or through general dependence of small suppliers on large or monopsonist buyers.

In CMEs, employer and sectoral associations are better organized and more encompassing, and they perform crucial coordinating functions such as bargaining collectively, managing vocational training programs, and negotiating sectoral standards. Relations with suppliers are based on long-term, negotiated relations that often involve joint efforts at upgrading. Relations with government are also likely to be mediated by strong business associations. As noted earlier, Hall and Soskice (2001) distinguish this formal, industry based coordination in Europe from the more informal, group-based coordination in Japan, or NMEs in my typology.[11]

In NMEs, crucial coordination also takes place through informal networks of firms, best typified by the keiretsu in Japan. Such network-based business groups are multisectoral and provide strong links across sectors. In practice, formal associations in network economies may also be important and help to mediate coordination within sectors, often with government support as in deliberation councils and publicly supported R&D consortia. However, in addition to formal association ties, informal networks also permeate sectoral relations among firms, in "intra-industry loops" (Witt 2006). Relations with

[9] In a Coasian perspective, supplier relations are also dependent on sectoral and product characteristics. Where transaction costs are high (and contracts therefore difficult to write), buyers will shy away from market relations and favor longer-term networks, ongoing negotiations, or outright hierarchy. However, in the grayer, more uncertain range of make-or-buy decisions, an institutional perspective would expect more cross-national variation, with suppliers relations tending to be closer and longer term in NMEs and CMEs, and vertical integration more widespread in HMEs.

[10] On hierarchical relations among firms in Chile, see Taylor (2006, chap. 6), and for those in France, see Hancké (1998).

[11] Among others who draw distinctions between Japanese and European capitalism, see Kitschelt et al. (1999), Streeck (2001), Yamamura and Streeck (2003), Pontusson (2005), and Whitley (1999).

TABLE 2.3. *Labor Relations and Skills*

|  | Liberal (LME) | Coordinated (CME) | Network (NME) | Hierarchical (HME) |
|---|---|---|---|---|
| Employment relations | short term, market | long term, negotiated | life time employment | short term, market |
| Industrial relations | fewer unions | encompassing unions | company unions | few unions |
| Labor-management committees | no | yes | yes | no |
| Skills | general | sector specific | firm specific | low |

suppliers are often long term with formal negotiation, but there are additional network and informal relations (as in the practice of shifting employees from buyer to supplier firms).

On the labor side, there is a greater resemblance between liberal and hierarchical capitalism, on the one hand, and coordinated and network capitalism, on the other (Table 2.3). In hierarchical and market varieties, employment relations (for the majority of workers outside the small labor elite) are short term and unmediated by unions that are generally few or absent. Workers therefore lack incentives to invest in sector or firm specific skills, and invest, if they do invest, in more general skills. In CMEs and NMEs, in contrast, employment relations are longer term, and employees therefore have greater incentives to invest in sector-specific skills. The difference between CMEs and NMEs derives largely from expectations of longer-term employment (as in Japan) where employees trust that they will be able to amortize investment in firm specific skills. In CMEs, training is organized on a sectoral basis and government policies such as generous unemployment benefits allow laid-off workers to wait for jobs that match their skills and therefore allow them to amortize sector specific training (Estevez-Abe et al. 2001; Iversen and Soskice 2001).

In the abstract, unions do not mesh well with the organizing principles in market and hierarchical varieties, and in practice, large majorities of workers in purer cases of each do not belong to unions. Beyond, or alongside, unions, there is a further issue of additional forums for consultation and negotiation over work organization and other shop-floor issues. On this dimension, both theoretical expectations and practice are more black and white: LMEs and HMEs have none whereas CMEs and NMEs have a range of different forms of ongoing consultation between management and labor, including statutory bodies like works councils (codetermination), representation on company boards, and shop-floor work teams.

Overall, each variety has distinctive strengths and weaknesses (Table 2.4). For Hall and Soskice (2001), the adaptability of LMEs combined with high-level skills in cutting-edge technology and service sectors promotes radical innovation in new products and businesses. CMEs and NMEs, in contrast, manage

TABLE 2.4. *Comparative Institutional Advantage and Empirical Cases*

|  | Liberal (LME) | Coordinated (CME) | Network (NME) | Hierarchical (HME) |
| --- | --- | --- | --- | --- |
| Comparative institutional advantages | radical innovation, services | incremental innovation, manufacturing | incremental innovation, manufacturing | commodities, simple manufacturing |
| Cases | United States Great Britain Estonia | Germany Scandinavia Slovenia | Japan Taiwan | Latin America (South East Asia?) |

through longer-term relationships to innovate incrementally, especially in manufacturing, and to make constant improvements in quality and productivity in more established lines of activity. HMEs lack both of these kinds of innovative capacities due to lower skills overall and short-term hierarchical relations that impede collaborative shop-floor relations needed to promote incremental production innovation. Firms in hierarchical capitalism develop instead competitive advantages in commodity production, often based on natural resources and low-complexity manufacturing in sectors such as agro-industry (pulp and paper, vegetable oils, fish and meat packing, and ethanol), minerals and metals (steel, aluminum, copper, and cement), and more industrial commodities (textiles, electronic components, and auto parts) in which the design and marketing are located in developed countries and production is subcontracted to firms in developing countries through global production networks (Gereffi et al. 2005).

Table 2.4 categorizes some major empirical cases, based primarily on the leading sectors and big firms in each country. The LME, CME, and NME classifications follow the conventional wisdom on developed countries that most closely approximate each ideal type and add in some emerging cases of each. Many of the larger, middle-income developing countries approximate the HME variety. The economies of large countries of Latin America and Southeast Asia, as well as countries such as Turkey and South Africa, have many hierarchical business groups and MNCs, short job tenure, and lower skills, and generally weak labor unions that lack capacity to negotiate effectively (on Turkey, see Özel 2011). Section III and later chapters provide more empirical and comparative indicators.

Among the emerging capitalist economies of East Europe and the former Soviet Union, some governments adopted more or less explicit programs of transition to a particular variety, other countries gravitated towards particular models, and others are still in transition or at least not yet recognizable as one of the four varieties. The Baltic countries (Lithuania, Latvia, and Estonia) adopted the most extreme market reforms, pushing them in a liberal direction, whereas Slovenia stands out for the sustained reliance on CME kinds of institutions such as strong business associations, labor unions, and tripartite negotiations (Bohle and Greskovits 2007).[12] Russia and some of the other former Soviet Republics seemed to be moving toward hierarchical capitalism, but several cases have ended up better classified as state or patrimonial capitalism (discussed later).

Among the rising industrial economies of East Asia, Korea, Taiwan, and China seem to hover between CMEs and NMEs, and on some dimensions drift over to HMEs (however, they are pretty clearly not LMEs).[13] Taiwan, for example, had extensive business networks but also strong business associations that coordinated CME-style standards, R&D, and exports (Cheng 1996; Fields 1997). Taiwanese business groups were smaller and relied more on network ties to buyers and suppliers (S.-J. Chang 2006; Feenstra and Hamilton 2006). In contrast to Taiwanese groups, chaebol in Korea tended to be more vertically integrated and hierarchical. Because of the apparent similarities between keiretsu and chaebol, Japan and Korea are often classified together as group-based CMEs (Kitschelt et al. 1999; Soskice 1999). However, chaebol and keiretsu rely on quite different coordinating mechanisms: loose, informal networks in keiretsu, and rigid hierarchical control in chaebol (see Whitley 1990). To the extent that Korean business associations perform important coordinating functions among chaebol and that Korean labor unions are less company based than in Japan, then Korea starts to look more like a European-style CME (however, with faster labor turnover). Moreover, in the late 1990s, the Korean government mandated that all large firms create internal labor-management committees (Haagh 2004), and by the 2000s, CME-style firm-level dialogue had emerged in several leading chaebol (Kong 2011).

The ideal typical distinctions also help identify significant within case deviations and combinations. In the United States, for example, networks are crucial to Silicon Valley as well as smaller niche sectors like diamonds and fashion design (see Uzzi 1996). Moreover, some privately held firms in the United States (some in commodities like Cargill) resemble hierarchical HME business groups. In the case of the other three varieties, the growing service sector has many LME features: general skills, smaller firms without network or association ties, and shorter-term employment. Lastly, some firms in HMEs (some of the best known cases are Embraer (aircraft, Brazil) and Techint (steel tubes, Argentina), have managed to create pockets of lasting investment in skills and well-mediated employment relations and consequently look more like CME firms. For the most part, these anomalies are exceptions that prove the rule, and their exceptionalism can often be traced to peculiar and determined efforts not

[12] Feldmann (2007) provides a detailed analysis of Estonia and Slovenia as prime examples of, respectively, new LMEs and CMEs. Poland and Hungary (and other countries of Central Eastern Europe) are dominated by MNCs and foreign banks. King (2007) calls these cases of "liberal dependent post-communist capitalism." Nölke and Vliegenthart (2009) call them DMEs (dependent market economies). See also Bohle and Greskovits (2012).

[13] China has not only networked groups like keiretsu but also shorter-term employment relations and many MNCs that are characteristic of hierarchical capitalism (Keister 2000). For arguments that China is trending in a more liberal direction, see Steinfeld (2010).

to conform to the prevailing complementarities, as, for example, was the state's long-term subsidization of skill development in Embraer (Goldstein 2002), or the decisions of family-owned hierarchical business groups in the United States not to list their firms.

This section would be incomplete without a foray into the controversy over the appropriate place of the state in defining types of capitalism (see Coates 2000; Schmidt 2002; Boyer 2005; and Hancké et al. 2007a). For other analytic purposes, it may be more useful to start with categories based on the state's role in the economy as, for example, in comparisons of welfare states (Esping-Anderson 1990) or of development strategies in poor countries (Woo-Cumings 1999). However, these characteristics of different states do not necessarily correlate with the kinds of relations – especially among firms and between firms and workers – that are at the core of the "varieties of capitalism" framework.[14] States are, of course, the primary actors in regulating many of these relations, and impeding, enabling, or shaping their evolution, as discussed in the next sections. But the fact that states are crucial to the emergence and functioning of any capitalist system does not in itself create an analytic imperative to incorporate state features or aspects of relations between business and governments into typologies of capitalism (see Hancké et al. 2007b). Moreover, leaving the state out of the typology facilitates subsequent analysis of the impact of the state on the emergence, institutionalization, or unraveling of particular types of capitalism.

However, states in some developing countries so overwhelm the economy that it is less appropriate to use an ME (market economy) suffix to describe them. There may be enough private property or private profits to merit calling them capitalist, but markets are not primary factors in distributing gains. Common names for these state dominated economies include rentier capitalism, predatory states, petro-states, developmental states, crony capitalism, or just state capitalism. For the most part, these statist types belong under Weber's umbrella concept of political capitalism where private profits depend more on politics than markets (Gerth and Mills 1958, 66). In such extreme cases of state dominance, the nature of the state is more important than the organization of private firms in determining the type of political economy.

Among varieties of political capitalism, three general types stand out: state capitalism, developmental states, and patrimonial capitalism. In instances of state capitalism, the public control of the economy, especially in the largest firms and sectors, exceeds the private sector, either by virtue of public property (as in China through the 1990s) or by natural resource rents (see Musacchio

---

[14] Although most CMEs in northern Europe have large welfare states, welfare spending among LMEs varies greatly. Similarly, although state intervention through industrial policy and credit markets has been substantial in France and Japan, such intervention was also vast in pre-Thatcher Great Britain through public enterprises or in the United States technology policy during the Cold War (see Crouch 2005).

and Lazzarini forthcoming). In the latter case (rentier or petro states), the state, by virtue of its control massive natural resource rents, dominates economic activity and forecloses the emergence of a large, independent private sector (Karl 1997). Second, at extreme levels of intervention, developmental states (perhaps in Taiwan and Korea in the 1960s and 1970s) regulate so much of economic activity that they can be considered cases of political capitalism (Amsden 1989; Schneider 1999).[15] Third, political leaders may favor particular businesses in what is variously termed crony, clientelist, booty, or patrimonial capitalism.[16] Patrimonial capitalism is often associated with natural resource rents, but political leaders can also engage in clientelism without them. In the wake of market reform and globalization in the 1990s, political capitalism faded, but the subsequent commodity boom and renewed state intervention after the 2008–09 crisis brought it back. In Latin America, it is most evident in Venezuela, Bolivia, and Ecuador (though these countries account for only a small part of the region's economy).

The goal of this section was to lay out the main static differences among the four varieties and examine how distinct principles of markets, negotiation, trust, and hierarchy generate different relations among firms, between owners and managers, and between workers and managers. In turn, reassembling these distinct sets of relations lays the foundation for four ideal-typical varieties of capitalism. The next sections turn from static differences to dynamic interactions, especially within hierarchical capitalism.

## III. Complementarities and Compatibilities

As introduced in Chapter 1, the glue holding different capitalisms together is institutional complementarities across different spheres of the economy where the presence of one institution increases returns to, or efficiency of, another institution, or where "one institution functions all the better because some other particular institutions or forms of organization are present" (Amable 2000, 647). The benefits of the complementarities approach are several. First, it incorporates linkages across different realms of the economy. Second, strong institutional complementarities generate a system where the whole is greater than the sum of the parts (suggesting skepticism of conceptions of capitalism that are just lists of factors or sums of parts). Third, institutional complementarities shape the preferences and strategies of economic agents (Hassel 2007). Fourth, as traced out empirically in Chapter 7, these distinctive preferences motivate economic agents to engage in politics and institution building and maintenance in ways that reinforce existing complementarities. Moreover, in a

---

[15] Among those who advocate for a statist variety, Weiss (2010) proposes a governed market economy (GME) similar to a developmental state.

[16] See King (2007) on patrimonial capitalism in Russia and other former Soviet republics. Hutchcroft (1998) uses the term "booty capitalism" to characterize banking in the Philippines.

less conscious and deliberate manner, institutional complementarities can also take alternative strategies off the table, thereby also reinforcing continuity in a more passive fashion. Tracing this process from institutions to complementarities to preferences and back to mobilization to reinforce the initial institutions is crucial to fend off charges of mechanistic equilibrium and functionalism.

Applied to the broader range of capitalisms considered here, the concept of complementarity requires some further elaboration and extension (see Crouch 2005, chap. 3; Deeg 2005; Höpner 2005). For one, institutional complementarities should include the possibility of negative outcomes or effects. Negative effects almost never come up in analyses of liberal and coordinated capitalism where the focus is the alternative institutional configurations that generate different competitive advantages.[17] For some, international competitiveness is a necessary element of a variety of capitalism (Nölke and Vliegenthart 2009). In other frameworks, appropriate institutional complementarities generate higher growth than in hybrid institutional mixes (Hall and Gingerich 2009). Limiting institutional complementarities only to the wealthiest, best performing economies does not though make analytic sense – complementarity in any abstract definition is neutral with respect to outcomes – and impedes our ability to understand poor and under performing economies. Moreover, in a last conceptual extension some connections across realms of the economy may fall short of complementarity, and should be better understood as compatibilities, where the existence of one institution does not interfere with or impede another (but may also foreclose other institutional alternatives; see Streeck 2005).

The real litmus test for identifying a distinct variety of capitalism is the existence of institutional complementarities that link separate realms of the economy together and shift the incentives of firms and workers; "complementarity is what makes taxonomies of capitalisms possible" (Jackson and Deeg 2008, 683). Yet, many of the new varieties proposed, such as statist (Schmidt 2003), dependent market economies (DMEs; Nölke and Vliegenthart 2009), mixed-market economies and emerging market economies (MMEs and EMEs; Hancké et al. 2007a), and governed market economies (GMEs; Weiss 2010) lack significant complementarities. As such, they are more descriptions of clusters of traits, and perhaps useful for other typologies, but they lack the coherent dynamics and self-reinforcing complementarities of a variety of capitalism.

Because the complementarities in CMEs, NMEs, and LMEs are well covered elsewhere (see, for example, Hall and Soskice 2001; Crouch et al. 2005), this section concentrates on complementarities in hierarchical capitalism. Then, to illustrate differences in complementarities across the four varieties, the last part of this section briefly contrasts one type of complementarity – between skill

---

[17] In one exception, Amable (2005, 374) mentions briefly possible negative effects and notes that institutional complementarities may also generate benefits only for a some groups, which is a useful point of departure as well for thinking about complementarities in hierarchical capitalism.

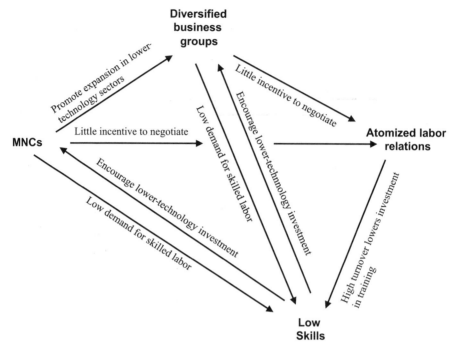

FIGURE 2.1. Core Complementarities in Hierarchical Capitalism

regimes and employment relations – across all four varieties. This set of comparisons highlights the particular negative complementarities in hierarchical capitalism.

In hierarchical capitalism, complementarities are strong, though variable across spheres, and work to reinforce hierarchical relations among and within firms and foreclose alternative interactions based on networks, markets, or negotiation (see Figure 2.1). The following discussion briefly considers the main pairwise complementarities, with empirical illustration from Latin America. Despite occasional apparent similarities with LMEs or CMEs, complementarities in HMEs have distinct logics, and the analysis highlights how these complementarities impede evolution away from hierarchical capitalism to another variety.

*MNCs and business groups.* MNC dominance of higher technology, complex manufacturing, and tradable sectors increased the returns to business groups to invest elsewhere in commodity, simple manufacturing, and nontradable sectors. In terms of interfirm relations, MNCs and hierarchical business groups both thwart coordination of the sort found in CMEs, especially in business associations. MNCs often join local business associations, but they tend to participate less actively and have difficulty coordinating with local firms because they are subject to hierarchical control and management decisions taken abroad. When managers are foreign, language, culture, and shorter time horizons further undermine potential coordination among firms. Subsidiaries of domestic business groups may also make unreliable interlocutors – top management is outside the sector and may ultimately decide to exit (or attempt, as often happens, to buy up competitors). Hierarchical business groups also lack the networks that promoted "group-based" coordination in NMEs. Put abstractly, sustained coordination, formal or informal, is unlikely among agents (in subsidiary firms) of distant hierarchical principals (MNCs or group owners) with opaque and diverse interests.[18]

*MNCs, business groups, and atomized labor.* In political economies where they negotiate frequently, business and labor have incentives to organize to match their counterparts (Schmitter and Streeck 1999). If labor is well organized, then returns to business investment in collective action are higher, and vice versa. In hierarchical capitalism (as in most LMEs), business and labor rarely negotiate, and the disorganization of one reduces returns to organization for the other. In Latin America, the relative disengagement of business and labor with each other means that both groups tend to organize more to engage the state (Collier and Collier 1991; Schneider 2004). Low union density and the absence of other intermediating forums like works councils or factory committees reduce the potential gains to managers from negotiation and thereby increase the relative returns to hierarchical employment relations.

*MNCs, business groups, and low skills.* The lasting, perverse complementarities of a low-skill trap or equilibrium are well known (Booth and Snower 1996). The basic coordination problem is that workers do not invest individually in acquiring skills because firms do not offer high-skill, high-wage jobs. Firms in turn have incentives to invest in production processes that do not require skilled labor because skilled workers are scarce. This low-skill trap held through the 2000s for most of Latin America where both MNCs and business groups have relatively low demand for skilled labor. As noted earlier, domestic business groups specialized in lower technology commodity sectors and services, and had fewer incentives to invest in R&D, hire scientists and engineers, or train highly skilled workers. In one survey of Latin America, "the most striking result [was] the low level of R&D conducted by firms" (de Ferranti et al. 2003, 5). R&D expenditures in Latin America rarely exceeded the comparatively low level of .5 percent of GDP and more than three-quarters of that was public (Katz 2001, 4). Even when they hired skilled workers, business groups did not hire very many; "with respect to other regions of the world, the large Latin American companies . . . generate little employment" (IDB 2001, 37).

---

[18] MNCs and business groups also supplant LME-type markets. Because they substitute for financial markets, MNCs and domestic business groups constitute nonmarket forms of organizing corporate governance, yet, in contrast to the effects of nonmarket coordination in CMEs, there are fewer institutional incentives for their investment to be patient. Nonmarket organization of investment in HMEs allows business groups and MNCs to respond flexibly and rapidly to market signals; both forms of corporate governance are well suited to managing swift entry and exit.

Some MNCs are prominent in higher technology sectors, but several factors limit their demand for highly skilled workers. Where manufacturing FDI was higher, as in Mexican maquiladoras, the new jobs were low skill (Berg, Ernst, and Auer 2006, 124). Moreover, MNCs keep their R&D at home. By the 2000s, MNCs were investing very little in R&D in Latin America (ECLAC 2005). Last, MNCs are not likely to be a force (voice) pushing for upgrading education and skills in any given country because they have so many options in other countries (exit). In sectors characterized by low transport costs and decentralized production – automobiles, for example – MNCs can locate plants with varying skill requirements in areas where skills are already available. Moreover, MNCs pay higher wages than local firms (Berg 2006), so MNCs can easily poach skilled workers, which depresses even further the incentives for domestic firms to invest in training.

*Atomistic labor relations and low skills.* Median job tenure in Latin America was only 3 years, compared to 5 years in LMEs and 7.4 years in CMEs (including Japan; see Chapter 5). Changing jobs also often means changing sectors. For example, among Chilean workers who changed jobs in the 1990s, more than half switched from one sector to another (Sehnbruch 2006). Moreover, the frequent movement of workers between formal and informal employment presumably involves shifting among sectors with different skill requirements. This rapid turnover also reduces the incentives for both labor and management to put energy into improving plant- and firm-level intermediation, let alone establish the bases for longer-term trust and personal loyalties characteristic of NMEs. The crucial negative complementarity is that short job-tenure reduces returns to investing in skills.

*Low skills and business groups and MNCs.* In turn, the absence of large pools of skilled workers in hierarchical capitalism further discouraged domestic firms from investing in upgrading their production or in other higher technology sectors. Studies in the United States, for example, have shown that technology acquisition did not lead firms to upgrade training and skills, but rather firms that already had skilled workers invested more in new technologies (IDB 2003, 188). MNCs base decisions on new investment in part on the skills available in particular economies and can always move new investment to different countries (exit) rather than upgrade in an economy where they already operate. As Paus put it, "human capital is the single most important factor in attracting high-tech FDI to a small latecomer" (2005, 158).[19] Low technology investment coupled with high labor turnover may also facilitate diversification. That is, lower technology investment and the management of homogeneous flows of temporary, unskilled workers can become elements of, and increase returns to, economies of scope. Once a firm develops a successful strategy for borrowing

---

[19] Decisions based on skills are most important for efficiency-seeking FDI. MNCs may undertake market-seeking or especially resource-seeking FDI with less regard for available skills. See Chapter 4.

one technology and using it successfully with a flow of unskilled workers, then the barriers for replicating this strategy in other sectors are lower (see Amsden 1989). Last, the fewer skills workers have, along with high levels of turnover in the labor market (as well as a pervasive informal sector), the more easily workers can be replaced. This vulnerability to substitution on the labor side further bolsters hierarchical employment relations.

In sum, a range of complementary dynamics across multiple spheres of the economy reinforces core components of hierarchical capitalism. Later chapters elaborate on the brief summaries provided here. Most complementarities in HMEs reinforce, or increase returns to, hierarchical arrangements and encourage economic agents to extend hierarchy throughout their relations with managers, other firms, and workers. And, though insufficient to fix a stable equilibrium, these complementarities stem movement toward any of the other three varieties.

The issue of skills provides a revealing dimension for comparing complementarities across the four varieties of capitalism. In liberal economies, short-term employment and greater labor market mobility encourage incremental investment in general skills, while the returns to workers are lower for investments in sector and firm-specific skills (Estevez-Abe et al. 2001; Hall and Soskice 2001). For LME firms, the wide availability of general skills encouraged (i.e., increased returns to) new start-ups (and associated markets for venture capital) drawing on high-end general skills (as well as low-end service sectors like restaurants and retail that relied on low-wage, short-term employment). In hierarchical capitalism, as just noted, the complementarities were negative: short-term employment, and low demand for skills generally, discouraged worker investment in human capital overall. For employers in HMEs, the lack of high-end skills discouraged investment in complex manufacturing and services and favored instead concentrating in commodity production.

In CMEs, longer worker tenure encourages up-front investment in sector specific skills (and generous unemployment benefits reduce the risk of this investment). Moreover, multiple and encompassing forums for bargaining – industrial unions and plant level representation for workers through institutions like codetermination – provide opportunities for negotiating the distribution of gains in productivity from investment in training. These negotiations also give employers some assurance that, if they invest in workers' skills, skilled workers will not later exploit their (hold up) leverage over the firm. For employers then, investments in skill-intensive manufacturing and long-term incremental innovation have higher returns. In NMEs, the outcome, in terms of returns to investment in high-skill manufacturing are similar, but the logic is different because NMEs lack similar mechanisms for negotiation. Instead, trust-based expectations of lifetime employment and seniority-based pay increased returns to workers from investing in firm-specific skills (see Dore 2000; Thelen 2004).

Beyond the issue of skills, Hall and Soskice (2001, 18) argue further that the internal logics of different varieties of capitalism encourage stakeholders over time to adopt the full package of complementary institutions: economies with coordination or with markets in several spheres of the economy will tend to develop more of the same in other spheres. Once workers or employers in CMEs, for example, realize the benefits of coordination in one realm, they are more likely (and have the organizational capacity) to extend coordination to other areas, as well as to push the state to help them achieve coordination. This process of recognizing joint gains and extending them is also a plausible mechanism for isomorphism across institutions in NMEs.

However, isomorphism has a different dynamic in market and hierarchical capitalism where economic agents are not realizing joint gains through bargaining or trust.[20] Rather, managers and owners in LMEs and HMEs use their power and autonomy to push for, respectively, markets and hierarchies in other realms. Managers in liberal economies seek greater flexibility, and in fighting external restrictions, coming from either government or unions, they push for market relations in other realms. Managers in LMEs (who themselves have relatively brief tenure) are subject to the short-term monitoring of the stock market, and want maximum flexibility to meet immediate targets. In hierarchical capitalism, the goal is less market flexibility and more managerial control; however, the process and politics often look similar to LMEs as owners and managers work to restrict interference by unions and government in order to maximize returns to private hierarchy.

Similarly, the process of institutional maintenance differs across varieties. Over time, the institutional foundations of CMEs and NMEs such as business associations, keiretsu networks, labor unions, and codetermination require continual investment and repeated commitment by the stakeholders, as well as the state, to sustain them (Thelen 2001). In contrast, markets and hierarchies have greater institutional inertia and need less active support to persist. Moreover, it requires less effort to shift from coordination to markets and hierarchies than vice versa (Hall and Soskice 2001, 63). In most realms, it is more difficult to build networks of trust or institutionalized negotiation in LMEs and HMEs than it is to introduce markets and hierarchy to undermine or displace networks and bargaining in NMEs and CMEs.[21]

Overall, however, these various pressures for isomorphism are uneven and limited, and have not pushed all countries towards purer types. Many countries sustain anomalous features (strong unions, for example, in liberal countries like Great Britain [historically], Ireland, and Australia) for long periods despite employer pressures to make them more institutionally compatible. Other countries maintain clearer hybrid mixtures of institutions over long periods (what

---

[20] See Höpner (2005) for a full review of different theories of institutional coherence.

[21] On the weakening of networks and coordination and the increase in market forces especially in equity and labor markets in Japan and Germany, see Yamamura and Streeck (2003), Lincoln and Gerlach (2004), and Lincoln and Shimotani (2010).

Hall and Soskice call the Mediterranean variety including France and Italy).[22] Moreover, other pressures may counter isomorphism. For instance, the recent expansion in stock market activity (spurred in part by the entry of foreign portfolio investment) is displacing banks and cross-shareholding, reducing blockholding, and, in the process, making many CME and NME economies resemble LMEs more, at least on the dimension of corporate ownership (Lane 2003; Streeck 2009). However, some of these same exogenous pressures, especially increasing capital flows, as well as high demand for commodities, seem to reinforce isomorphism in LMEs and HMEs, which underscores the main point that the sources of isomorphism are variable across types.

In sum, a range of different kinds of complementarities and compatibilities give coherence and continuity, though not stable equilibria, to each of the four varieties. Capitalist systems are always evolving; complementarities make that evolution incremental and path dependent rather than abrupt and radical. In individual cases, complementarities are among a range of pressures that shape a process of constant evolution, alongside a series of large exogenous shocks, from economic crises of the twentieth century to globalization pressures of the twenty-first century, that have reverberated through all varieties of capitalist economies. However, to the extent that economies sustain divergent institutional configurations, their respective complementarities are a large part of the story.

## IV. Conclusions and Comparisons

My analysis has stressed commonalities among the larger countries of Latin America on the core features of hierarchical capitalism, but the region is quite heterogeneous, and some countries deviate sufficiently from the mean to warrant consideration for separate classification. Venezuela's oil rents, for example, make it an outlier, especially in terms of the weight and role of the state in the economy. Venezuela still shared many HME features such as low skills and large business groups, but analytically it may have more in common with other large petro states such as Indonesia and Russia in a variety of political capitalism (Karl 1997). Oil and gas rents in Ecuador and Bolivia pushed their political economies in a similar direction.

Another change that affected some of the larger countries was a significant expansion in equity markets in the 2000s (Stallings 2006). One hypothesis would be that the countries at the vanguard of this expansion, Chile and Brazil, would be trending toward LME forms of corporate governance. Although there are signs of more dispersed ownership and greater participation by institutional investors, both foreign and domestic, nearly all companies in both countries still have controlling blockholders, in most cases families. Overall, these variations –

---

[22] For a stronger argument that purer types generate higher growth than do hybrids, see Hall and Gingerich (2009).

more of degree than of kind – do not yet warrant excluding countries from the category of hierarchical capitalism, but they do help identify potential sources of future change and movement away from HME complementarities toward other possible types of capitalism. Chapter 8 returns to an analysis of intraregional variation.

Outside Latin America, the core features of hierarchical capitalism also seem prominent in some other middle-income countries. However, East Asia (especially Taiwan and Korea) differs greatly from Latin America along all four dimensions of HMEs. East Asia had higher educational and skill levels and lower levels of FDI and socioeconomic inequality. Diversified business groups dominate the domestic private sector in both regions, but, as discussed in the next chapter, Asian business groups were more active in manufacturing and ultimately moved into higher-technology sectors (Schneider 2009b). A last difference is the stronger role in East Asia of business associations and other forms of interfirm cooperation, usually enforced or subsidized by the state. Despite some interregional similarities, countries such as Korea and Taiwan differ significantly enough to exclude them from the HME category. The general point, examined further in Part II, is that not all developing countries have hierarchical capitalism, nor is hierarchical capitalism a necessary consequence of low levels of development.

For now, to recapitulate, this chapter sought to make four contributions to the debate on comparative capitalisms. First, it proposed ideal types structured by four guiding principles – markets, bargaining, trust, and hierarchy – that consistently inform a diverse set of relations among stakeholders. Second, this fourfold typology introduced a new principle, hierarchy, that was missing from earlier debates in comparative capitalism, but that has long been a basis for a wide range of nonmarket relations in capitalist systems. Third, the inclusion of hierarchy allows a broader consideration of types of firms, especially MNCs and diversified business groups, that dominate production in much of the world. Bringing MNCs back in as more than simple institution takers is crucial to understanding the potential impact of globalization, economic integration, and the evolution of economies outside the developed world. Last, the incorporation of HMEs extends the potential geographic scope of the varieties of capitalism perspective to include many developing countries.

PART II

BUSINESS, LABOR, AND INSTITUTIONAL
COMPLEMENTARITIES

# 3

# Corporate Governance and Diversified Business Groups

## Adaptable Giants

## I. Introduction

In 1980, the largest private domestic firm in Mexico, Banamex, was a sprawling, highly diversified (with dozens of subsidiaries), closely owned, and family-controlled business group, also known as a *grupo económico* or just grupo. Twenty-five years later, the Banamex group was long gone, and many observers expected that decades of profound economic and political liberalization would have transformed the rest of the corporate landscape as well. Yet, by the mid-2000s, the largest private firm in Mexico, and for that matter in all of Latin America, the grupo Carso, was a similarly sprawling, widely diversified (nearly 200 subsidiaries), family-controlled business group (Grosse 2007). The names may change, but the corporate form lives on. Similar comparisons could be made for the other large countries of the region. In fact, for the last 50 years, scholarship on large domestic firms has consistently documented the dominance of family-owned, diversified business groups (Schneider 2005).

In the absence of deep equity and credit markets, business groups, along with MNCs, have been the main private institutions for mobilizing large-scale investment.[1] Latin America businesses could not finance investment through domestic bank finance (as in CMEs) or stock markets (as in LMEs) and relied instead on retained earnings, international loans, or loans from state agencies (see Figure 3.1). By one estimate, even companies listed on the Brazilian stock exchange relied on retained earnings for about 75 percent of their financing

---

[1] Financial markets in Latin America were "in fact very small ... On average the ratio of credit to the private sector to GDP in the 1990 s was close to 35 percent, roughly a third of the size of the average credit markets in East Asia and the developed countries" (IDB 2001, 57). Despite significant growth through the 2000s, financial markets remained small compared to other developing regions and relative to Latin America's level of development (de la Torre, Ize, and Schmukler 2012).

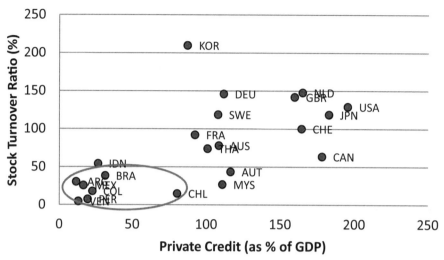

FIGURE 3.1. Private Credit and Stock Market Turnover Ratio. *Note:* The other measure for stock markets is often the value of total capitalization. The relative ranking of countries is similar to that for turnover, but some countries such as Chile have much higher rankings by capitalization. However, turnover is usually a better measure because it gauges how active markets are. The measure of private credit in this figure includes consumer and mortgage credit, and so is not a precise measure for assessing firm financing. Another measure of the percentage of firms using banks to finance investment shows pronounced differences among Mexico (3 percent) and Argentina (7 percent) versus Chile (29 percent), Colombia (31 percent), and Brazil (48 percent; World Bank Enterprise Surveys, data.worldbank.org/indicator/IC.FRM.BNKS.ZS, accessed 23 August 2011).

needs (Claessens, Klingebiel, and Lubrano 2000). Early analyses of business groups emphasized their crucial role in pooling capital and acting as internal capital markets (Leff 1978). Moreover, individual and institutional investors and banks did not own large enough shares to get on boards (save pension funds in a few companies in the 2000s). Markets for corporate control did not exist, and business groups passed instead within families from one generation to the next.

By some measures, stock markets in Latin America grew a lot after 1990, especially measured by total market capitalization which more than quadrupled from 8 percent of GDP in 1990 (on average for the seven largest economies) to 34 percent in 2003. However, during the same period, turnover fell from 30 to 20 percent, and the number of firms listed actually dropped from 1,624 to 1,238. In contrast, during the same period in seven developing countries of East and Southeast Asia, market capitalization almost doubled to 80 percent of GDP, turnover increased slightly to 152 percent, and the number of listed firms more than doubled (Stallings 2006, 124). Even where stock markets had grown substantially, as in Brazil and Chile, the largest markets (proportionally) in the region, they were in fact smaller than traditional measures would indicate. For example, in Chile, stock market capitalization surged in 2003 to 119 percent of GDP, however, many listed firms traded only a small portion of their total value, liquidity was low, and the turnover ratio was only 8 percent, which is "very low by international standards" (Stallings 2006, 158–59) and well below even regional averages.

The relative absence of external financing and powerful outside investors makes for a stark contrast with liberal and coordinated capitalisms. Flourishing equity markets are a hallmark of liberal capitalism in Great Britain and the United States and the strategic relationship uppermost in the minds of most managers of listed firms. The crucial comparable relationship for managers in coordinated capitalism, at least in the twentieth century, was with banks that held both long-term credits and significant equity stakes, which put bankers on the boards of many companies. In hierarchical capitalism, neither equity markets (and associated stake holders like institutional investors and stock analysts) nor private banks have much if any influence over large firms, nor are relations with these external financial sectors and their agents among the most important for managers of MNCs and business groups. Instead, the key strategic relationships for managers in hierarchical capitalism are with those who own the firm: families for most business groups and MNC headquarters. Consequently, rather than examine equity markets and banking systems in Latin America to make direct comparisons to the literature on comparative capitalism, this chapter and the next focus on the corporate structures and the direct owners of large firms to understand the origins of firm strategy and behavior.

Despite their prominence, systematic, long-term, cross-national data on the size, structure, and behavior of business groups are lacking in part because controlling shares are obscured, and many firms are unlisted and therefore publish no financial information. For scholars who do undertake the painstaking work of estimating the size and reach of business groups, the results are consistently large.

- In Mexico by the 1980s, there were 121 major diversified groups (Camp 1989, 174). By the mid-1990s, the 59 largest business groups accounted for 15 percent of GDP (Amsden 2001, 231).
- In Chile in the 1950s, the 11 largest business groups controlled nearly 300 firms (Lagos 1961 cited in Johnson 1967, 47). The holdings of the Edwards group for example included a bank, a newspaper, the beer monopoly, coal and gold mining, a real estate firm, and an insurance company that in turn controlled other industrial firms (Johnson 1967, 53). By the 2000s, the 20 largest firms in Chile produced half of GDP (Waissbluth 2011, 37).
- In Colombia, the four largest business groups (accounting for 20 percent of GDP) controlled 278 firms in 1998 and had minority holdings in other

firms (Rettberg 2000, chap. 3, p. 16). In 2006, 90 percent of the largest
523 nonfinancial firms belonged to twenty-eight business groups (and most
of the fifty-one nongroup firms were subsidiaries of MNCs). More than
half these firms belonged to the five largest business groups that operated on average in seven different sectors (González et al. 2011a, 7, 1,
22).

* In Argentina in the 1990s, the forty largest groups participated in about 700
  firms, most of which were on the list of the 1,000 largest firms in the country
  (Bisang 1998, 151, 156).[2]

These calculations come from different periods and use different methods,
but at a minimum, they show that any attempt to characterize capitalism in
Latin America has to devote considerable attention to business groups as key
institutions for corporate governance and mobilizing investment, technology,
and managerial talent.

Changes in recent decades brought additional reasons to focus on big business. The disputes of the 1990s pitted markets against states with the often-
explicit claim that once state intervention was reduced, markets would lead
development. In fact, the main protagonists are not markets but businesses;
the opposite of state-led development is not market-led development but rather
business-led development. Exports, investment, R&D, productivity, and potential movement toward knowledge economies came to depend by the 2000s primarily on private business. Even when, as in much of the region, governments
in the late 2000s began intervening more, policy success depended heavily on
the capacity of private firms to respond to policy incentives. Among the hundreds of thousands of firms in Latin America, the largest hundreds, or, in many
instances, the largest dozens, are crucial. Although they account for a minority
share of GDP, this share leads in terms of investment, R&D, and innovation.[3]
Historically, large firms defined development trajectories in many rich countries (Chandler, Amatori, and Hikino 1997). Large firms in Latin America are
even more prominent given the comparative scarcity and underperformance of
medium-sized firms (Karcher and Schneider 2012).

Although scholarship in Latin America has long focused on business groups,
they rarely came up in English publications. This neglect shifted in the 2000s
with a new cottage industry – among consulting firms, business press, and some
academic studies – that focused on the aggressive internationalizing by some

---

[2] On business groups and diversification in Venezuela and Ecuador, see, respectively Naím and
Francés (1995, 166–67) and Conaghan (1988, table 2, 46, see also 33–45).

[3] In earlier developers, big business made four contributions to growth: (1) exploiting economies
of scale; (2) firms became the "locus of learning for the initial development and continued
enhancement of their product-specific intangible organizational assets"; (3) big business was
the core of "network of suppliers, equipment makers, retailers, advertisers, designers..."; and
(4) "primary driver of technological advancement through their heavy investment in research
and development activities" (Chandler and Hikino 1997, 26). See also Herrera and Lora (2005).

business groups from Latin America.[4] This reporting, some of it breathless, gives the mistaken impression that all business groups are surging abroad. But, this reporting has a severe selection bias; these studies sample only on those firms succeeding abroad with little attention to business groups that are not. Understanding the subset of internationalizing business groups and what is driving them abroad is important, but it is not the full story. This chapter tries to redress this bias and so starts with some empirical background on business groups. In addition, the main goals of this chapter are to show (1) the resilience of business groups in Latin America and their expansion on the heels of the commodity boom; (2) major differences among types of business groups – organic, portfolio, and policy induced – with contrasts between business groups in Latin America and Asia; and (3) the limitations of business groups in Latin America in generating innovation and high-skill employment.

## II. Structures and Functions

Business groups in Latin America are characterized by concentrated owner-ship, family control, and multisectoral diversification. In terms of *ownership concentration*, virtually all listed firms in Latin America have a controlling shareholder, usually owning well above the common threshold for blockhold-ing of 20 percent. Sometimes, the ultimate ownership is obscured by pyra-mid schemes and nonvoting shares, but studies that unravel these complex structures invariably find in the end a single controlling shareholder, family, or controlling bloc. In addition, many large firms are privately held and are not listed on stock exchanges. Business groups place a high value on con-trol and pay high premia when acquiring control of a firm. The premia for block and voting purchases (which confer control rights) over the market value to minority shareholders were, respectively, 34 and 36 percent in Mexico, 15 and 23 percent in Chile, 65 and 23 percent in Brazil, 16 and 29 per-cent in Korea, but only 2 and 2 percent in the United States (World Bank 2007, 51).

*Family capitalism* is endemic in Latin America (see IDE 2004). In the 2000s, more than 90 percent of the 32 largest business groups in Latin America were controlled by families and most had several family members in top management positions (Schneider 2005). Families owned most business groups in Central America (Segovia 2005, 24), and families controlled 27 of the 28 largest busi-ness groups in Colombia.[5] In a study of the ownership structure in the mid

---

4  On the business press side, this chapter cites a number of business school case studies as well as reports from the Boston Consulting Group on "Global Challengers." In the academic press, see, among others, Goldstein (2007), Fleury and Fleury (2011), Beausang (2003), and Ramamurti and Singh 2009.

5  Personal communication from Maximiliano González, 9 December 2011. See González et al. (2011a, 2011b). Moreover, thousands of large nonlisted firms in Latin America are presumably family owned (Garrido and Peres 1998, 32). In the United States, in contrast, only a third of

1990s of the 20 largest firms in 27 countries, the two Latin American countries in the sample, Mexico and Argentina, ranked first and third in terms
of the highest proportion of firms controlled by families, 100 percent and
65 percent, respectively (La Porta et al. 1999, 492, 494). The average for
the whole sample of 27 countries, almost all developed countries, was only
30 percent family owned (where one family owned at least 20 percent of the
firm). Family ownership usually means hands-on management by the family.
The 34 largest private domestic firms in Mexico were all family owned, and all
had family members on the board and in top management positions (Hoshino
2006, 166). In the Grupo Carso, the largest business group in Latin America,
Carlos Slim filled eight of the top 21 management positions with relatives (three
sons, one son-in-law, and four other relatives; Elizondo 2011, 199).

*Multisectoral diversification* and conglomeration among large domestic corporations are long-standing traditions in Latin America. Although many business groups in Latin America did rationalize their diverse holdings after the
1990s, they did not get swept up in the de-conglomeration fad that took hold
in the United States in the 1980s.[6] For many business groups, the scope of diversification covers not just one or two sectors but many of the main sectors of the
economy, and conglomerate subsidiaries regularly have little market or technological relation to one another (Garrido and Peres 1998, 13). In the 1990s,
across eight countries of Latin America, 34 of the 40 largest business groups had
diversified into four or five different sectors (out of five total: primary, manufacturing, construction, services, and finance; Durand 1996, 93). In my survey, the
largest groups had on average subsidiaries in over three of seven different sectors, and only about a quarter specialized more narrowly in one or two sectors
(Schneider 2008).[7] The average diversification was lower (fewer than three sectors) in the largest countries (Mexico and Brazil), which had more specialized
firms, compared to an average closer to four sectors for business groups in Chile,
Colombia, and Argentina. In Central America, business groups are "exceed-
ingly" (*sumamente*) diversified usually across sectors like finance, transportation, tourism, construction, commerce, and agro-industry (Segovia 2005, 21).

the largest, *Fortune* 500 firms were family controlled (Colli and Rose 2003, 339). By another
calculation, the percentage of inheritors in command of big businesses in Great Britain, France,
and Germany ranged from 15 to 35 percent in the early decades of the twentieth century but
dropped below 10 percent by the end of the century (Cassis 1997, 126). For my sample of groups
in Latin America, the proportion of controlling heirs is over three quarters (Schneider 2008).

[6] In the United States, conglomeration was popular in the 1960s and 1970s, but by the 1980s was
vilified as "the biggest collective error ever made by American business" (Davis, Diekman, and
Tinsley 1994, 563). The subsequent specializing shift in the United States to "core competencies,"
"refocusing," and "back-to-basics" did not catch on in Latin America (or most of the rest of the
developing world; Knoke 2001, 117–19).

[7] In Chile "on average, almost 80% of large listed firms are affiliated to an economic group"
(Lefort 2005, 8). Even within sectors, firms in Latin America tended to diversify more than
similar firms in developed countries, largely in response to fluctuations in demand. See, for
example, Edmund Amann (2000, especially 233–48) on the capital goods industry in Brazil.

Were de-conglomeration a natural response to market reform, we would expect to find it well advanced in Chile, the country with the longest neoliberal orientation. In fact, in Chile, "groups are the predominant form of corporate structure." Some 50 conglomerates control "91 percent of the assets of listed non-financial companies in Chile. There is no clear decreasing trend in these figures," (Lefort and Walker 2004, 4). Diversified conglomeration in Chile was the predominant form of corporate organization under a succession of very different development strategies: ISI (1950s and 1960s), radical neoliberal reform (late 1970s), and pragmatic neoliberalism (1980s on; see Silva 1996; Lefort 2005). Each period offered some peculiar incentives to diversify, and different business groups dominated in successive periods, yet what stands out is the enduring popularity of the business-group form.

The history of the Luksic group illustrates well this progression. Founded in the 1950s in copper mining, the group expanded broadly into metal processing, electricity, manufacturing, shipping, fishing, forestry, and agriculture. During the socialist government of the early 1970s, the Luksic group expanded abroad into Argentina, Brazil, and Colombia. After the military coup in 1973, the group resumed investment in Chile and diversified into telecommunications, hotels, banking, beer, and railways. Much of the more recent diversification in Luksic and other business groups had a defensive quality, as business groups moved into naturally protected, nontradable, and service sectors. By the late 1990s, about three-quarters of business groups ($N = 33$) had subsidiaries in sectors not subject to competition from imports, perhaps a more predictable, risk-averse response to trade opening (Schneider 2008). As noted earlier, business groups in Central America were concentrated in nontradable sectors like construction, tourism, and finance (Segovia 2005, 21).

Throughout most of the twentieth century, uncertainty prevailed along major economic indicators like growth, government spending, inflation, exchange rates, and interest rates (IDB 2003, 116, 133). These uncertainties encouraged defensive diversification precisely into unrelated sectors – a trademark of Latin American business groups – in order that some part of the group would be spared any given economic shock. For example, in announcing in 2005 the establishment of a construction subsidiary, Juan Rebelledo, the vice president of the huge mining firm, Grupo México, explained that "the construction firm has the advantage, the same as with the railroad firm [another subsidiary], of being countercyclical to copper, so that when the prices of that metal go down a lot, these firms can provide liquidity, and that is the advantage of having a relatively diversified and controlled portfolio" (*Reforma* online, 23 August 2005). Or, as a manager at the Brazilian conglomerate Camargo Corrêa put it more starkly: "if we had stayed only in construction, we'd be dead by now" (interview, 2 August 2006).[8] Volatility also encourages blockholding as

---

[8] See Schneider (2008) on other motives for diversification ranging from small financial and stock markets to ideas. Diversification is common even in the United States among privately held,

owners seek to maintain tight control in order to be able to adjust rapidly to changing circumstances (Silva 2002, 66; Garrido and Peres 1998, 32). Lastly, as is discussed in Chapters 5 and 6, within particular firms and plants, volatility encouraged managers to maintain flexibility with regard to labor and payroll (given expectations that abrupt downsizing could be required at regular intervals), which reduced incentives for long-term employment arrangements, for investing in worker training, and for establishing enduring institutions for ongoing intermediation with employees.

Given arguments that dispersed ownership in LME corporations is a functional adaptation to the larger policy swings associated with majoritarian governments in LMEs (Hall and Soskice 2001; Gourevitch and Shinn 2005, 10), one might expect policy instability to push developing countries toward dispersed ownership. In fact, HMEs are as well adapted as LMEs to respond to short-term swings in policy and macroeconomic volatility. Centralized corporate control in hierarchical capitalism allows business groups and MNCs to respond flexibly and rapidly to market signals; both corporate forms are well suited to managing swift entry and exit (Andrade, Barra, and Elstrodt 2001, 83; Grosse 2007). In some ways, hierarchy may be an even better adaptation for managing volatility, because controlling families do not have to consult with corporate boards or worry about the reaction of the stock market, as managers in liberal economies do.

A last advantage that many business groups enjoy over potential competitors is that they operate in sectors with high barriers to entry, either natural or regulatory. A first set of markets in which groups dominate tends naturally to oligopoly or monopoly. At first glance, it is puzzling that so many business groups such as Cemex (Mexico), Loma Negra (Argentina), Votorantim (Brazil), Briones (Chile), and Sindicato Antioqueño (Colombia) grew out of cement and continue to have large operations there. However, because transportation costs are high, it is fairly easy for firms to capture large shares of regional markets and to use oligopolistic pricing to generate the cash flow to expand elsewhere. Cemex is the most famous case in this sector (Marchand, Chung, and Paddack 2002; Schrank 2005). Cemex controls around two-thirds of the Mexican market (and large shares of other markets in Latin America), and Mexican consumers pay double what U.S. customers pay (Schrank 2005, 109). In the early 2000s, the Mexican market accounted for one-third of Cemex's revenues but two-thirds of its operating income. This cash flow helped bankroll Cemex's aggressive strategy of foreign acquisitions. Many other business groups grew out of beer and soft drinks (Ambev, Cisneros, Modelo, Femsa, Ardilla Lülle, and Santo Domingo), baked goods (Bimbo and Gruma), or processed foods (Brazil Foods). These products all require extensive and expensive distribution networks. These distribution networks in themselves raise barriers

family-controlled groups such as Pritzker and Cargill that are not subject to the specializing pressures of the stock market (see Ward 2004; Granovetter 2005, 430).

to entry, but the barriers can be prohibitive if producers can force retailers, formally or informally, into exclusive arrangements not to sell other brands.[9]

Another set of business groups operate in markets with regulatory barriers to entry. Several domestic newcomers to the ranks of the largest firms are airlines: TAM, Gol, and especially LAN. These are successful and sometimes innovative airlines, but they would have had difficulties growing as fast as they did in the absence of government regulations that limit the access of foreign carriers and prohibit foreign carriers from operating domestic routes. In broadcasting, all governments regulate airwaves, and several business groups (Globo, Cisneros, and Azteca) started in the early days of television and grew with the medium. Other groups started in other sectors and later acquired television and radio operations (Santo Domingo, Luksic, Ardilla Lülle, and Loma Negra). Even when regulators allow new entrants, market leaders have rarely been displaced. Last, some groups benefit from barriers to entry by virtue of the natural resources they own. Although new discoveries are always possible, owners of large mines, prime agricultural land, or forests block others who might want to enter the sector. Oligopoly, regulatory protection, and barriers to entry all reduce competitive pressures and can allow business groups to reduce their efforts to invest and improve efficiency (as discussed later).

For the most part, I treat the three features of business group structure – concentrated blockholding, family control, and multisectoral diversification – as a composite whole because they occur so regularly together. However, it is also worth considering the micro complementarities among them, where the presence of one increases the returns from, or incentives for, the other two (see Figure 3.2). Thus, as noted earlier, the fact that the business group provides income and wealth over the long run to family members means that the incentives to diversify are greater than if the owners were dispersed investors or large institutional blockholders that have diversified portfolios outside any one firm (arrow 1 in Figure 3.2). Moreover, if families are owners, then diversification can ease succession crises and family relations generally by offering opportunities for multiple heirs to manage separate pieces of the business group (interview, José Ermírio de Moraes Neto, Votorantim, 9 December 2005) (Lansberg and Perrow 1991, 130). On a slightly different dimension (of positive emotional, but negative economic, returns), family owners may hold on longer to subsidiaries for sentimental reasons where professional managers might be more inclined to sell (interviews with top managers at Camargo Correa and Itaú, 2–3 August 2006).

At the same time, diversification can increase the returns to family over professional management. Diversification raises information costs and asymmetries and thereby exacerbates principal/agent problems for which family

---

[9] In 1998, the flour and tortilla giant Gruma tried to challenge Bimbo in the market for packaged bread. Bimbo retaliated by impeding the expansion of Gruma's distribution network. In the end, Gruma sold its bread operations to Bimbo (Elizondo 2011, 162).

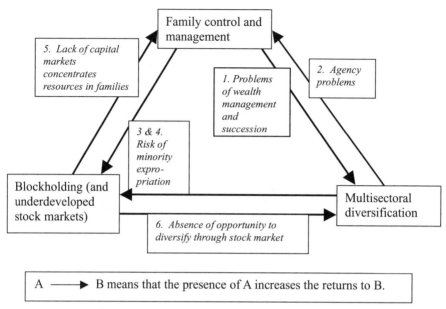

FIGURE 3.2. Complementarities among Blockholding, Family Control, and Diversification (Schneider 2008: 389).

management is one solution (arrow 2 in Figure 3.2; Khanna and Palepu 1999, 280). Furthermore, if diversification does not require cutting-edge technological or managerial expertise, then professional talent is potentially less valuable than is strong principal control over agents of the sort provided by kinship ties (see Granovetter 1995, 108–09). Moreover, if imperfections (like the oligopolies common in many countries) generate rents in particular markets, they create further incentives to diversify as well as additional transparency and agency problems between owners and managers, making tight hierarchical and/or family control again attractive options (Gourevitch 2003).[10]

Both family control and diversification in turn increase the returns to blockholding by increasing the discount that potential minority investors would demand (arrows 3 and 4 in Figure 3.2). Diversification raises information costs to outside investors, and the resulting organizational complexity increases opportunities for majority shareholders to expropriate them. Similarly, outside investors are wary of family firms, in part because families have tax and other incentives to extract maximum salaries, benefits, and consumption from the business group (interview, José Luis Osorio, 5 December 2005; see IIF 2004, 7).

---

[10]  Roe (2003) argues that less competitive markets offer opportunities for managers and workers to seek rents and thus encourage owners to counter with concentrated ownership and close oversight.

From the family perspective, if outsiders are unwilling to pay what business-group owners think their shares are worth, then why sell them? Furthermore, as noted earlier, the dominance of blockholding, of which the underdevelopment of the stock market is both cause and consequence, favors family control and diversification (arrow 5 in Figure 3.2). The absence of opportunities for diversifying through stock markets increases the returns to internal conglomerate diversification (arrow 6 in Figure 3.2; Schneider 2008). Last, the lack of well-developed financial intermediation through banks, bonds, stocks, and other means does not so much increase the returns to family control as make it the default.

Complementarities and background factors often support institutional maintenance through incentives not to press for change rather than active support for the institutional status quo. For example, conglomeration and family capitalism were encouraged by high transaction costs (weak legal framework, threats from state, underdeveloped capital markets, etc.), and in a vicious cycle, once business groups overcame these costs, they had competitive advantages over other kinds of firms. Once the largest firms found solutions to problems of volatility, finding capital, and access to technology, they then had few incentives to press for reforms to mitigate these problems thereby giving smaller, non-conglomerated firms a better chance to compete with them. So, for example, because they had internal funds, MNCs and conglomerates reduced overall demand for capital through stock markets, and they had few incentives to pressure governments to expand stock markets.

## III. Comparative Perspectives on Strategy[11]

Cross-nationally, business groups vary substantially in size. Overall, larger business groups tend to come from larger economies, especially within Latin America, though some behemoths emerged in small countries such as Singapore and Sweden, and many of the largest business groups from developing countries came from medium-sized Korea (Amsden 2001). A stronger relationship to geography emerges when the measure is the share of GDP; business groups in smaller countries tend to account for a bigger share of their smaller economies (Schneider 2009b, table 1).

Beyond country size, the major explanations for variation in group size are political and policy related. In one sample comparing the sales of the top ten business groups in 1995 in four Asian and four Latin American countries, the average share of GDP for the largest Asian groups (25 percent) was nearly double the share of the top ten in Latin America (14 percent; calculated from Guillén 2001, 72). Policy and development strategy provide a first explanation. In the twentieth century, export promotion policies in East Asia allowed firms to grow, whereas ISI in Latin America limited the markets business groups

---

[11] This section draws on Schneider (2009b), which provides more data and detail.

produced for. Moreover, as discussed in the following, policies promoting the large presence of MNCs and state enterprises in Latin America further restricted opportunities for business groups there to expand. Lastly, Amsden (2001, 225–32) argues that greater levels of inequality in Latin America (compared to East Asia) undermined the legitimacy of big business groups and prompted governments to restrain their growth. In a global survey, the IDB (2001, 35, 40) found that "the largest firms in Latin America are very small in comparison with other regions in the world. Among seven regions, Latin America comes in last in average size in terms of total assets of the countries' 25 largest companies." It found that the three variables that explained 85 percent of the variance were country size, size of the financial sector, and quality of infrastructure.

Business groups also vary in overall strategies for diversification that, simplifying, revolve around two main economic incentives – economies of scope and risk reduction – as well as policy measures that directly or indirectly encourage diversification.[12] Economies of scope offer business groups opportunities to transfer existing organizational models, market strategies, and experienced personnel to new activities in ways that tend to flatten learning curves and reduce costs. Korean chaebol found economies of scope in the process of licensing production technologies and starting up new plants to use them (Amsden 1989). The teams that worked in executing one project could then be mobilized to implement the next one. The sharing of "management know-how" was crucial for the chaebol overall and especially when entering new businesses (S.-J. Chang 2003, 90).[13] Other diversified firms generate expertise in multiple sectors where new products have long gestation periods and high development costs. So, for example, General Electric and Siemens both produced complicated, costly machinery like locomotives, jet engines, and electric turbines. Other groups find economies of scope not on the front end of product development but rather on the delivery end. Proctor and Gamble has economies of scope in branding, marketing, and managing relations with advertisers and retailers that can lower costs across a range of different products. Similarly, groups that produce outputs that are measured in millions of tons such as processed metals (e.g., steel, aluminum, or copper), cement, and other minerals, develop expertise in bulk logistics that can be applied to a variety of commodities. The Brazilian group Votorantim, for example, produces cement, aluminum, pulp and paper, and orange juice. The production technologies and markets for

---

[12] For discussions of a range of other economic incentives to diversify based largely on market imperfections and transaction costs such as underdeveloped capital markets, legal systems, and informational intermediaries, see Leff (1978), Khanna and Palepu (1997), Khanna and Yafeh (2007), and Grosse 2007. These incentives are more related to how companies adapt to their institutional environments and are less germane to the overall corporate strategies analyzed in this section.

[13] The Tata group in India had a deliberate long-term strategy for recruiting and training managers, promoting their mobility and communication across group firms, and assembling 'star teams' to solve problems in particular subsidiaries (Khanna and Palepu 1997, 49).

these products are quite different, but production in each case requires figuring out how to transport and process millions of tons of inputs and outputs.

A second main strategy for diversifying is risk management where business groups seek out subsidiaries that are subject to different market cycles. Historically, this was a major motivation for diversification in Turkish groups (Bugra 1994, 188). In Brazil, by the 2000s, some business groups were using sophisticated computer models to calculate precisely how countercyclical investment in a new sector might be, as well as to generate an overall indicator of a group's protection from market volatility (interview with manager at Camargo Correa, 2 August 2006). In contrast to economies of scope, risk reduction leads business groups to diversify into sectors that are as unrelated as possible, like hotels and mining, or steel and cattle. Risk reduction is a more intense motivation in business groups with core activities subject to wide price and demand fluctuations such as raw materials, industrial commodities (metals), construction, and capital goods. And, as noted earlier, volatility has generally been much higher in Latin America than in Asia and Europe, which gives business groups in Latin America more reasons for unrelated, risk-reducing diversification.

Beyond these economic strategies for diversification, policy makers sometimes directly push, or entice, business groups into new sectors. When the Park regime in Korea embarked on the drive in heavy and chemical industries (HCI) in the 1970s, planners called on existing chaebol to develop new sectors. For example, the government "chose Hyundai and Daewoo to develop power plant facilities and Hyundai, Samsung, and Daewoo to build ships" (S.-J. Chang 2003, 54). In Latin America, when governments decided in the 1990s to privatize state enterprises, the only buyers with sufficient resources were local business groups or MNCs, and governments often preferred domestic buyers (Manzetti 1999). In a more diffuse fashion, tax incentives in Taiwan in the 1960s encouraged businesses to establish new firms rather than to expand existing ones, and these new firms had lasting effects on the structure and diversity of Taiwanese business groups for decades afterward (Chung 2001). Other policies provided more indirect incentives for diversification. Under ISI, for example, firms rarely exported, so once domestic markets were saturated in particular product lines, firms had nowhere to invest but in new sectors.

These various economic and political motives can be recombined to distinguish conceptually among three ideal types of diversified business groups: organic, portfolio, and policy induced (see Table 3.1). *Organic business groups*, develop largely according to the logics of economies of scope and vertical integration, and their subsidiaries are thus likely to have stronger synergies in organization, personnel, and expertise. New investments are more likely to be greenfield plants. For example, from 1938 to 1993, Samsung created 62 new firms, nearly double the number it acquired, and most of the acquisitions came in the early decades and the establishment of new firms in the later decades. Moreover, many of the acquisitions were horizontal while the creation of firms was in new sectors (Kang, 1997, 37). Forays into new sectors through greenfield

TABLE 3.1. *Three Types of Diversified Business Groups*

|  | Organic | Portfolio | Policy Induced |
|---|---|---|---|
| Core motivations | economies of scope (and vertical integration) | risk management | government incentives |
| Scope of diversification | narrower | broadest | broad |
| Integration of management | high | variable | variable |
| Group ties to subsidiary | longer term | shorter term | shorter term |
| Examples | General Electric (United States), Votorantim (Brazil), Samsung (Korea), Techint (Argentina), Formosa (Taiwan) | bank centered groups, Banamex (Mexico), Pritzker (United States), Camargo Correa (Brazil), Luksic (Chile), Wallenberg (Sweden) | Chaebol (1970s), privatization acquisitions, Israeli defense contractors, Carso (Mexico), Suharto-linked groups (Indonesia) |

investment require long lead times and tend to occur incrementally and sequentially, and the resulting subsidiaries are likely to remain in business groups for long periods or forever. Management connections across member firms tend to be denser and closer, especially in projects tapping economies of scope that rely on the transfer of personnel among subsidiaries.

*Portfolio business groups* diversify to manage risk and to maximize returns buying and selling firms. Managing risk focuses the attention of owners of business groups in more volatile sectors or countries while opportunistic acquisitions are likely to inform group strategies in more stable environments. Portfolio business groups are more likely to buy firms rather than to build them from the ground up, and to spin off firms if they run into trouble. Bank-centered business groups tend naturally to develop as portfolio groups. Because portfolio business groups often expressly buy subsidiaries in sectors completely unrelated to core group firms, the technological incentives to integrate management are lower, and business group owners, especially in developed countries, often allow subsidiary managers considerable autonomy. However, as noted earlier, broad diversification raises problems of agency and information asymmetries, especially in less competitive markets and in developing countries, that can encourage greater management integration (often through kinship networks).

Last, *policy-induced business groups* diversify in response to government incentives or directives. As noted earlier, these policies can range from direct industrial promotion, such as the Korean HCI, to privatizations that draw firms into new sectors, to more indirect effects of tariff and other protections. This category would also include a subset of patrimonial business groups that arise in cases of purer political or crony capitalism under long-standing personal dictatorships such as those headed by Suharto, Marcos, or Putin, where governments determine the structure of groups more directly by distributing concessions to family, friends, and supporters (see, for example, Rivera [2003] on the Philippines).[14] Patrimonial groups may coexist with other groups; in Indonesia in 1996, the sales of "Suharto-linked groups" were nearly double those of "independent groups" (Hanani 2006, 188). In patrimonial groups, the pattern of diversification depends less on any market logic than on government created rents.

As ideal types, portfolio, organic, and policy-induced groups can be analytically distinguished, and countries or periods identified with the predominance of a particular type. In practice, however, some business groups may mix these strategies by combining, for example, a core set of organic subsidiaries with another set of risk-balancing portfolio investments. In other cases, organic or portfolio groups may be induced by particular policies to enter new sectors, especially during periods of rapid policy change. Over time, individual business groups may shift their predominant strategies. Samsung started out in the 1940s and 1950s under ISI as a bank-centered portfolio group, then shifted to a more policy-induced group after the military government took away its banks, but along the way, it developed economies of scope in project execution that helped it shift by the 1980s and 1990s to an organic group focused more on electronics technologies (Kang 1997, 37–45).

Despite this empirical complexity, the typology is still useful in identifying broad trends or clustering across countries and periods. According to one index, business groups in Taiwan and Korea were less diversified (1.65) than those in Southeast Asia (2.9) and Latin America (3.1) and were less likely to have financial subsidies (Khanna and Yafeh 2007, 334). These data fit with the view that groups in East Asia, especially Japan, Taiwan, and Korea, have tended to be more organic and clustered in manufacturing sectors with greater economies of scope (Amsden 2001). In contrast, countries with long-standing personal dictatorships (as in some countries in Southeast Asia and Central America) tend to generate more policy-induced, patrimonial groups, as do politicized processes of sweeping privatization (as in Chile in the 1970s), Argentina, and many countries of Eastern Europe. And portfolio groups tend to predominate when business groups grow out of banks or raw material commodities or in countries where volatility and uncertainty have been greater, as has been common in Southeast Asia and Latin America.

---

[14] The emerging capitalist economies of Russia, the Ukraine, and Romania have been characterized as patrimonial overall and dominated by "parasitic financial-industrial groups" (King and Szelényi 2005, 213). For a detailed case study of the rise of a patrimonial group in Bulgaria, the dominant Multigroup conglomerate, see Ganev (2001).

The discussion so far has focused largely on internal logics of diversification. These internal logics are the primary, often exclusive, focus in much of the literature on business groups that consequently misses the crucial external constraints or parameters that decisively shape group structure. Government policies established significant external boundaries for group expansion by setting the terms of group interaction with MNCs, state enterprises, and banks.[15] That is, when governments reserved certain sectors for state enterprises or MNCs, or put banks off limits, then business groups had to find other areas into which they could expand.

Countries vary a great deal in terms of the sectoral distribution and proportion of the production accounted for by MNCs. Among developed countries, as noted earlier, MNCs are rare in Japan, but more common in the United States and large countries of Europe. For most of the twentieth century, Swedish governments of varying ideological persuasions imposed severe restrictions on foreign ownership to protect national business groups from being taken over (Högfeldt 2004, 15). Among developing countries, governments excluded MNCs from many sectors in Korea and India but welcomed them in Latin America and Southeast Asia. In all these cases, government policy heavily conditioned, if not directly regulated, the presence of MNCs. For business groups, the most important impact of MNCs comes in terms of the opportunities they close off or leave open (see Chapter 4). In the formative decades of the 1960s and 1970s, the heavy presence of MNCs in Latin American manufacturing closed off opportunities and pushed business groups into services and commodities, whereas the relative absence of MNCs in Korea left open more possibilities for chaebol expansion in manufacturing (Maman 2002). There is nothing automatic about groups taking advantage of opportunities; however, once MNCs are established in particular sectors, domestic firms tend to avoid direct competition.

State enterprises also closed off some opportunities for business groups and expanded others. Cross-regional variations were similar to MNC presence, with state enterprises typically occupying larger slices of economies in Europe and Latin America than in Asia. State enterprises in most countries were concentrated in public utilities, mining, oil, and capital-intensive manufacturing sectors such as steel. Also, parallel to the story of MNCs, governments sometimes adopted policies in which state enterprises had to invest together with domestic firms or buy inputs from local suppliers which drew business groups into new sectors (Evans 1979). Last, as discussed later, the eventual privatization of many state enterprises after the 1980s opened previously closed options for business-group diversification.

---

[15] In one extreme example of setting parameters, Russian legislation in the 1990s stipulated that "banks could participate in only one financial-industrial group; banks could own no more than 10 percent of the stock of any company in the FIG; there could be no more than 20 firms in each FIG; there could be no more than 25000 workers at each firm; and there could be no more than 100000 workers overall" (Johnson 1997, 335).

Finally, differences in banking regulation had profound impacts on business-group evolution. Where banks faced few regulatory restrictions, they were usually core group enterprises. For example, the two largest business groups in Sweden, the Wallenberg and Handelsbank groups, grew in the early twentieth century out of their respective banks (Collin 1998, 726). In Latin America, through much of the twentieth century, banks were pivotal in the formation and evolution of business groups. In Central America, 16 of 28 business groups had operations in finance (calculated from Segovia 2005, 21–24).[16] Business groups without banks are more common in countries with legal and regulatory restrictions on business groups owning banks and on banks owning nonfinancial firms or lending to firms that are part of the same business group, as in the United States, Korea, India, Taiwan (pre-1980s), and Chile (post-1980s). Also, most governments around the world regulate foreign ownership of banks, so MNC purchases of domestic banks that once belonged to business groups are usually the result of government reforms to open the financial sector, as was common in Latin America in the 1990s and 2000s (Martinez-Diaz 2009).

In sum, government policies on these three kinds of ownership – MNCs, state enterprises, and banks (of or by other nonfinancial firms) – set clear limits on the range of diversification possible and hence explain a great deal of cross-national variation in business-group structure. Business groups may devise diversification strategies based on economies of scope or risk reduction, but they are ultimately constrained by the boundaries established by government policies. These three policy boundaries though differ in their effects over time. Banking regulations and state ownership (nationalization or privatization) can change quickly, sometimes overnight, and business groups can adjust just as quickly by buying (or relinquishing) banks and state enterprises. In contrast, MNC entry, especially in manufacturing, establishes a path-dependent boundary that is subject to much less change in the short run and has a decisive long-term impact on business-group strategy.

## IV. Responses to Liberalization and Globalization

Business groups also differed in their responses to financial shocks, market-oriented reforms, and globalization. Some business groups collapsed, from Daewoo, one of the largest chaebol, to many of the major groups in Peru. Several diversified business groups radically reinvented themselves as specialized firms. The sprawling Argentine conglomerate Bunge y Born underwent one of the most spectacular transformations as it sold off all but its core agribusiness interests and moved its headquarters to New York. Other business groups

---

[16] Similarly, the six largest Chinese-Filipino groups either started in finance or bought large financial firms after growing large in manufacturing (Rivera 2003, 95–97). And, four of the six largest South African groups in the 20th century either started in finance (especially insurance) or acquired major financial firms (Goldstein 2000, table 1).

were partially displaced by MNCs or by new kinds of leading firms (as in India; Goswami 2003). Most business groups streamlined operations, and divested at least some peripheral subsidiaries, and at the same time established new subsidiaries abroad. Not surprisingly, the comprehensive policy shifts of the 1990s had the greatest impact on policy-induced kinds of groups, and many of these went through massive restructuring. However, overall, globalization did not, as many expected, sound the death knell for diversified groups, and market reforms in some cases opened new opportunities for policy-induced diversification (see Schneider 2008).

Privatization programs, for example, gave many business groups opportunities to grow and diversify. The story of the Mexican group Carso, the largest in Latin America, is illustrative. Carlos Slim had made a fortune on the stock market in the 1980s but then started moving out of finance and, in the 1990s, bought Telmex, the fixed-line telephone monopoly, when the government put it up for sale. He acquired subsidiaries in many other sectors, but made telecommunications a new core business and leveraged it into an ambitious program of international expansion. Similarly, in Argentina in the early 1990s, one or more of the top 10 business groups participated in 32 of 54 firms privatized, usually in consortia with MNCs (Guillén 2001, 83). Governments often designed privatization programs to exclude foreign investors, thereby favoring domestic business groups. In Mexico, only five of dozens of major privatizations permitted the participation of foreign capital (World Bank 2007, 47–49).

Other market reforms increased pressures to de-diversify. The end of many promotion policies and trade protection removed the incentives for policy-induced holdings that business groups subsequently divested. For domestic business groups, the new wave of MNC entry after the 1990s closed off more sectors and options for diversification, especially in complex manufacturing and services. However, de-diversification did not go as far as many expected nor as far as the de-conglomeration wave in the United States in the 1980s. Chile embarked on radical economic liberalization in the 1970s, well ahead of most developing countries. However, by 1988, the average range of diversification for 10 groups was 7 different sectors, and the average number of subsidiaries was 9. Moreover, as free markets consolidated in the 1990s, the same 10 groups in fact increased their diversification to 8 sectors and 13 firms by 1996 (Khanna and Palepu 2000, 275). In Colombia, the five largest nonfinancial business groups streamlined only slightly from 1996 to 2006, following market reforms, reducing the number of subsidiaries from an average of 50 per group to 44 per group, operating in an average of 8 sectors in 1996 and 6.6 sectors in 2006 (calculated from González et al. 2011a, 22).[17]

---

[17] De-diversification did not go far in Asia either. From 1985 to 1997, the top 30 chaebol increased their extent of unrelated diversification. The index of diversification dropped rapidly in the post crisis restructuring after 1997, but by 2000, the index had dropped back only to the already high levels of 1985. As one disappointed observer put it, globalization "required chaebols to

Across the region, business groups in smaller countries tended to be more diversified than were those in larger countries. Among 33 business groups, the average number of sectors per group (using a different metric) was 4.5 in Chile, Colombia, and Argentina, compared to 2.5 sectors per business group in Mexico and 2.8 in Brazil (see Schneider 2008). Of the few large specialized firms in Latin American, most are either Mexican or Brazilian. Geographic proximity to the United States may also play some role in encouraging specialization in that Mexican firms, especially those initially based in the northern city of Monterrey such as Femsa (beverages), Vitro (glass), and Cemex, were more specialized and more likely to have adopted a U.S. style discourse on "core competence."[18] Overall, firms in large countries are bigger and may therefore find it easier to make acquisitions abroad in their core sectors, whereas business groups in smaller countries lack scale and opt instead to diversify domestically. This trend was especially apparent in Central America where business groups were very diversified (Segovia 2005).[19]

Family capitalism has evolved, albeit slowly and incrementally, since the 1990s. Among all types of large firms, family enterprises lost some ground in the 1990s to MNCs and scattered institutionally owned firms (especially ex-state enterprises; Goldstein and Schneider 2004, 61). However, the great majority of large, private domestic firms, remained family controlled, and even new business groups adopted traditional styles of family management.[20] In terms of direct family control, many firms shifted gradually to more professional management by hiring more outside managers, shifting family members out of formal management positions on to company boards, and sending heirs to get MBAs abroad (Miceli 2006). The process of moving families to the board was pronounced in Brazil and Chile, where general programs in improving corporate governance were also quite visible. However, it is still an open empirical question as to just how much control families really relinquished. For example, some family "board members" continued to work daily alongside professional

narrow their business focus to a few core competencies... [but] Chaebols failed to make this transition" (S.-J. Chang 2003, 78). In Taiwan, various diversification indicators for the largest 100 groups remained steady or increased after the liberalization of the 1980s and 1990s (Chung and Mahmood 2006, 80).

[18] See, for example, the management messages in Vitro's 2004 Annual Report, http://library .corporate-ir.net/library/10/108/108614/items/144715/general04.pdf.

[19] Despite its relatively small size, Chile has a disproportionate number of large firms, some of which (especially in retail and LAN) were specialized and internationalized. Other more traditional Chilean groups (Angelini, Matte, and Luksic for example) are however still quite diversified.

[20] Carlos Slim, the owner of the largest business group in Latin America, placed many relatives in management. So committed was he to family capitalism that in 2003, Slim invited, at his expense, the heads of several dozen of the largest firms throughout Latin America – and their children – to meet in Mexico for three days to talk about family firms (see Schneider 2004, xxii). Wealthy group-owning families have since made this an annual retreat in different countries each year (interview Carlos Julio Ardila, 10 August 2011).

managers, and in other cases, the board met very frequently, even weekly, to keep management on a short tether (interview with Horacio Lafer Piva,14 September 2007). In sum, despite piecemeal moves toward professionalization and separation of ownership and management, families maintained tight control over the great majority of the largest business groups.

The most significant response to globalization by business groups, especially from developing countries, was international expansion, though the extent and type of internationalization varied significantly across regions and types of groups (see Goldstein 2007). Among developing countries, Latin American MNCs, also known as Translatins or multilatinas, grew more slowly than MNCs from developing Asia: of the 50 nonfinancial MNCs from developing countries with the most assets abroad, only seven were from Latin America (and one of the largest of these was state owned; ECLAC 2006, 65).[21] Despite the press (and the case studies at the Harvard Business School) devoted to a handful of sophisticated, aggressive Translatins like Cemex and Embraer, what stands out overall is a comparatively hesitant effort by domestic firms to expand abroad. Translatins mostly stayed within the region, bought up existing firms in neighboring countries, and sometimes later sold out to MNCs (though see Chapter 8 on internationalization by Brazilian business groups).

Moreover, the type or strategy of internationalization varied. Most FDI follows one of three main logics: market seeking, resource seeking, or efficiency seeking (Aykut and Goldstein 2006; ECLAC 2006). Efficiency enhancing investments (designed mostly to reduce labor costs) often move production offshore for export to third markets or back to home-country plants for further processing or assembly. Internationalization by more organic Asian groups was predominantly efficiency seeking (ECLAC 2006). As rapid development and democratization in countries like Korea and Taiwan drove wages up, business groups sought out lower-wage production sites in Asia, especially China after the 1980s.

In contrast, groups in Latin America, especially portfolio groups, relied primarily on market seeking investment, buying competitors in foreign markets in order to secure market share, without linkages back to home-country production. Commodity firms, especially in mining, undertook resource-seeking investments by buying mines and other resource assets abroad. Outside these resource investments, foreign investments by Translatins were rarely for export to third markets and almost never for offshoring component production, in large part because most Translatins are not in manufacturing but rather commodities and consumer services, which do not offer many opportunities for backward or forward integration. Some of the most aggressive Translatins were more specialized firms like Cemex (cement, Mexico), Gerdau (steel, Brazil),

---

[21] Similarly, in 2004 only 12 of the 100 largest MNCs from developing countries were from Latin America. Of the rest 77 were from Asia, with just 11 from India and China (though their numbers have grown since) (Rugraff, Sánchez-Ancochea, and Sumner 2009, 23).

or Falabella (retail, Chile), whereas many of the more diversified firms like Votorantim in Brazil, Ardila Lülle in Colombia, or Luksic in Chile have fewer and smaller subsidiaries abroad. New opportunities for internationalization may in effect offer an alternative strategy for managing risk: some firms diversify internationally by acquiring firms abroad in their core sectors; others diversify domestically by acquiring firms at home in different sectors. Cemex, for instance, diversified geographically in order "to balance risk in one region with stability in another," according to CEO Lorenzo Zambrano, who added, "we need to be in many markets to survive" (*Business Week* [International, online], 26 October 1998).[22]

These different strategies may have responded to immediate economic opportunities, but the capacities of groups to take advantage of these opportunities derived in large measure from the longer-term evolution of business groups in the two regions and the government policies that promoted or constrained them. That Asian business groups were guided by efficiency motives was related to the fact that they started as export industries and grew large by exporting lower-cost (and later higher-quality) goods. Translatins, in contrast, started much smaller because of the limits of ISI and other policy constraints on growth, and they were less interested in offshore production to enhance efficiency because they had been boxed out of higher-technology manufacturing by MNCs. Overall, the incentives for internationalizing were generally stronger among the organic groups common in East Asia than in the portfolio groups in Latin America.

Governments in Brazil and Chile in the 1990s and 2000s enacted significant reforms of their domestic stock markets with the goal of drawing in more investors and investment and thereby increasing capital available to firms (Amann 2009). For the period 2004–09, firms in Brazil raised capital equivalent to 1.8 percent of GDP (*Valor Econômico*, 29 October 2010, via email summary by Radiobrás). IPOs in Chile were far fewer than in Brazil, and only large firms were able to tap into the stock market. Expanding stock markets have the potential to change fundamental features of hierarchical capitalism, and to do so much more quickly than changes on other dimensions (as considered further in Chapter 8).[23] For one, if business groups issue more shares, they may dilute their strong hierarchical control. Few firms have done this yet, but it may become an alternative route for families to cash out (alternative to selling out to another group or MNC). Possibly more important, to the extent that small firms raise investment capital on stock markets, it undermines the

---

[22] Acquiring subsidiaries in developed countries had additional advantages in allowing business groups to access cheaper international finance.

[23] Outside Latin America, corporate finance may also be the component of LMEs and CMEs that is least sticky. In Germany and Japan, for example, cross shareholding, and long-term bank financing and share ownership in firms – the famous patient capital – dominant in the late twentieth century has shifted somewhat to more arm's length, market-based relationships (see Chapter 2; Streeck 2009; Lincoln and Shimotani 2010; Culpepper 2005).

advantages business groups have in the cost of capital, and thereby lowers barriers to entry. By the mid-2000s, most business groups were also raising capital on Wall Street through ADRs (American Depository Receipts). Although the business groups that issued ADRs did have to comply with stricter reporting requirements, they did not change fundamental patterns of diversification, blockholding, and family control (Schneider 2008).[24]

The commodity boom of the 2000s shook up the ranks of the top business groups and shifted intragroup investments toward commodity sectors. JBS was a large meat packer in the early 2000s but ranked only fifty-eighth in terms of sales in 2004 (when it was known as Friboi; *Valor Econômico* 2005, 58). Through a string of aggressive and rapid acquisitions, foreign and domestic, JBS catapulted itself into the ranks of Brazil's largest firms and became the world's biggest beef producer. The rapid growth of meat exports from Brazil, especially to Asia, helped fuel JBS's expansion, but the BNDES added a crucial policy-induced component by financing several of JBS's large foreign acquisitions. The soy boom in Argentina also contributed to the emergence of new business groups like los Grobo. In Chile, business groups were already in the main commodity sectors, so the boom only helped to consolidate their dominance. Mexico was less affected by the commodity boom, which consequently had less of an impact on recasting dominant business groups (Chapter 8 provides more detail on these recent shifts).

The 1990s and 2000s were exciting times of change and transformation of business groups in Latin America. Market reforms and globalization churned the ranks of the top business groups (save in Colombia), forcing out old stalwarts and promoting new entrants. Remaining business groups streamlined activities and professionalized management. Yet, when the dust settled, the list of top domestic firms was still mostly concentrated, family-owned and managed, diversified business groups.

## V. The Downside for Development

The large literature on the performance effects of business groups is inconclusive in part because it assesses the performance of group subsidiaries rather than the group as a whole (Carney et al. 2011). The different strategies of portfolio, organic, and policy-induced groups, and their different sectors of operation, give few grounds to think that their impact is either universally positive or negative. A risk-taking exporting organic business group focused largely on manufacturing should have a very different impact from a risk-averse portfolio business group concentrated in nontraded oligopolistic sectors. The upside of the growth of EMNCs from Latin America has been well documented

---

[24] Studies of European and Mexican firms that listed in the United States also found little change in governance (Davis and Marquis 2005; Siegel 2006).

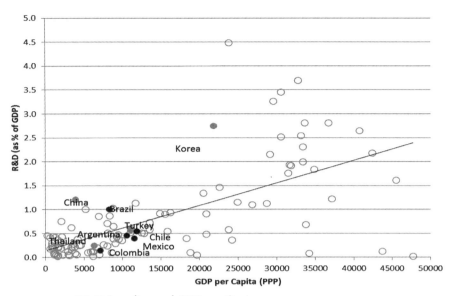

FIGURE 3.3. R&D Spending and GDP per Capita

(see Goldstein 2007; Fleury and Fleury 2009; Ramamurti and Singh 2009). Without denying the success stories, this section focuses on remaining weaknesses of business groups in promoting development and movement toward a high-skill, knowledge economy, especially on three dimensions: R&D, family management, and anticompetitive practices.

R&D is a central challenge for Latin America, and strategies to accelerate the transition to a knowledge economy have been much debated (see, for example, Kuznetsov and Dahlman 2008; Rodríguez, Dahlman, and Salmi 2008). Most countries in Latin America, with the notable exception of Brazil, have rates of R&D investment below what would be expected for their income levels (Figure 3.3). Moreover, in developed countries, the majority of investment in R&D comes from business, but in Latin America, governments still account for the lion's share. Reversing these proportions in Latin America requires significant investment by the largest firms.[25]

Although investing often in acquisitions, at home and abroad, business groups in Latin America have not put commensurate effort into R&D, technology, and innovation generally (Grosse 2007). Famous exceptions such as

[25] In their volume, *Big Business and the Wealth of Nations*, that focused primarily on the history of growth in the OECD countries, Chandler and Hikino conclude that "the large industrial enterprise has remained *a* central institution in the dynamics of modern economic growth. Its essential role has been to drive technological advance" (1997, 56). In contrast, in their comprehensive study of post-reform development, Stallings and Peres conclude that "what is notable about Latin America is the absence of important investments directed toward developing strategic assets, particularly technology" (2000, 172).

TABLE 3.2. *Research and Development by Business Groups in Brazil, 2009–10 (percentage of sales)*

| | Sector | 2009 | 2010 | Average |
|---|---|---|---|---|
| Vale | Mining | 4.1 | 1.9 | 3.0 |
| Odebrecht/Braskem | Construction & petrochemicals | .39 | .31 | .35 |
| Itaú (Duratex + Itautec) | Building materials & informatics | 3.4 | 2.2 | 2.8 |
| Oi/Telemar | Telecommunications | .06 | .04 | .05 |
| Gerdau | Steel | .48 | .68 | .58 |
| Camargo Correa | Diversified | .09 | .11 | .10 |
| Cosan | Sugar & ethanol | .04 | .04 | .04 |
| Usiminas | Steel | .08 | .16 | .12 |
| **Median** | | .24 | .24 | .23 |

*Sources*: Company reports, SEC filings, and personal communications for 8 of largest 20 business groups in Brazil that reported some R&D expenditure.

Cemex (Mexico), Techint (Argentina), LAN (Chile), and Embraer (Brazil) serve mostly to underscore the rule. In Mexico, the private sector invested only .17 percent of GDP in R&D in 2007. The flagship firms of the Grupo Carso, América Móvil (the fifth-largest mobile telephone company in the world), and Telmex, despite their size, have not registered any patents recently (Elizondo 2011, 159–60). The increasing concentration of business groups in commodities does not generally offer promising opportunities for expanding R&D. In sectors like mining, basic metals, meatpacking, cement, and pulp and paper, firms have few opportunities for product innovation or expanding skilled employment (McMillan and Rodrik 2011, 3). Innovation in these sectors comes more through management and logistics that bolster firm productivity – and the international success of many business groups – but they do not generate large R&D departments nor demand for highly skilled labor more generally.[26]

Table 3.2 shows R&D expenditures for eight of the largest nonfinancial business groups in Brazil (out of the top 20) that reported R&D expenditures in their annual reports.[27] Besides the two outliers of Vale and Itautec/Duratex

[26] R&D is, of course, only one measure of the innovative capacity in business and is not usually reported in service firms. By the 2000s, some business groups in Latin America were very successful in logistics and transportation: EBX, Claro, Vale, LAN, Odebrecht, and Sidgo Koppers, among others. However, R&D is still a useful metric for considering employment effects. Only small numbers of high-skill employees work in R&D departments; however, firms that invest a lot in R&D also rely on suppliers with high-skilled workers and need higher-skill workers in their own production plants where they are introducing new products and processes. This employment effect is important for the analysis of demand for skills in Chapter 6.
[27] Of the 12 groups that did not report any R&D, some were in services like retail (Pão de Açucar) or air transportation (TAM) while others were in food and commodities (JBS, Marfrig, Brazil Foods, CSN, and Votorantim).

(small parts of Itaú), R&D was minimal with a median level of .23 percent of sales. Although Vale shows that commodity production does not necessarily lead to low R&D, the other firms in sugar and steel fit the common pattern of low investment. Given that total private R&D was higher in Brazil than elsewhere in the region, spending by business groups in other countries would likely show similarly low levels of R&D.

Internationalization also makes it easier for business groups to conduct R&D or other high-skill operations abroad where the skills already exist. For example, Cemex's pioneering and very successful application of IT to its cement operations led Cemex to spin off a separate logistics subsidiary, Neoris, to offer consulting services to other firms. However, the potential benefits for the Mexican economy and labor market were reduced when Cemex moved Neoris's headquarters to Miami. More generally, as Brazilian firms internationalized, they also invested in R&D abroad. Among 100 Brazilian MNCs, none conducted R&D outside Brazil in 2002 but one-third of them did in 2008 (Arbix and Caseiro 2011, 599).

On the second dimension, family management brings advantages and disadvantages (Amsden 2001, 192). While family management can bring benefits such as loyalty, long-term commitment, and often generations of experience, genetics are hardly the best basis for recruiting raw managerial talent, especially for firms that can afford to pay top dollar. Moreover, family firms are subject to vicious, sometimes fatal, succession crises as heirs battle one another for control. One major study found that only 20 percent of family firms lasted more than 60 years, and of the surviving firms, two-thirds had stopped growing (Ward 2004, 6). Another study found that firms with dispersed ownership were best managed, followed by firms run by their founders, but "worst of all were family-owned firms run by the founder's eldest son" (*Economist*, 13 November 2007).[28]

However, families may be well suited to managing diversified business groups, and the world financial crisis of the late 2000s certainly tainted the reputation of the alternative of professional management in widely held corporations. Other studies find that family managers often take a longer-term view of firm strategy but at the same time may adopt more conservative strategies designed to maximize steady family income (a longer-term perspective also gives family firms a leg up in politics that is examined further in Chapter 7). Some evidence shows that family firms also hire workers for longer periods and are less likely to fire them in downturns (Ellul et al. 2011). Families, scholars, consultants, and business schools have in recent decades begun to think more systematically about how to avoid the pitfalls of family capitalism. Business

---

[28] An *Economist* (13 November 2007) article stated that this was "further proof of the wisdom of Warren Buffett's opposition to the hereditary principle, which he calls the "lucky sperm club," and describes as akin to "choosing the 2020 Olympic team by picking the eldest sons of the gold-medal winners in the 2000 Olympics."

schools offer classes on family business, consulting firms help devise new modes of governance and succession plans, and Latin America's wealthiest families exchange experiences in the annual meetings started in the early 2000s by Carlos Slim. Nonetheless, genetics and family dysfunctions will continue to interject challenges into management that professionally managed firms do not face.

The last area in which business group behavior can raise problems for development is in oligopoly, distorted regulation, and anticompetitive behavior. Chile, for example, was a leader among developing countries in liberalizing its economy and is also a leader in the concentration of corporate control. As noted earlier, the 20 largest firms account for half of GDP, meaning that a small number of hierarchies controlled a large proportion of economic activity.[29] When asked what sectors of the economy were subject to potential abuses of market power, the director of the Chilean antitrust agency said "almost all sectors" (interview, December 2010). These are problems created by any type of large firm, yet they are more acute with business groups in Latin America. As noted earlier, many business groups made it an explicit strategy to enter or stay in nontradable, protected, or regulated sectors. So, business groups were more concentrated in problematic sectors. In addition, outside Brazil, the national economies of other countries are relatively small and have certainly grown less than business groups that have expanded exponentially through acquisitions.[30] This size asymmetry creates practical difficulties in antitrust and other regulation, but, more important, it creates political opportunities for business groups to influence legislation, policy making, regulation, and the judiciary, especially in contexts like Latin America where institutions are relatively weak and changeable (as analyzed further in Chapter 7).

Table 3.3 provides some scattered estimates of where business groups have significant market share that would in theory allow them some leverage over product pricing and, as near monopsonists, over supplier prices. Low tariff barriers reduce the margin for significant abuses in tradable sectors, though less so for products with low price to weight ratios like cement, soft drinks, and food. In the best-documented cases, Telmex and Telcel, in Mexico, have decreased consumer welfare and have been a drag on the development of telecommunications which in turn is central to overall development in the twenty-first century (see Chapter 8). By one calculation, in Mexico, "31% of total household spending is in markets that are monopolised or suffer from

---

[29]  By another measure, the sales of the 63 largest firms in 2006 equaled 87 percent of GDP. These figures exaggerate the proportion of GDP controlled by large firms because they include foreign sales. At the same time, it underestimates the degree of concentration because some of these firms belong to an even smaller number of business groups (*América Economia*, 9 July 2007, p. 67).

[30]  As noted earlier, empirical studies have shown that business groups pay very large premia to acquire firms that give them market dominance.

TABLE 3.3. *Market Concentration and Business Groups in Selected Sectors*

| Business Group and Country | Sector | Domestic Market Share |
|---|---|---|
| **Argentina** | | |
| Arcor | candy | 70 |
| | chewing gum | 98 |
| **Brazil** | | |
| Brazil Foods | frozen foods | 60–80 |
| | margarine | 50 |
| Ambev | beer | 63 |
| Votorantim | cement | 41 |
| **Chile** | | |
| Angelini | fuel distribution | 64 |
| Luksic | beer | 86 |
| Angelini & Matte | forestry | 60 |
| Concha y Toro, Santa Rita, San Pedro Tarapaca | wine | 85 |
| Briones | cement | 30 |
| **Colombia** | | |
| Sindicato Antioqueño (1991) | Tobacco | 66 |
| | pulp & paper | 41 |
| | cement | 64 |
| | textiles | 39 |
| 3 business groups | insurance | 55 |
| **Mexico** | | |
| Bimbo | packaged bread | 40 |
| Carso | fixed phone | 92 |
| | mobile phone | 76 |
| | broadband internet | 68 |
| Cemex | cement | 65 |
| Femsa | soft drinks | 73 |
| Televisa | television (non subscriber) | 62 |
| TV Azteca | television (non subscriber) | 35 |

Sources online at http://www.cambridge.org/HCLA

limited competition while Mexican businesses face high input prices."[31] That business groups cluster in sectors that have significant market power at least raises suspicions that they are not as concerned about efficiency and low prices

---

[31] OECD, accessed on 16 February 2011 http://www.oecd.org/document/34/03343,en_2649_40381664_44948578_1_1_1_1,00.html. In addition, the share of assets of the five largest banks rose from 74 to 88 percent. By the late 2000s, Mexico had one of the "most concentrated banking systems in the world" (World Bank 2007, 42; however, by then, it was also mostly foreign owned).

as firms in more competitive markets would be. At a minimum, operating in less competitive markets reduces pressure on business groups to invest overall and in innovation in particular; at the same time, it increases incentives to invest in politics.[32]

This section was not intended to provide a full review of the advantages and disadvantages of private sectors dominated by business groups but rather to highlight three main areas of concern – low investment in R&D, family management, and oligopoly. Policy can counter some of these weaknesses, most directly, of course, through already existing competition agencies, though governments can do little to effect changes in family management. Policy interventions appear most promising in the area of R&D. Korean chaebol, Japanese keiretsu, and Scandinavian business groups have shown that business groups can bet their corporate strategies on high R&D (Amsden 2001; Sabel 2009). In fact, business groups are well suited to shift profits (and commodity rents) from some member firms into R&D in others. Yet, to date, few policies in Latin America have attempted to push business groups to make this transfer to R&D.

## VI. Conclusion

This is a chapter about business groups, but telling their story without the state is like staging *Othello* without Iago. Looking back historically on the global variation among business groups in structure and strategy usually leads back to prior state actions and policies. The promotion by the Korean state, for instance, of domestic manufacturing in large firms was an integral part of the development of economies of scope in emerging chaebol. Conversely, domestic politics in Latin America generated a lot of the macroeconomic instability that encouraged portfolio groups. Moreover, states intervened directly to promote or restrict the growth of business groups as well as to set the terms of their interaction with banks, MNCs, and state enterprises. Last, governments pursued changing development strategies from ISI to market reform and economic integration that had deep effects on group strategy and structure.

The major theoretical implication of these multiple empirical routes to the establishment of diversified business groups would be a caution against efforts to construct a single explanation or logic for business group formation, behavior, and potential contribution to development. And if, historically, business groups arose in different circumstances, developed distinct internal logics, and adapted to diverse government-imposed constraints, then there is little reason

---

[32] Concentration and oligopoly can facilitate collusion on price, but there is little evidence that it promotes coordination on other dimensions, and at least some evidence suggests that large firms tend to dominate business associations and impede coordination. The general point is that leading firms with market power insert a degree of hierarchy into markets, especially from the perspective of smaller firms.

to expect them to respond the same way to later exogenous shocks and market opportunities. Beyond theory, the major practical and policy implication is that states have many ways to influence the structure and strategies of business groups.

The range of different business groups considered in this chapter should also make it clear why it is difficult to say whether business groups are, always and everywhere, good or bad for development. Features like diversification or family management can be good for some aspects of performance, bad for others. Overall, though, to the extent that business groups in Latin America have competitive advantage and export potential, it is not in manufacturing or services but rather in commodities. Diversification offers business groups in Latin America several advantages. It helps them survive volatility in policy, politics, and world commodity markets, and allows firms to adjust quickly to shifting policy environments and new business opportunities (Grosse 2007). This agility makes business groups potentially valuable partners for new policy ventures. Given their pooled internal resources, business groups are well placed to transfer rents internally from commodity production, where windfall rents have been running high, to more knowledge intensive activities, though in practice such transfers have not been common, and governments have yet to figure out how to encourage them effectively.

Business groups offer a central example of why, contra North (1990), it is essential to problematize organizations in institutional analysis. Incentives, preferences, practices, and strategies vary widely across firms depending on whether they are parts of business groups, and, if so, what sort of business group and whether it is run by family members or professional managers, or, as discussed in the next chapter, whether the firm is owned by a foreign MNC. Much of the cross-national variation among organic, portfolio, and policy-induced business groups results from government actions and strategies – or rules – yet even within countries, business group responses to these rules vary. Within Brazil, a fairly specialized and internationalized steel company (Gerdau), a widely diversified portfolio group (Camargo Correa), and a business group in oil, mining, and logistics operating almost exclusively in Brazil (EBX), all faced the same rules but adopted different strategies (Goldstein and Schneider 2004), giving them different capacities to contribute to development.

Various subtypes of groups exhibit distinctive complementarities with labor markets. Organic groups, of the sort more common in manufacturing in Asia, are more likely to invest in R&D, to hire more engineers and technical personnel, and to place higher value on long-term skilled employment. In contrast, groups that emerge from commodity production are more likely to evolve into portfolio groups in which the incentives for investing in research and development are lower, as is the demand for skilled technicians and workers and for longer-term employment relations. The direct connections between big business and labor market dynamics are of course only partial since smaller firms account for the lion's share of total employment. However, large firms are likely to set the standard for labor relations and provide the strongest signals on demand for higher skills, especially once multiplier effects on upstream buyers and downstream suppliers are factored in. In labor markets, to return to the issues at the beginning of the chapter, the kinds of firms countries have affects the kinds of jobs that are likely to be abundant. Chapters 5 and 6 take up these labor and skill issues in greater depth.

# 4

## Corporate Governance and Multinational Corporations

### How Ownership Still Matters

## I. Introduction

Analyses of liberal, coordinated, and most other varieties of capitalism focus on large national firms. In Latin America, such a purely domestic focus would miss major players; in most countries, MNCs constitute a third to a half of the largest firms. In terms of complementarities, MNCs often have patterns of interactions with other firms, workers, and governments that do not resemble patterns of domestic business groups. MNCs cannot be assumed to be "institution takers" that come to countries and blend into the corporate landscape (Pauly and Reich 1997).

Debates continue about whether and how MNCs contribute to host country development, human capital, and technological progress. Although more radical views, for and against, persist, a more nuanced middle ground contends that the impact of MNCs depends on the context and that "the search for universal relationships is futile" (Lipsey and Sjöholm 2005, 40). The range of relevant contextual factors is wide, but generally, FDI is more likely to have positive effects in an economy characterized by more-developed financial markets (Alfaro et al. 2004), more technologically advanced local firms, more competitive markets (both locally and internationally), fewer restrictions on FDI flows, and higher stocks of human capital (Moran, Graham, and Blomström 2005).[1] This range of contextual factors begins to shade into the core

---

[1] Although used interchangeably in this book, precise definitions of FDI and MNCs vary somewhat. In most definitions, MNCs have a controlling interest (50 percent or more of the shares) in subsidiaries abroad, whereas FDI flows are defined as a lower level of 10 percent or more. FDI is thus a more inclusive measure and a portion, usually relatively small, of FDI goes into minority shareholding though with the presumption that it grants some management influence. However, FDI does not include often short-term portfolio investments of companies into foreign stock markets. For full discussions of conceptual and measurement issues, see OECD (2005, 2010a).

complementarities in the literature on varieties of capitalism, and this chapter thus takes the contextual analysis a step further to analyze how MNCs fit into hierarchical capitalism.

Ultimately, however, understanding the impact of FDI on local firms, labor relations, and skills requires looking beyond immediate spillover effects – the focus of most contemporary research on MNCs – to longer-term path dependence in the evolution of business groups and labor markets. Most empirical studies of FDI assess a fairly short time span using either cross sectional or short-term panel data. On the firm side, these studies look mostly at the impacts on firms directly connected to MNCs, either competitors or suppliers, to assess whether their behavior changed on dimensions like sales, investment, productivity, and R&D. What is missing is a longer-term path-dependent analysis of how MNC entry shapes the evolution of leading domestic firms that are deliberately not suppliers or competitors. On the labor side, existing empirical research again focuses mostly on short-term impacts on wages and skills of workers in MNCs or on competing or supplier firms. What is missing is a longer-term analysis of how MNC strategies such as in-house training or poaching of skilled workers from other firms affect the ongoing strategies of domestic firms and workers to invest in human capital. For example, the fact that MNCs pay higher wages and employ more-skilled workers seems like a plus in the immediate run (especially if competing firms follow suit), but widespread poaching drives down incentives for domestic firms to invest in training.

MNC investment varies greatly across countries, regions, and varieties of capitalism (Table 4.1). Averages for Latin America approximate those of LMEs, but are way above averages for CMEs and East Asia.[2] FDI flows as a percentage of total investment are also much higher in Latin America than in other varieties or in Asia (in part because total domestic investment in Latin America is relatively low) (H.-J. Chang 2003, 253; Kohli 2009). Stocks of FDI have more than tripled across all varieties and regions (quintupled in the large CMEs), which suggests that close attention to MNCs should be more central to analyzing all varieties of capitalism.

The predominance of MNCs in postcommunist Eastern Europe prompted debate about whether it contributed to new models of capitalism (Bohle and Greskovits 2007). Nölke and Vliegenthart (2009) argue that distinctive DMEs

---

The focus in this chapter is primarily on majority control through MNCs and not on minority stakes or portfolio investment. At the same time FDI accounting might include some investment flows not undertaken by MNCs and their majority owned subsidiaries, FDI also does not capture all MNC investment, some of which is done by already established MNC subsidiaries that use domestic finance (credit or retained earnings; Agosin and Machado 2005).

[2] FDI stocks are generally much higher in small countries (populations around 10 million and fewer), especially small CMEs (Belgium and Scandinavian countries), so they are excluded from Table 4.1.

TABLE 4.1. *FDI Stock as a Percentage of GDP across Varieties of Capitalism and Regions*

|  | 1980 | 1990 | 2000 | 2010 |
|---|---|---|---|---|
| Large CMEs | 2.2 | 3.4 | 7.7 | 12.1 |
| LMEs | 12.2 | 18.3 | 29.0 | 36.8 |
| Latin America | 10.0 | 14.0 | 31.5 | 29.5 |
| East Asia | 2.6 | 4.3 | 10.1 | 12.4 |
| South East Asia | 8.0 | 12.3 | 29.9 | 28.3 |
| **Other Countries** | | | | |
| Turkey | 9.5 | 5.5 | 7.2 | 24.3 |
| South Africa | 20.4 | 8.2 | 32.7 | 36.6 |
| India | 0.2 | 0.5 | 3.5 | 12.2 |

*Note*: Averages are unweighted. CMES (Japan and Germany); LMEs (United States, United Kingdom, Australia, Canada); Latin America (Argentina, Bolivia, Brazil, Chile, Ecuador, Colombia, Mexico, Peru, Venezuela); East Asia (Korea, Taiwan, China); Southeast Asia (Philippines, Malaysia, Indonesia, Thailand).
*Source*: http://unctadstat.unctad.org/TableViewer/tableView.aspx.

(dependent market economies) are characterized by hegemonic MNCs (virtually no large domestic firms), relatively high skills, competitive advantages in medium technology, and integration into global production networks. The key cases are the countries of East Europe closest to West Europe: Poland, Hungary, Czech Republic, and Slovakia. The main coordination mechanism in this new variety is hierarchy.[3] Beyond this common allocation mechanism of hierarchy, the DME model has less relevance in Latin America because workers' skills in East Europe are higher and business groups rare. However, the DME is a useful comparative construct to bear in mind. For example, Argentina might be trending toward a DME with mostly MNCs, few large domestic firms, and higher levels of education, though (due to geography) less integrated into global production networks. Or, if large domestic business groups emerge in East Europe and skill levels decline (as Nölke and Vliegenthart worry), DMEs could transition toward hierarchical capitalism.

In sum, MNCs merit scrutiny for both theoretical reasons and practical concerns as MNCs, along with diversified business groups, were the key conduits in the private sector for organizing access to capital, technology, and markets through Coasian internalization and global hierarchies. Section II turns next to consider briefly patterns of FDI in recent decades with a special focus on acquisitions that added new hierarchies in the control of large firms in Latin America,

---

[3] Amsden (2009, 410) emphasizes hierarchy as well: "the multinational, operating through its subsidiary, is inherently a bureaucratic animal. Strategic decisions must filter from headquarters, then to regional offices, and then to subsidiaries, making three levels of bureaucracy right there. Professional management is one side of the multinational's coin, but bureaucracy and rule-bound decision making is the other."

as well as the extension of hierarchy through global production networks. Section III singles out some negative consequences of FDI on the evolution of the domestic private sector, R&D, skills, and training. Section IV analyzes some of the political consequences of the large presence of MNCs especially the fragmentation of business representation and the passivity of MNCs in general politics.

## II. Trends in FDI in the 1990s and 2000s

As noted in Chapter 1, MNCs have been central economic protagonists throughout Latin America for more than a century, but some trends in FDI shifted in recent decades including the huge growth of aggregate flows after the mid 1990s, the shift from greenfield investment to brownfield acquisitions, and the growing incorporation of domestic manufacturing into global production networks through both FDI and MNC subcontracting of local firms. Overall, these trends resulted in the growth of the MNC share of the largest firms throughout the region and dramatically in Argentina. MNC strategies differed across the region: largely efficiency seeking (lower labor costs) in manufacturing along the southern periphery of the United States (Mexico, Central America, and the Caribbean), resource seeking in smaller Andean economies (Chile, Ecuador, Bolivia, and Peru), and market seeking, especially in services, in the four largest economies of Colombia, Argentina, Brazil, and Mexico (ECLAC/CEPAL 2002, 35). These were modal trends, but large countries received FDI of all sorts, and market-seeking investment in services was ubiquitous throughout the region. Through the 2000s, about half of all FDI in Latin America went into services, about 30 percent into manufacturing, and about 20 percent into natural resources (ECLAC 2010, 9). About 90 percent of FDI continued to come from developed countries (Cruz 1995, 23–24; Izquierdo and Talvi 2011, 23–24). These trends were part of the global boom in FDI that extended a multitude of new hierarchies throughout the world. The number of foreign subsidiaries of MNCs grew from 170,000 in 1990 to 690,000 in 2004, half of them in developing countries (UNCTAD 2005 cited in Chudnovsky and López 2007, 8).

The growth of MNCs was especially apparent in the ranks of the largest firms in Latin America: MNCs went from 27 percent of the 500 largest firms in 1991 to 39 percent in 2001 (Santiso 2008, 21). By another calculation, among the largest firms, MNCs accounted for 48 percent of sales in Venezuela, 57 percent in Brazil, and 73 percent in Argentina (as a proportion of the total sales of the 100 largest firms) (Andrade et al. 2001, 83). The jump in FDI was especially dramatic in some countries and sectors. In Brazilian manufacturing from 1996 to 2000, the participation of foreign firms in total sales rose from 27 to 42 percent (Lazzarini 2011, 18). And among the top 100 nonfinancial firms in Brazil, MNCs increased their share of the revenues from 26 percent in 1990 to 40 percent in 1998 (Goldstein and Schneider 2004, 61).

Before 1990, MNCs usually entered Latin America with greenfield investments in new plants and operations. In the 1990s, most FDI went into brownfield acquisitions of existing firms, in part through massive privatization programs, which accounted for about half of FDI acquisitions (Calderón, Loayza, and Servén 2004, 8). In addition, new Translatinas or multilatinas (business groups that expanded into other countries of the region) further contributed to the wave of mergers and acquisitions. The irony, some might say perverse, is that by the 1990s, ISI had succeeded in creating many medium-sized firms that offered attractive acquisition targets and reduced the need for MNCs to undertake greenfield investments. The other irony is that trade liberalization reduced the value of firms subject to international competition with MNCs and thereby made them less expensive takeover targets. In this sense, trade liberalization led not to more competition through the entry of new firms into previously closed markets but to more hierarchy and concentration.[4]

Many MNC acquisitions of private industrial firms further reinforced MNC dominance in manufacturing and the overall division of labor with remaining business groups. The auto parts sector, especially in Brazil, is emblematic. Pre-1990 restrictions on FDI and domestic content requirements forced the big auto assemblers to buy from locally owned suppliers and thereby created a significant pole of domestic manufacturers. With the lifting of these requirements and restrictions in the 1990s, MNCs encouraged their host country suppliers to buy up local producers in Latin America. In Brazil, the auto parts sector rapidly denationalized in the 1990s and 2000s (Diniz 2011). The few domestic suppliers that survived did well, including some connected to business groups (Alfa and Desc in Mexico) and other medium-sized firms, especially in Brazil (see Chapter 8).

In the 2000s, privatization programs wound down, and MNCs returned to more greenfield investments, for example, in natural resources where acquisition targets became scarcer (ECLAC 2010, 40–41, 45). Cross-border acquisitions though continued; the Translatinas, or Latin MNCs, still focused almost exclusively on brownfield acquisitions (Santiso 2008; Hiratuka 2009). As large domestic business groups ventured abroad, they mostly started (and many stayed) in neighboring Latin American countries.[5] These acquisitions were rarely in manufacturing, where rich country MNCs continued to dominate, but rather in commodity and service sectors such as beer, steel, retailing, mining, cement, and telecommunications. The Brazilian biofuels sector provides an illustrative case of brownfield investment and denationalization as foreign

---

[4] Prior to 1990s, U.S. MNCs commonly entered joint venture arrangements abroad. These ventures declined rapidly thereafter due to changes in U.S. tax policy, host country restrictions, and the growing dependence of MNCs on intra firm trade (Desai, Foley, and Hines 2004). The result was fewer partnerships and more hierarchy.

[5] By the 2000s, some Mexican and many Brazilian MNCs were acquiring more firms in developed countries (Arbix and Caseiro 2011).

firms bought up nearly a quarter of productive capacity by the late 2000s. The foreign share of the sector rose from 4 percent in 2003 to 26 percent in 2010; foreign firms controlled two of the three largest firms in the sector, and the largest firm, Cosan, created a complex merger with Shell (Freitas 2010, 94). In parallel, in 2008, Monsanto bought CanaVialis and Allelyx, the main biotechnology firms working in the biofuels sector, from Votorantim's venture capital subsidiary (Matsuoka, Ferro, and Arruda 2009, 379).

Argentina represents an extreme case of MNC acquisitions and near complete denationalization of large firms. By 1993, 60 percent of the sales of the 500 largest firms came from MNCs (compared to 43 percent for Brazil), and by 2003, MNCs accounted for a remarkable 82 percent of sales and a similar share of exports (Chudnovsky and López 2007, 11, 16). Two trends accelerated this shift. First, MNCs bought many privatized firms, especially utilities, and banks in the early 1990s. Second, in the late 1990s, several domestic groups sold all or part of their conglomerates to Brazilian buyers (e.g., Pérez Companc to Petrobrás, Loma Negra to Camargo Corrêa, and Quilmes to Ambev). By the early 2000s, the number of surviving large domestic business groups, the erstwhile "captains of industry" so prominent in the 1980s, could be counted on one hand: Techint (steel), Arcor (candy), and several others. By the late 2000s, several new big groups, especially several close to the Kirschners, were emerging but had yet to reach the size and scope of their predecessors from the 1980s or to shift the balance of large firms toward a greater Argentine share (see Chapter 8).

What is the impact of these shifting patterns of greenfield and brownfield investment on the investment behavior of local firms? At first glance, host countries seem to benefit more from greenfield than brownfield investment because greenfield investment creates new jobs and productive capacity that did not exist before. However, regular year-by-year entry of new greenfield investments could have a negative collateral effect of depressing local investment. That is, if domestic investors fear that MNCs might in the future set up competing greenfield plants, then that greenfield threat discourages local investment in sectors in which FDI is common. As seen in the previous chapter, many of largest business groups in Latin America in fact grew out of commodity sectors such as cement or protected services (banking) where FDI was rare. If, in contrast, brownfield acquisitions are more common than are greenfield investments, and local investors think MNCs may buy their firms, then local business has more incentives to invest in start-ups (such as the biotechnology ventures in Brazil). In the past, venture capital sorts of investments were stymied by the absence of an exit option through IPOs in local stock markets. In this sense, MNC acquisitions of local startups are a functional substitute for IPOs, and could thus encourage local investors to put more funds into startups.

Another overlapping view of the impact of foreign firms focuses on the integration of local firms into subordinate positions in global production networks (also known as global commodity or value chains) created as manufacturers in developed countries shift production, or parts of the productive chain, offshore (see Gereffi et al. 2005). Much of this integration occurs within MNC hierarchies as MNCs move production offshore into foreign subsidiaries. Domestically owned suppliers range in a gray zone between market and hierarchy; however, most cluster toward the hierarchy end of the spectrum. Although formally independent in terms of ownership, dependence on single buyers can reduce local management autonomy to a fairly hierarchical relationship. In Latin America, these production networks have had a greater impact on smaller countries and partner countries in regional trade agreements (NAFTA and, to a lesser extent, Mercosul).

Global production networks are more common in some sectors (such as consumer electronics, apparel, and automobiles) than in others (services, commodities, and higher-technology niches). Some of the most dramatic geographic dispersions of production networks came in textiles and automobiles. For example, in the 1990s, global production networks rapidly transformed the apparel industry in Mexico and elsewhere in Central America and the Caribbean. Employment in apparel manufacturing in Mexican *maquila* firms grew from 64,000 workers in 1993 to 270,000 in 2000 (Bair and Gereffi 2001, 1889).[6] Automobile MNCs such as Ford, General Motors (GM), and Volkswagen have long figured among the largest private firms, especially in Brazil and Mexico. Established initially behind tariff walls to produce final products for small domestic markets, after the 1970s, auto and parts producers began integrating into global production networks (Moran 1998). Beginning in the 1970s, a convergence of Mexican and Brazilian policies to promote exports with competitive pressures from Japanese imports in U.S. markets, pushed U.S. firms, led by GM, to invest in component production (starting in a big way in engine manufacturing), first in Mexico and soon after in Brazil. By the mid 1990s, Mexico was the largest exporter among developing countries in the automotive sector with $14 billion in exports (and employment of 364,000; Moran 1998, 56). Exports peaked in 2000 at $16 billion, after which exports of final cars dropped in response to the U.S. recession though parts exports continued to grow and accounted for a third of total automotive exports by 2003. Brazilian exports also grew rapidly in the 1990s, reaching $4.3 billion in 2004, however, in contrast to Mexico, parts exports as a proportion of total automotive exports fell from nearly 50 percent in 1997 to slightly more than a third in 2004.[7]

These and other sectoral and regional stories highlight a number of general features of global production networks. First, relatively small decisions in MNC

---

[6] In the blue jeans segment clustered in Torreón, production grew 12-fold (from 500,000 to 6 million garments per week) and employment over 6-fold (from 12,000 to 75,000) over the eight years from 1993 to 2001. Most of the major suppliers were family owned Mexican firms, but they produced alongside some large MNC subsidiaries.

[7] United Nations Commodity Trade Statistics Database, http://unstats.un.org/unsd/comtrade.

headquarters can have large impacts, negative or positive, on local economies. Second, local manufacturers were mostly MNC subsidiaries or smaller, more specialized domestic firms. Only about a third of the largest business groups in the region had major subsidiaries that were integrated into global production networks in sectors like textiles and auto parts (Schneider 2008). Third, more stable integration into global value chains, especially higher value chains, usually depended on long-term prior investment with state support, as in the auto industry in Brazil and Mexico. Last, as analyzed in Chapter 6, the extension of global production chains created a lot of unskilled and semiskilled jobs, thereby lowering the relative demand for more highly skilled workers, especially in concentrated regional markets such as northern Mexico.

The next section turns to some of the main consequences of increased FDI. For now, suffice it to note the visible consequence of increasing hierarchy as more firms in the region became integrated into global hierarchies.

## III. Consequences and Complementarities

Nathan Jensen (2003, 587) summarizes the conventional positive wisdom on the benefits of FDI:

FDI is an engine of employment, technological progress, productivity improvements, and ultimately economic growth. FDI provides both physical capital and employment possibilities that may not be available in the host market. More importantly, FDI is a mechanism of technology transfer between countries, particularly to the less-developed nations.

Jensen further claims that "few scholars dispute the aggregate economic benefits of FDI" (2003, 587). But, to the contrary, a good deal of research does question this rosy hegemony.[8] The findings of the many empirical studies of the effects of MNCs – on growth, investment, or spillover effects on domestic firms – are mostly equivocal, ambiguous, or contingent on the type of investments or conditions in receiving countries. Moreover, a full assessment needs to go beyond an exclusive focus on the net present benefits of FDI to incorporate an analysis of the longer-term impact of FDI on business-group structure and strategy.

At a macro level, the effects of FDI on growth and investment are not generally strong or unidirectional. For example, Alfaro (2003) finds that aggregate FDI has an ambiguous effect on growth. However, breaking FDI down by sector reveals a positive effect of manufacturing FDI, negative by natural resource FDI, and ambiguous with FDI in services. The effect of FDI is also contingent on the prior development of financial markets; when financial markets are large, FDI has a greater positive effect on growth (Alfaro et al. 2004). Total

---

[8] For reviews of inconclusive findings on benefits, see Calderón et al. (2004), Kohli (2009), and Rugraff, Sánchez-Ancochea, and Sumner (2009a).

investment rates in Latin America, despite the large inflows of FDI, remained around 20 percent, much lower than the 30+ percent investment rates in Asia. The wave of foreign acquisitions, of course, would not be expected to add much to total investment, however, it is surprising that increased greenfield FDI did not make a net addition to ongoing domestic investment. One study in fact found crowding out, where FDI "displaced domestic investment in Latin America" over the three decades from 1971 to 2000, in contrast to Africa and Asia where the impact of FDI was neutral (Agosin and Machado 2005, 159).[9]

Another perspective on the economic consequences of FDI looks at the potential spillover effects on productivity in domestic firms. Positive effects could come through three channels: (1) human capital (MNCs train people who later go to work for domestic firms), (2) horizontal spillovers (MNC entry makes markets more competitive and forces everyone to lower costs and improve quality), or (3) vertical spillovers (MNCs induce domestic suppliers to upgrade). The first channel has not been researched much, but horizontal and vertical spillovers have been subjected to greater econometric scrutiny. Earlier studies showed mostly positive spillovers, but more-recent studies with more sophisticated methodologies have found few or equivocal effects, though the case for less studied vertical spillovers is stronger (Chudnovsky and López 2007, 14; Hiratuka 2009). Studies that disaggregate the effect by type of firm generally find that MNC entry can have an invigorating horizontal effect on firms that are already productive and innovative but can be debilitating for less productive firms.[10] Other research examines what happens in the local subsidiary after a foreign acquisition. In Argentina, foreign takeovers resulted in more skilled workforces, higher labor productivity, more exports and imports, and the adoption of new products or processes. However, these takeovers did not produce any increase in total employment or R&D and did not have positive vertical or horizontal spillovers (Chudnovsky, López, and Orlicki 2007, 7).

One immediate consequence of foreign investment is that MNCs come to control a large share of international trade. Although difficult to measure precisely, estimates of intrafirm trade between Latin America and the United States vary between one-third and two-thirds (Zeile 1997; Petras and Veltmeyer 1999).[11] In Brazil in 2000, 38 percent of total exports and 33 percent of

---

[9] Another study of a shorter, more recent period (1999–2002) found a slightly positive relationship between FDI and total investment (gross fixed capital formation [GFCF]) in Latin America. But fluctuations over time in the larger economies of Brazil, Argentina, Chile, and Mexico showed that substantial increases in FDI were not associated with large increases in GFCF (UNCTAD 2004, 11).

[10] In Argentina, for example, FDI had no spillover effects in aggregate, but did have positive effects on firms with more absorptive capacity (that invested more in R&D and training) (Chudnovsky, López, and Rossi 2008).

[11] By 1994, 29 percent of U.S. imports from Latin America came through intrafirm trade. For US trade as a whole, 36 percent of total exports and 43 percent of total imports came through intrafirm trade (Zeile 1997, 24). Across regions, the average for imports from Latin America

imports were intrafirm, and MNCs accounted for 63 percent of total exports and 57 percent of imports (Hiratuka and De Negri 2004, 133). Although the patterns are similar for other regions, it is important to note that this trade is not a market exchange between independent buyers and sellers, but more shipping orders between members of the same corporate organization. In addition, as noted earlier, many export firms in Latin America are dependent on one or two international buyers in closely linked global commodity chains in which the interfirm relationship is more vertical than horizontal. Although not counted as intrafirm trade, it is often just as controlled by foreign firms.

MNCs account for a lot of exports, especially manufactured exports, from Latin America. MNCs also import a lot. In Argentina in the 1990s, firms acquired by MNCs exported and imported more than the firms they acquired and more than comparable domestic firms, and a study of 54,000 firms in Brazil in the late 1990s, found that MNCs exported 70 percent more than domestic firms and imported 290 percent more (Chudnovsky and López 2007, 15). On one hand, external sourcing of inputs can lower costs and improve quality. On the other hand, however, it breaks up the internal supply chain, which has deeper backward linkages to other sectors. At an extreme, this delinkage from the domestic economy can create MNC enclaves, such as many maquila operations in Mexico, with minimal multiplier effects (Gallagher and Zarsky 2007). External sourcing also reduces the positive vertical spillover effects that some advocates hope FDI will have on domestic suppliers.

The fundamental, longer-term consequence of FDI in Latin America was to box domestic firms out of most dynamic manufacturing sectors like electronics and automobiles. The early penetration of MNCs in these sectors, from the 1950s on, meant that business groups emerging then and in later periods did not enter these sectors (Amsden 2009). Already by the 1970s, the foreign share of manufacturing was 24 percent in Argentina, 50 percent in Brazil, 30 percent in Chile, 43 percent in Colombia, 44 percent in Peru, and 14 percent in Venezuela (Cunningham 1986, 46). The percentages were usually higher in sectors such as chemicals, electrical equipment, and transport equipment than in consumer nondurables such as food, beverages, textiles, and clothing. In comparative terms, by one calculation, the median "penetration measure" for MNCs in 1967 was 6,137 for Latin America versus only 1,372 for Asia.[12] By the 2000s, among the largest firms in Latin America, only one was in high technology manufacturing, Embraer. In contrast, the largest firms of developing Asia were concentrated in manufacturing. India, China, and Korea all have domestic auto

was lower than the averages for Europe (47 percent) and Asia (42 percent) (Zeile 1997, 33), probably because Latin America exports more commodities. So, for noncommodity trade, the proportion of intrafirm trade from Latin America would be much higher.

[12] The penetration measure is the stock of FDI weighted by the total capital stock and population of the country. The average measures were somewhat closer: 6,593 for nine countries of Latin America compared to 2,772 for seven countries of Asia, but the average for Asia is inflated by one outlier, Malaysia (Bornschier and Chase-Dunn 1985, 91, 156–59; Kohli 2009, table 4).

producers; Latin America has none. The result in Latin America is that domestic business groups are concentrated in lower-skill, lower-technology sectors (see Chapter 3).[13]

Contention over the distribution of foreign, state, and local private investment across various sectors was central to development policy in Latin America through most of the twentieth century. During early industrialization through the first half of the twentieth century, the disputes in petroleum, mining, and heavy industry and in utilities such as electricity and telephones pitted state enterprises against MNCs, with state enterprises ultimately winning most of the battles. Later, after the 1950s, with the arrival of manufacturing MNCs, domestic business was also a protagonist in some debates, especially in policies to promote domestic content (as in domestic parts suppliers to MNC auto producers) and to encourage joint ventures between MNCs and local firms (Evans 1979). Although policy debates and negotiations among firms were continuous over decades, generally speaking state enterprises took over sectors with resource rents, natural monopolies, and high capital investments (steel), MNCs dominated higher-technology sectors (where policy makers decided that domestic firms could not compete), and domestic business groups ended up with everything else.

Of course, there were major variations over time and across countries in government decisions favoring MNCs, state enterprises, or business groups, depending heavily on the leftist and nationalist leanings of governments, as well as their dependence on local business for coalition support. The main point is that these decisions had long-term path-dependent consequences for the development of MNCs and local business groups. The story of oil in Chile is exceptional and illustrative (Bucheli [2010] provides the full story). It is exceptional because the state did not nationalize oil as states did in other large countries. It is exceptional and illustrative in that governments, starting in the 1930s, broke up an MNC duopoly and forced the creation of a local private oil company (one of the few in the region). With strong government backing, Copec thrived (in distribution, not exploration) in subsequent decades and became the core of a series of major business groups. Coming through the turbulent 1970s, Copec became a core subsidiary of the Cruzat-Larrain group. When this business group collapsed in 1982, Angelini bought Copec and made it one of the main firms in his rising business group, which it remained into the 2000s. In sum, the fact that major Chilean business groups were in the oil industry while their counterparts elsewhere were not is the direct result of government decisions on dividing the national market with MNCs (and later resisting proposals to nationalize the whole sector).

---

[13] In one calculation of spillover effects, when MNCs force local firms out of business, it can have a positive effect by increasing the average productivity in the sector (Lipsey and Sjöholm 2005, 40). However, the longer-term consequence is to restrict the range of sectors where domestic firms enter and grow.

MNCs are presumed to be operating on the technological frontier, but there are several reasons that they may not operate as "engines of technological progress" (Jensen 2003, 587). First, they may not in fact transfer much of their own technology, and much more technology transfer may happen through domestic firms that buy or license technology abroad (Amsden 2001, 238). Second, MNCs have historically done little of their R&D outside of their home countries and rarely in Latin America. In the 2000s, more than two-thirds of FDI in Latin America went to sectors with low and medium-low technology intensity, and less than 1 percent of FDI (2003–09) involved R&D projects (ECLAC 2010, 52, 55). In 2005, Latin America and the Caribbean ranked "last out of all the world's regions in terms of percentage of research and development investment companies have made in the last three years or expect to make in the next three years" (ECLAC 2005, 17).[14] Overall, according to ECLAC (2010, 10), FDI has "a stronger impact as a source of financing than as a transmitter of knowledge and technology or a catalyst of structural change in the economies of the region." Amsden's critique is characteristically more caustic. Historically, MNCs abetted technological underdevelopment, because they kept R&D activities "overwhelmingly at home" (Amsden 2001, 207). Consequently, MNC contribution to host country R&D was "virtually nil": less than 1 percent of total R&D in Korea, Taiwan, Mexico, and Brazil and about 2 percent in Argentina (Amsden 2001, 14, 207). Moreover, the share of FDI in total capital formation correlates *negatively* with a number of other indicators of technological development, including spending on R&D, patents received, and scientific publications (Amsden 2001, 208).

On the dimension of R&D, Brazil emerged in the 2000s as the major exception in the region. MNCs like Dupont, IBM, GE, auto parts companies, and Monsanto all opened or expanded R&D centers. U.S. MNCs invested $2 billion in R&D activities in Brazil from 2002 to 2006 (Oliveira 2010, 20). By 2006, U.S. MNCs were investing $571 million a year in R&D in Brazil, up 185 percent from 2001 (Brito Cruz and Chaimovich 2010, 108). Brazil ranked second among developing countries as a destination for R&D investment, though sixteenth overall among all countries, and Brazil's share was less than 2 percent of all R&D investment abroad. This surge in R&D FDI is promising, but it involves only a small group of MNCs. The bulk of FDI is still market seeking and not export or innovation intensive (Egan 2011, 7).

Among the factors that most attracted MNCs to Brazil, MNC managers ranked availability of skilled labor and low cost as most important. On the skills side, the major factor was the larger pool of PhDs (more than 10,000 new PhD candidates graduate every year). However, among the factors that most impeded investment in R&D, MNC managers listed again skills and costs;

---

[14] U.S. MNCs increased R&D in Mexico from $183 million in 1994 to $284 million in 2002, but Mexico's share of total R&D by subsidiaries of U.S. MNCs worldwide fell from 1.5 to 1.3 percent (Sargent and Matthews 2008, 545).

however, on this negative ledger, it was the lack of engineers and high costs of regulation and importing goods. Among university graduates, only 5 percent are engineers, compared to 31 percent in China and 25 percent in South Korea (Oliveira 2010, 18–19). Chapter 8 considers further this exceptional MNC investment in R&D in Brazil; for now, the point to emphasize is that R&D investment by MNCs was minimal in other countries of the region.[15]

Advocates of FDI, as well as policy makers subsidizing FDI, are often mostly enthusiastic about the jobs it creates. In the immediate run, it seems clear that greenfield FDI creates jobs that did not exist, but over the longer term, the positive employment effect depends on a counterfactual that is difficult to prove, namely, that no domestic firm would have created those jobs, or even more jobs, in the absence of FDI. In a policy environment favorable to FDI, domestic business will rationally shy away from areas where MNCs might enter (Amsden 2001; Agosin and Machado 2005). Conversely, and comparatively, when in Asia, governments declared certain areas off limits for foreign investors, domestic businesses moved in (with additional support from the government).

A more fruitful approach is to ask what are the effects, once established, of a larger MNC presence on labor market dynamics.[16] At first glance, MNCs seem to increase the demand for skilled workers to whom they pay very well. In Brazil, for example, blue-collar workers in MNCs had on average 9 years of schooling (versus 7 years in national firms), 5.5 years of average tenure (versus 3 years in national firms), and earn 2.5 times more than do workers in national firms (Hiratuka 2009, 13). However, MNCs do not provide much of an overall boost to incentives for investing in human capital (beyond minimum credentialing like completed secondary education), in part because they do not hire many workers. Also, when MNCs hire, they often take on unskilled workers whom they then train (interviews with human resource managers, see the Appendix), but the signal then to potential workers is that investing in prior training is unnecessary. Moreover, when MNCs do hire skilled workers, they often poach them from local firms. The signal to domestic firms then is that their investments in training are at greater risk, thereby increasing the disincentives to train. These complementarities are analyzed further in Chapter 6.

Many studies of the economic impact of FDI conclude that it is neither negative or positive in itself; it depends usually on the type of investment (high versus lower technology, for example) and, more important, on the conditions in the receiving country, both economic (size of market, pool skilled workers, etc.)

---

[15] In 1996, U.S. MNCs invested $666 million in R&D in Latin America: 73 percent in Brazil, 17 percent in Mexico, 6 percent in Argentina, and 3 percent in the rest of Latin America (Hill 2000, 5). Moreover, what MNCs count as R&D in many developing countries is often just tinkering to adapt products and processes to local markets and conditions.

[16] The literature on MNCs (outside the auto industry) has little coverage of skills, training, labor relations, or labor markets overall. For exceptions, see Berg et al. (2006), Berg (2006), and Mosley (2010).

and policy related (as in support for R&D; Alfaro and Charlton 2007). For Latin America, these conclusions mean that impacts are heterogeneous across countries of the region. Basically, Brazil benefits the most (and it is the only country with significant MNC investments in R&D) largely because of the large pool of skilled workers (especially PhDs), dynamic industrial and IT sectors, and favorable government policies (Chudnovsky and López 2007, 21).

In sum, MNCs brought a lot of capital, created jobs, and transferred some technologies. However, the broader and longer-term contributions were uneven. FDI did not increase overall investment, tended not to develop backward linkages, extended MNC control over trade, and, outside Brazil, did not bring much in investment in R&D. Over the longer term, in two of the main institutional complementarities, MNCs boxed domestic firms out of several sectors and generally depressed demand for skilled workers.

## IV. Political Consequences: The Costs of Mousiness[17]

While many of the economic effects of MNCs are indirect and difficult to measure, the political consequences are more readily apparent. In general, MNCs are less engaged in politics than are domestic business groups, and fragment and weaken the voice of big business overall. A first impact of MNCs is to splinter the organization of the business elite (Schneider 2004). The existence of foreign chambers of commerce, especially the ubiquitous Amchams (American Chambers of Commerce), provide a first visible indicator of the organizational fragmentation. Sectors with only MNCs (like autos) or only domestic firms (such as cement, historically) are spared these divisions. In sectors with more evenly divided production, sectoral associations can usually come to some modus vivendi between foreign and domestic firms, though sometimes the two groups will have separate caucuses within the same association. In other cases, foreign and domestic firms split to form separate organizations (as in mining in Chile and banking in Argentina).[18]

Even when MNCs are incorporated into sectoral associations, they are usually not well represented in encompassing, multisectoral associations. Earlier corporatist regulations often barred foreigners from leadership positions. Powerful associations of only large firms usually excluded foreigners as did encompassing business–government councils (Schneider 2004). One of the strongest business associations in Latin America, the Mexican Council of Businessmen (CMHN) excludes MNCs by statute (Schneider 2002). Argentina is an

---

[17] Hirschman was one of the first to worry about MNCs and politics: "The trouble with the foreign investor may well be not that he is so meddlesome, but that he is so mousy! It is the foreign investor's mousiness which deprives the policy makers of the guidance, pressures, and support they badly need to push through critically required development decisions and policies amid a welter of conflicting and antagonistic interests" (1971, 231).

[18] MNCs also fragmented business organization in Spain (Molina and Rhodes 2007, 238).

interesting exception in this regard as exclusive associations of large firms – CEA (Consejo Empresario Argentino) and later AEA (Asociación Empresaria Argentina) – included many MNCs.[19] The main point for associations is that big business rarely spoke with one voice and usually lacked institutional means for reconciling preferences and negotiating joint positions between foreign and national firms.

In terms of networks, political actors know that MNC managers are more temporary (even when they are nationals) and so are less valuable in developing longer-term networks. MNCs can hire local lobbyists and enlist their home country embassies, but to the extent networks with policy makers matter, short-term MNC managers are at a disadvantage especially compared with established families that own the largest domestic business groups (Schneider 2010b). Moreover, home country regulations limit the ability of some MNCs to make informal contributions, side payments, and direct bribes (Elizondo 2011, 200). In addition, electoral laws mostly prohibit foreign campaign contributions (see Chapter 7).

Hirschman argued that FDI, at middle levels of development, crowded out domestic entrepreneurs and sapped political support for accelerated development because policy making is not "invigorated by the influence normally emanating from a strong, confident, and assertive group of industrialists" (Hirschman 1971, 231). The counterfactual question of what would business politics in Latin America have looked like had MNCs not been a third or more or the largest firms raises contrasts with countries such as Japan, India, Korea, and to a lesser extent Turkey, that all had stronger, nationalist capitalist coalitions (Kohli 2004).

Because MNCs already have competitive advantages in international markets, they are less interested in national development strategies and more interventionist states. However, if states offer benefits and subsidies congruent with MNC investment strategies, MNCs will take full advantage, and, once established, MNCs become strong supporters of continued subsidies and protection (Egan 2010). When not directly benefiting from government largesse, MNCs generally have more liberal preferences on policy (interview Amcham, Buenos Aires, July 2010). MNCs are also less likely than domestic exporters to oppose the currency over valuations that have been historically common in Latin America and detrimental to both macro stability and manufactured exports (Steinberg 2010). As noted in Chapter 1, the many MNCs among the region's top exporters (a third of the 200 largest exporters in 2004; ECLAC 2006, 11) control much of the intrafirm trade. Currency appreciation in one country is thus more likely to provoke exit than voice. Rather than join a

[19] When Lula created CDES (Conselho de Desenvolvimento Econômico e Social) he invited five CEOs of MNCs, all Brazilians. Of the 82 members of the council, half were from business, so MNCs accounted for 12 percent of business representatives and 6 percent of all members (Ayala 2003).

costly coalition to press for devaluation, MNCs can shift exports to another country. For example, in response to the appreciation of the Brazilian Real, Bosch reduced exports from Brazil to the United States from $800 million in 2005 to $500 million in 2007 and made up the difference with exports from Mexico. Similarly, Massey Ferguson cut tractor exports from Brazil by a third and sourced them from Asia instead (*Valor Econômico*, 5 October 2007, pp. 1, A6, Radiobrás e-mail summary).

In sum, a range of factors weakens MNC engagement in local politics from the lack of political resources like networks and associations to the lack of intense policy preferences due to their ability to exit. This is not to deny occasional episodes of coup conspiracies in the mid-twentieth century nor instances of major corruption, but rather to highlight MNC absence from normal politics and engagement in, or debates about, national development strategies (see also Chapter 7). In some respects, this absence weakens domestic business by depriving it of a potential ally, but in other ways it leaves business groups in a stronger position by clearing the political arena of potential rivals.

## V. Conclusion

By the late 2000s, heavy annual inflows of FDI were normal, expected, and central components of development strategies of most governments of the region (outside of the left populist petro states). Much of this investment created jobs, increased productivity, and brought new products and technologies. However, at the same time, MNCs had several drawbacks in that they did no R&D (outside Brazil), often hired skilled workers away from other firms, and brought more trade and economic activity under hierarchical control. Most importantly, from a longer term, variety of capitalism perspective, MNCs shifted incentives for local economic agents, both big business and skilled workers. This chapter has noted several ways MNCs connect with labor markets, and these complementarities will be more fully elaborated in Chapters 5 and 6. The key complementarity examined here was between MNCs and domestic business groups. MNCs and business groups are connected through a myriad of commercial ties – joint ventures, suppliers, buyers, subcontractors, and so on – but the key complementarity is that the existence of MNCs in particular sectors increases the returns to business groups to investing elsewhere.

Just as all business groups are not alike, nor are all MNCs. In both cases, it is essential, as argued in Chapter 1, to problematize the organization and make organizational analysis an integral part of overall institutional analysis. Rather than assume preferences and strategies, the analysis needs to pry inside to see empirically what MNC strategies are. At a minimum, those strategies vary according to whether the firm is seeking resources, market access, cheap labor, or skilled labor. The deeper, development impacts of, for example, R&D FDI in Brazil, retail FDI in Peru, or maquila investment in Mexico are completely different. Given these diverse organizations and strategies, and their uneven distribution across countries of the region, it makes little sense (echoing studies cited in the Introduction) to attempt to assess the aggregate, universal impact of FDI on outcomes like growth, exports, or investment.

However, broad aggregate trends in FDI do seem to contribute to within-variety heterogeneity (see Morgan 2009). Much of the distribution of FDI is driven by geography: large populations draw market-seeking MNCs, resource-seeking FDI goes where it can find natural resources, and efficiency-seeking MNCs concentrate near the rest of the production chain or the destination market in the United States. As such, FDI constitutes an exogenous shock, mostly unmediated by local institutions (though flows slowed in the 2000s to countries with populist left presidents).[20] However, all types of FDI fit well with hierarchical capitalism (save R&D FDI in Brazil), and generally do not push labor markets and skills away from the low skill equilibrium. As discussed in Chapter 6, efficiency-seeking FDI draws mostly on unskilled labor, whereas resource-seeking FDI employs small numbers of workers. Market seeking FDI may employ more skilled workers (as in automobile production), though without shaking up skills markets overall because MNCs can poach workers or train their own.

---

[20] FDI in Germany in contrast is endogenous and driven more by institutions as MNCs seek out advantages of CMEs in manufacturing. In 2004, FDI went disproportionally into manufacturing: 60 percent of employment in FDI (Morgan 2009, 591).

# 5

# Labor

*Atomized Relations and Segmented Markets*

## I. Introduction[1]

Through the mid-2000s, observers of labor markets in Latin America generally agreed that performance in recent decades had been disappointing, for some, in fact, "perhaps the greatest disappointment of the new development strategy" (Berg et al. 2006, 1). This disappointment is not restricted to social scientists, as public opinion surveys "confirm that employment is people's primary concern in almost all countries" (Pagés, Pierre, and Scarpetta 2009, 1). Employment levels picked up during the 2000s, but often in low productivity activities or what a World Bank study called "growthless jobs" (Pagés et al. 2009, 2).

However, the diagnoses and resulting policy prescriptions for how to fix labor markets vary greatly. For the International Labour Organization (ILO), for example, a core problem is informality, which accounts for about half of all employment and half of new jobs created in the 2000s. A central policy recommendation is therefore for more and better enforcement as well as "social dialogue" among representatives of workers, employers, and the government (ILO 2006, 12, 19; see also IDB 2003, 118, 277). Others, in contrast, blame rigidity and over-regulation of labor markets and its "many undesirable side effects," and call for deregulation and more flexibility (World Bank 2004a, 35, 37–38). Another group focuses on comparatively low levels of education and skills. These studies usually recommend greater investment in education as well as additional policies to reform training institutes (IDB 2003, 276), to expose firms to greater competition (de Ferranti et al. 2003, 9), or promote diffusion of information on the high returns to education (Menezes-Filho 2003, 143). Returns to education have been a central concern of scholars who analyze

[1] This chapter draws heavily on Schneider and Karcher (2010), which provides more empirical detail and data sources.

how shifts in labor markets in the 1990s exacerbated already high levels of inequality, both because wages of skilled workers rose relative to wages of unskilled workers and because the returns to education are higher for rich students than for poor students (Perry et al. 2005; Di Gropello 2006, 76–77). Policy prescriptions tend to emphasize reducing obstacles and enhancing access to secondary, postsecondary, and vocational education.

The case for each of these proposed reforms is compelling, but individually their impact is likely to be muted unless they take into account the broader interactions among core institutions of labor markets and their interactions with strategies and structures of business groups and MNCs analyzed in previous chapters. Expanding programs in vocational education, for example, is designed to raise skill levels in the workforce. However, the usefulness of these skills and the incentives of workers to invest time in acquiring them depend on the likelihood of remaining in jobs that require these skills, a condition that is difficult to meet in labor markets in Latin America where median job tenure is only three years. This low tenure rate in turn is associated in part with high regulation and a large informal sector. In short, the effectiveness of training depends on a range of other factors beyond the actual training programs themselves.

A more encompassing analysis entails an examination of five core features or institutions – extensive labor market regulation, a low-skills regime, rapid turnover, sparse unions, and pervasive informality – and the reinforcing interactions among them that distinguish labor markets in Latin America from labor markets in most other regions. Other scholars have looked at some of these connections, but none has put together all these pieces. In particular, rapid turnover, and its negative effects on human capital and social dialogue, has received little attention. In fact, to the extent researchers look at turnover, it is often viewed in positive terms as an indicator of smooth adjustment to changing market opportunities (see World Bank 2004b, chap. 7).

Political factors further reinforce some of these economic interactions. Political contention over issues such as informality, high employment protection, or low skills cannot be fully understood in isolation from one another. Moreover, understanding these interactions helps flesh out the politics of labor market regulation by adding to the analysis of the active support for the status quo an understanding of the weakness of potential sources of support for would-be reformers. So, for example, the potential coalition for reforming the informal sector (forcing more workers onto the books) is difficult to mobilize in part because the informal sector does not threaten existing unions, provides a default safety net for workers who are laid off on a regular basis, and offers employers ways to circumvent costly regulations.

Labor markets everywhere are segmented by salary levels, employment contracts, professional qualifications, and labor relations, but the five core features of labor markets in Latin America segment labor markets in distinctive ways. In addition to the formal/informal divide, formal workers fall into two main segments: (1) a large segment characterized by high turnover, precarious employment conditions, no union or other representation, and low skills and (2) a much smaller segment, a labor elite, in which workers have long job tenure, union representation, full protection under high labor regulation, and high skills.[2] Demarcations among the three segments are more gray zones than sharp lines, because workers move across boundaries (especially between formal and informal jobs) and because each boundary has workers in intermediate positions such as partially formal work (when, for instance, not all hours are reported or all benefits paid).

In rough average terms though, the informal sector accounts for about 40 to 50 percent of employment; the high turnover, formal segment for 30 to 40 percent; and the long tenure, labor elite for 10 to 20 percent. The second, high turnover segment resembles LME labor markets, but the other two segments – the informal and highly regulated, elite segments – make labor markets in hierarchical capitalism differ from those in liberal capitalism where informality and regulation are much less. In a descriptive sense, labor relations in Latin America are more hierarchical because employment in the two largest segments is so precarious (and workers lack representation) that it gives employers greater power over workers. In addition, the state intervenes hierarchically to impose restrictive regulations on employers of long-tenure workers.

By way of a road map, this chapter focuses primarily on dynamics internal to labor markets. The following Chapter 6 uses the analysis of skills to demonstrate the complementarities among MNCs, business groups, and labor markets. However, it is important to bear in mind the basic strategies of business for hiring unskilled labor and sometimes small numbers of skilled workers (mainly trained by firms) as outlined in previous chapters. These firm strategies are compatible with the five core features of labor markets in Latin America: low skill levels, high labor regulation, short job tenure, a large informal sector, and small, politicized unions that lack plant-level representation. Section II elaborates on the distinctive traits of labor markets in Latin America and briefly catalogs how labor markets in Latin America differ in most respects from both liberal and coordinated economies. Section III turns to an examination of the complementarities among the core institutions. Section IV analyzes additional political complementarities.

## II. Labor Markets in Liberal, Coordinated, and Hierarchical Capitalism

The box-and-whiskers plots in Figures 5.1 through 5.4 provide a first overview of how labor markets in Latin America differ on all dimensions from coordinated and liberal economies: informality and labor market regulation are

---

[2] These segments do not include public employment (which has a significant component similar to the high tenure segment) except workers in state-owned enterprises.

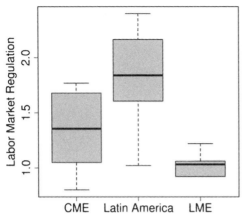

FIGURE 5.1. Regulation. *Sources*: Data for 1997 from Botero et al. (2003).

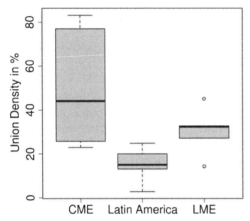

FIGURE 5.2. Union Density. *Sources*: Data for 1991–95 for Latin America from IDB (2003); for CMEs and LMEs for 1995, from OECD (2010b).

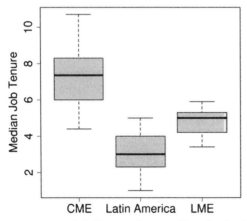

FIGURE 5.3. Job Tenure. *Sources*: Data for Latin America 1999–2001, except for Chile (1996) from IDB (2003). Data for CMEs and LMEs for 1995 from Estevez Abe et al. (2001) using OECD data.

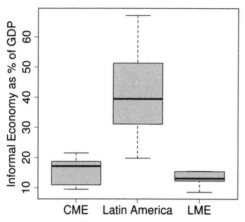

FIGURE 5.4. Informality. *Sources*: Data for 2002/2003 from Schneider (2005).

higher than in CMEs and LMEs; job tenure and union density are lower.[3] Across these four dimensions, there is almost no overlap between the boxes for Latin America and those for CMEs and LMEs. The box plots also show that Latin American countries not only are distinct from those in CMEs and LMEs, but are also quite similar to each other; the boxes and whiskers for union density, job tenure, and labor market regulation are just as narrow as those for the established varieties of capitalism. Although the box for Latin America is long for informality (which correlates more with GDP per capita), the region still forms a comparative cluster (with almost no overlap with the ranges for CMEs and LMEs). On these descriptive indicators, Latin American labor markets do appear to constitute a distinct variety, as the following discussions of each dimension spell out in greater detail.

1. *Labor market regulation.* Indices of regulation in Latin America are very high in comparative terms (Figure 5.1). These indices are also higher than in other developing regions (the median for developing Asia is close to the median for LMEs). Many countries in Latin America liberalized their labor legislations in the late 20th century in line with overall economic liberalization, yet these reforms were much more limited in extent than in other areas of the economy (Lora 2001). Particular to Latin America is a strong reliance on severance pay as a means of unemployment protection. The index on job security by Botero et al. (2003) used here does not weight severance pay heavily and may thus even understate the degree of regulation in Latin America. According to an

---

[3] In the box and whisker plots, the thick line shows the median for each group. The box contains all cases between the first and the third quartile. The "whiskers" include all cases within another 1.5 quartile ranges. For data sources, see Schneider and Karcher (2010). The patterns and interactions documented here may also exist in other developing and transition economics (Piore and Schrank 2008; Batt, Holman, and Holtgrewe 2009).

index of dismissal costs, regulation in every Latin American country is higher than in developed countries (Heckman and Pagés-Serra 2000).[4] At the same time, countries of Latin American have either no system of unemployment or social insurance or systems (as in the Southern Cone) where the benefits are relatively low, temporary, and restricted to small numbers of workers (Pagés et al. 2009).

2. *Labor unions* (Figure 5.2). Despite considerable variation, most labor unions in Latin America are comparatively small, and most have been shrinking. Rates of union density vary from 20 to 25 percent in Brazil, Argentina, and Mexico, to 10 to 15 percent in Peru, Colombia, and Chile, to negligible rates in some of the smaller, poorer countries (IDB 2003, 233).[5] Labor unions in Latin America are also more politicized than their counterparts elsewhere (Cook 1998, 314; Murillo 2001, 197). Earlier in the twentieth century, unions in Latin America, as well as in most developed countries, focused their mobilization strategies heavily on the state and political parties. However, unions in Europe retained a powerful organizational presence in the labor market and in many cases mobilized to bargain directly with well-organized employers' associations. Unions in Latin America had less autonomous organizational strength in labor markets, depended more on state and party leaders, and encountered fewer encompassing employers' associations with which they could bargain independently: "relatively few unions have the resources, the bargaining power, or the employer counterparts willing to engage in this kind of negotiation" (Cook 1998, 316). Unions focused on "political bargaining" with the government in contrast to the greater concentration in developed countries on economic (wage) bargaining with employers (Buchanan 1995; Cook 1998; Etchemendy and Collier 2007).[6]

---

[4] Although reforms in labor markets were not as significant as market reforms in other areas, several countries, especially Chile, Peru, and Argentina, undertook major flexibilizing reforms. The Botero et al. index captures the state of regulation after most of these reforms (see the online data appendix for Schneider and Karcher 2010).

[5] By some estimates, unionization among wage earners fell over the 1990s from 67 to 39 percent in Argentina, from 60 to 43 percent in Mexico, and from 18 to 5 percent in Peru (Marshall 2000, 12).

[6] For example, in pre-Chávez Venezuela, the four confederations of unions were closely tied with political parties, and "labor representatives used the clout of the major political parties to win favorable terms from management in contract negotiations. Since 1984, in fact, the union confederations have focused on achieving blanket salary raises by government decree . . . , shifting their activity from negotiating with business to government lobbying" (Enright, Francés, and Saavedra 1996, 218–19). Observers in Chile have criticized the CUT for focusing on traditional political and ethical concerns and attacking the neoliberal development model, rather than attending to more immediate, tractable worker concerns. However, CUT is legally prohibited from collective bargaining, which is completely decentralized to the firm level (Berg 2006, 50). See also Murillo and Schrank (2010, 249).

In instances where unions in Latin America do negotiate employment contracts, the level of centralization varies across countries and over time but tends to take place mostly at the firm or local level.[7] In Argentina, most contracts were by sector until 1993, then decentralized to the firm level for a decade, before recentralizing at the sectoral level in the wake of the economic boom of the 2000s (Etchemendy and Collier 2007). In Mexico, most, and in Chile all, contracts are negotiated at the firm level (Berg et al. 2006, 197–98; Haagh 2002). However, despite this trend toward decentralized wage bargaining, union representation at the plant and shop-floor levels is rare.[8] For example, in two-thirds of Chilean firms, "there exists no formal mechanism for the workers to participate in dialogue with management, either as a union or some other alternative" (Berg 2006, 49).

In sum, the general picture of bargaining in Latin America is of small, truncated unions, circumscribed in scope and confined to an intermediate or lower level of bargaining with major political, organizational, and legal constraints both on centralized bargaining and on shop-floor representation. Sympathetic governments may occasionally bolster union negotiators, but in recent decades, such support has rarely had lasting institutionalized consequences, especially on the shop floor. The absence of plant-level representation, and certainly anything formal like German-style works councils, is crucial in foreclosing possibilities for negotiations over skills and work organization that is the norm in coordinated capitalism.

3. *Job tenure.* By a variety of measures, job tenure is long in CMEs, short in LMEs, and really short in Latin America. The median tenure was 7.4 years in CMEs, 5 in LMEs, and only 3 in Latin America (Figure 5.3). Mean tenure rates show similar differences and a declining trend. Among major countries in Latin America, mean tenure in Argentina was 6.7 years in 2001 (down from 7.1 years in 1992) and 5 years in Brazil. In the wake of flexibilizing reforms in Peru in the 1990s, mean tenure fell by almost half from 5.8 years in 1991 to 3.3 years in 1999 (Cook 2007, 125). In contrast, mean tenure was 6.6 years in the United States in 1998, 12.2 years in Japan, and 10.7 years in Germany (Berg et al. 2006, 38).

In Brazil, among formal sector workers in the 1990s, annual turnover was 33 percent. Turnover was lower for workers who were older, had more education,

---

[7] Murillo and Schrank (2010, 253) list the dominant level of collective bargaining as follows: Argentina (industry), Brazil (local), Chile (firm), Colombia (firm/craft), Mexico (industry/local), Peru (firm), Uruguay (industry), and Venezuela (local/industry).

[8] Measures of the proportion of workers covered by collective bargains are not available for most countries. In Argentina coverage rose to 80 to 90 percent of workers in the mid 2000s (Etchemendy and Collier 2007). In Chile, in contrast, coverage was less than 10 percent in the 1990s (Haagh 2002, p. 92). But even in Argentina, unions are only weakly represented on the shop floor. In the comparatively well-organized metal sector, less than 20 percent of the firms that are covered by sectoral bargaining have union delegates (Karcher forthcoming).

and worked in larger firms (Gonzaga 2003, 179). For a later period (1997–2002), annual turnover was 40 percent (Gonzaga 2003, 180). A 2004 survey of several hundred, mostly lower-income workers in São Paulo, found that the average duration of their last employment was just over two years and for nearly three-quarters their last job lasted fewer than two years (Haagh 2011, 7). The exceptionally high turnover in Latin America is rarely central in analyses of labor markets and labor politics, but deserves greater emphasis on its own as a defining feature of work in Latin America, and especially, as discussed later, in relation to skills, regulation, and union organizing. Job tenure is also crucial for differentiating the high-turnover from low-turnover segment (labor elite).

4. *Informal employment* (Figure 5.4). Nonagricultural informal work has averaged more than 40 percent in the region for the last several decades (Pagés et al. 2009, 1). The range is wide within Latin America (from 25 percent (Chile) to 65 percent (Peru) (IDB 2003, 210) but still well above levels for CMEs and LMEs, both recently and historically, and somewhat higher than levels of informality in Asia. The largest share of the informal economy is accounted for by self-employed workers, or workers in micro-enterprises with fewer than five workers, but even for firms with more than 100 workers, almost 20 percent of workers are not covered by social security and can thus be considered informal (IDB 2003, 211). By the late 2000s, informality began to drop in Brazil, Argentina, and elsewhere, but overall levels remained comparatively high (Berg 2010).

The division in Latin America between formal and informal is permeable (Perry et al. 2007). Workers move rather frequently from informal to formal jobs, and back again. The absence of unemployment insurance (outside Brazil and Chile) means laid-off workers look to be rehired as soon as possible, which is usually easier in the informal sector. Data on age distribution across different kinds of jobs suggests a life-cycle pattern in which young workers entering the labor force start in informal jobs, mid-career workers are more likely to have formal jobs, and worker older than fifty are more likely to be self-employed, and thereby end up in the informal sector again (Perry et al. 2007, 7). In other words, although labor markets are segmented in terms of the types of jobs, workers in these segments are less likely to view themselves exclusively as one type of worker or another and are less sharply divided between insiders and outsiders, especially over the longer run.

5. *Skills and education.* Not surprisingly, given the income disparities, general education levels in Latin America are lower than in developed countries. In 2000, the average years of schooling among the adult population was 5.7 years in Latin America, 9.9 years in CMEs, and 11 years in LMEs. Controlling for income, educational attainment in Latin America was also comparatively low: "Latin American adults have 1.4 fewer years of education, and East Asian adults 0.4 years more than would be expected by their income levels" (de Ferranti et al. 2003, 3). More important though than years of schooling are actual educational outcomes (Table 5.1). Median reading scores for countries

TABLE 5.1. *Reading Proficiency among 15-Year-Old Students in 2009*

|  | Mean Reading Score | % of Boys below Level 2 |
|---|---|---|
| OECD average | 493 | 25 |
| **Selected Comparison Countries** | | |
| Korea | 539 | 9 |
| Finland | 536 | 13 |
| Slovenia | 483 | 31 |
| Austria | 470 | 35 |
| Turkey | 464 | 33 |
| Thailand | 421 | 55 |
| **Latin America** (median) | **413** | **54** |
| Chile | 449 | 36 |
| Mexico | 425 | 46 |
| Uruguay | 426 | 51 |
| Colombia | 413 | 50 |
| Brazil | 412 | 56 |
| Argentina | 398 | 59 |
| Panama | 371 | 72 |
| Peru | 370 | 70 |

*Source*: OECD (2010c, 11).

of Latin America that participated in PISA 2009 were 80 points lower than the OECD average (and the OECD now includes developing countries such as Mexico, Chile, and Turkey). Eighty points is roughly equivalent to two additional years of schooling. Disaggregating the mean, many students in Latin America fall below level 2, which is a minimum requirement for moving on to more training, education, and higher-skill employment.[9] Although Chile's 36 percent is on par with the lower-ranking OECD countries, the median for the rest of the region is more than half of 15-year-old students.

Moreover, Latin American governments invested little in training people once out of school: median spending on vocational training for the unemployed was .04 percent of GDP, compared to .23 percent in LMEs and .52 percent in CMEs (calculated from IDB 2003, 282). By another calculation, Venezuelan companies on average spent .2 percent of revenues on training, compared to

---

[9] For math, the average level of students in Latin America falling below level 2 is 63 percent (Elizondo 2011, 188). According to the OECD, "Level 2 is considered a baseline level of proficiency, at which students begin to demonstrate the reading skills that will enable them to participate effectively and productively in life" (OECD 2010c, 6) Students scoring below level 2 tend not to go on to postsecondary education and to have poorer labor market outcomes (OECD 2010d, 52).

2 percent in Germany and 3 percent in Japan (Enright et al. 1996, 215). Given this history of underinvestment in education and skills, it was not surprising that, as growth accelerated in the 2000s, skill shortages emerged as a growing constraint in several countries of the region (Pagés et al. 2009, 8–9). Chapter 6 analyzes skill issues in greater depth.

In sum, in a descriptive sense, labor markets in hierarchical capitalism are distinct rather than a subvariety of either liberal or coordinated economies. Some trends in Latin America – falling union density or higher turnover – make them appear to be heading in an LME direction. However, the convergence is partial and slow and is not matched on dimensions like regulation and informality, so for the time being, it does not seem appropriate to think of them as emerging LMEs. The decline of union density is one of the areas of greatest change, though this did not always imply a radical shift in the role of unions in labor markets because previously larger unions were often constrained by hostile and/or authoritarian governments, and many lacked routinized mechanisms for collective bargaining.

Other patterns have been more stable over time. On the regulation dimension, one comprehensive study of the labor reforms between 1990 and the mid-2000s documents reforms in 11 of the 17 countries in Latin America, but finds surprisingly little change in the standard labor contract (Vega Ruíz 2005, 12). Other authors studying Latin American labor reforms have argued that "early laws have proved particularly stable over time" (Carnes 2009; see also Cook 2007). ILO estimates point to an increasing informalization in Latin American through the mid 2000s, but even in the period between 1950 and 1980, four out of every ten jobs created were in the informal economy (Tokman 2001, 13). Low skill levels and a lack of training have been well-known issues in Latin America for decades, and, although schooling has improved somewhat, Latin America's relative position in the worldwide skill distribution has not. Evidence on turnover prior to the 1990s is scarce, but most partial data suggest that turnover was high (see, for example, Humphrey 1982).

This review of the five core features of labor markets focuses on the average tendencies in Latin America. The point is not that the countries of the region are all the same, but rather that labor market indices cluster in ways that justify classifying them as different from labor markets elsewhere. From a comparative perspective, what stands out is the relative absence of significant variation, compared both to other regions and to other dimensions of change in the political economies of Latin America. For other purposes, further disaggregation would be necessary to separate out, for example, groups of smaller, poorer countries in Central America and the Andean region where countries tend to have lower union density, lower education levels, and larger informal sectors than do the bigger, richer countries in South America. And, for the most part, the qualitative evidence for this chapter is drawn from this latter group.

Numerous calculations exist for the size of the informal sector. Although scholars differ on how exactly to measure the informal sector, their calculations

TABLE 5.2. *Labor Elite: Workers with 10 or More Years of Tenure (percentage)*

| | |
|---|---|
| Argentina | 25 |
| Bolivia | 19 |
| Chile | 21 |
| Honduras | 13 |
| Mexico | 19 |
| Nicaragua | 22 |
| Panama | 26 |
| Paraguay | 27 |
| Uruguay | 33 |
| **Latin America** (median) | 22 |
| OECD median | 35 |
| LME median | 30 |
| CME median | 39 |
| Mediterranean median | 43 |
| East Europe median | 33 |

*Sources*: for Latin America (except Mexico) (IDB 2003, statistical appendix) for various years in the late 1990s. For OECD countries (including Mexico), data are for early 2000s from http://stats.oecd.org/Index.aspx?DatasetCode =TENURE_DIS. OECD median is for 17 countries. LMEs: Australia, Canada, Ireland, and United Kingdom. CMEs: Austria, Belgium, Denmark, Finland, and Germany. Mediterranean: France, Greece, Italy, and Spain. East Europe: Czech Republic, Hungary, and Poland.

still rank countries and regions in the same way. What is harder to calculate is the size of the third segment, the formal, long-tenure, highly regulated, unionized, high-skill segment, or what used to be called the labor aristocracy (Table 5.2). One approach would be to look at economic activity. This third segment, or labor elite, is common in capital-intensive industries like automobiles and mining.[10] However, many in the third segment are also in minority positions in firms that otherwise have rapid turnover as, for example, with skilled mechanics responsible for equipment maintenance.

Another rough measure is the percentage of workers with long tenure (although this could also include some informal and unskilled workers). The median for Latin America of 22 percent of workers with more than 10 years of tenure (though data are lacking for large countries like Brazil and Colombia) is much lower than the proportion among OECD countries and various subsets of OECD countries (Table 5.2). Of workers with long tenure, many

---

[10] In the leading 4 percent of industrial firms in Brazil (about 1,000 out of 31,000 firms with more than 30 employees), workers were twice as productive, earned nearly twice as much, had on average two years more education, and two years more of average tenure (five versus three years) than were workers in industry as a whole (de Negri et al. 2010, 20, calculated from table 4).

are in the public sector (starting with millions of tenured teachers), so the proportion of workers with long tenure in the private sector is on average less than 22 percent median for Latin America. Another estimate would be the percentage of workers who are effectively protected by labor legislation (though this group could also include some short tenure and unskilled workers). In Chile, for example, only 28 percent of workers are eligible for severance pay (has an indefinite contract and has been working for more than a year) (Albornoz et al. 2011, 18). The labor elite would be a smaller subset of this group. The data are incomplete but point by several estimates to a labor elite on the order of 10 to 20 percent of the workforce.

## III. Complementarities in Labor Markets

Labor markets in Latin America are characterized by a number of institutional complementarities with negative outcomes. One of the better-known examples is the "low skills, bad jobs" trap, in which firms in countries with a large unskilled workforce "have little incentives to provide good jobs (requiring high skills and providing high wages), and if few good jobs are available, workers have little incentive to acquire skills" (Snower 1994, 1). Figure 5.5 sketches out economic complementarities and compatibilities among five core components of labor markets in Latin America. These complementarities structured incentives for sustaining the status quo (and as such constitute a constant cause type of path dependency; Mahoney 2000).

*Labor Unions.* The characteristics of Latin American labor unions – low density, strength in political bargaining, weakness in economic bargaining, and a lack of shop floor organization – reinforce several other labor market features. The weakness of unions, both nationally and on the shop floor, reinforces the low-skill equilibrium by impeding closer employer-union cooperation in skill upgrading. In earlier industrializers, unions were crucial in establishing vocational training systems (Thelen 2004), and later in enhancing the quality and quantity of training (Sehnbruch 2006, 208). In coordinated capitalism, the most successful vocational training systems are, in fact, administered jointly by unions and employers.

In Latin America, systems of vocational education sometimes provide for representation by labor unions on the national, local, and sometimes firm-level boards and committees responsible for planning training programs (IDB 2001, 139–40). But these boards are often pro forma councils charged with overseeing state-mandated spending, and most are distant from the shop floor (Ducci 2001, 272). In Chile, firms receive tax benefits for training workers, and even greater benefits if the training program is endorsed by a worker-management committee. Yet only 5 percent of the firms that provide training established such committees (Sehnbruch 2006, 185). In addition, the government expected a new apprenticeship program in the late 1980s to train 10,000 workers, but companies hired only about 500, in part because neither unions nor business

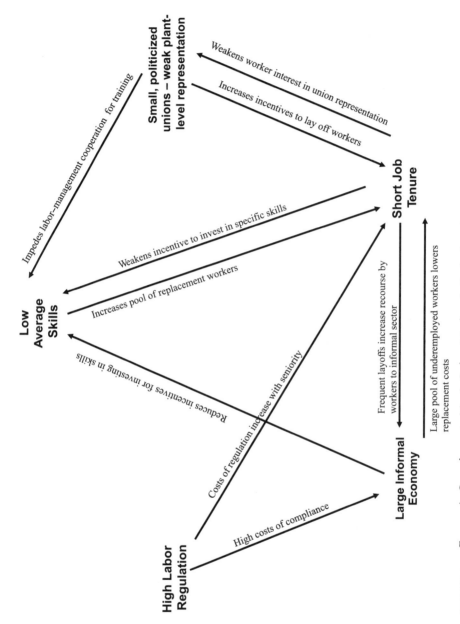

FIGURE 5.5. Economic Complementarities in Labor Markets in Latin America

Small, politicized unions – weak plant-level representation

Impedes labor-management cooperation for training

Weakens worker interest in union representation

Increases incentives to lay off workers

Short Job Tenure

Weakens incentive to invest in specific skills

Increases pool of replacement workers

Low Average Skills

Reduces incentives for investing in skills

Costs of regulation increase with seniority

Frequent layoffs increase recourse by workers to informal sector

Large pool of underemployed workers lowers replacement costs

Large Informal Economy

High costs of compliance

High Labor Regulation

associations were involved in designing or implementing the program (Sehnbruch 2006, 179). As noted earlier, Chilean labor law forbids unions from bargaining over nonwage issues.

The character of unions and generalized antagonism between unions and management may also contribute to low levels of job tenure. In the absence of important coordinating functions (as, for example, regarding training), "employers throughout the region have preferred the unilateral imposition of workplace changes" (Cook 1998, 316). From the union side, the absence of local opportunities for negotiation encourages a more national and militant orientation. The mutual disengagement at the firm and the plant level creates a climate of distrust between unions and employers and gives employers stronger incentives to accelerate turnover to foreclose possibilities of more vigorous union organizing on the shop floor.[11]

The IDB examined several surveys and concluded that industrial relations were "far from optimal" in the larger countries of Latin America. Among 47 countries surveyed, six Latin American countries mostly fell toward the bottom half, some near the bottom, of rankings by employers on whether industrial relations were more productive or hostile. Employees took an even dimmer view. Asked whether employers were honest, worker responses ranges from a high of only 25 percent in Mexico to a low of less than 5 percent in Argentina. Positive responses were similarly low to the answer of whether employees thought overall relations with employers were good (IDB 2001, 135–36).

As noted in the analysis of broader complementarities in Chapter 2, firm strategies – both business groups and MNCs – usually mean that few benefits can be gained from close negotiations with labor, and firms therefore have little interest in less atomized organization and representation by workers. In coordinated capitalism, in contrast, firms have strategies of high quality production and incremental innovation that consequently increase their interest in having well-organized unions and good shop-floor representation in order to have stable employment relations (without workplace disruptions), lasting settlements on gains from training, employee feedback to improve productivity and quality, and mechanisms for avoiding holdup by long-term workers with firm specific skills (Estevez-Abe et al. 2001; Hall and Soskice 2001; Thelen 2001). For MNCs and business groups in hierarchical capitalism that rely on unskilled labor, these incentives are lacking because the majority of workers are easily replaced, poorly paid, and short term. In this context, unions can impede the hiring and firing flexibility that is crucial to managing unskilled labor. Of course, MNCs and business groups have stronger incentives to negotiate with their labor elites (the higher-skilled, longer-term employees), but these minority

---

[11] In Chile, increasingly common temporary employment contracts legally prohibit workers from joining unions (Berg 2006, 55). In his account of Brazilian autoworkers, Humphrey describes how employers used regular layoffs – regardless of skill level or seniority – to control workers (1982, 118–21, 161).

relations can likely be better managed informally than with unions representing all workers. So, generally, firm strategies favor weaker unions and atomized labor relations.

*Informal Economy.* A large pool of informal workers enables high turnover rates. From a firm's point of view, the "reserve army" of informal workers facilitates quick replacement of laid-off workers. Many informal workers are waiting, "queuing" for formal jobs (Maloney 1997, 20). The fact that mainly salaried workers are queuing may even suggest that firms are able to fill vacant positions with employees already working in comparable (albeit informal) jobs. In general, there is a relatively large flow of informal workers into formal jobs – and back. Over a six-month period, the flow was about 10 percent of all workers in either direction in Argentina and 15 percent in Mexico (IDB 2003, 68, 76).

Additionally, high levels of informal work, especially in the form of self-employment and tiny firms, have a detrimental effect on the skill regime. As these micro enterprises are characterized by "poor capitalization and backward technology" (Portes, Castells, and Benton 1989, 300), they become part of the "low skill trap" where returns are low for additional training. The availability of employment opportunities in the informal sector, some of them well paid, lowers incentives for students to stay in school or for workers to invest more in skills (see Chapter 6). If we expand the concept of the informal sector across borders, then the option of well-paid, unskilled employment in a foreign informal sector (as for undocumented workers in the United States) further reduces incentives for training and formal schooling. Conversely, improving labor law enforcement – and thereby reducing informality – enhances skill levels (Almeida and Aterido 2008).

*Short Job Tenure.* The short average duration of job tenure in Latin America also undermines incentives to invest in education and training. In Peru, for example, high and increasing turnover in the 1990s, "had negative consequences for training and productivity" (Cook 2007, 125). More generally, the IDB concluded that "temporary contracts also seem to have negative effects on the accumulation of human capital" (IDB 2003, 220). Investments in specific skills are especially unlikely if both workers and employers face substantial risks of losing their investment (Estevez-Abe et al. 2001; Gonzaga 2003).[12]

For example, in Chile, though workers may receive some initial induction training in their first months on the job, training is generally more common for workers with longer tenure (Sehnbruch 2006, 191, 193). Moreover, not only

---

[12] In Venezuela, high turnover, fueled in part, as noted above, by the high cost of severance payments, "discourages firms from hiring people for the long-term, promoting them to higher levels of responsibility, or investing in their training or education. Managers of firms that place a high value on human resource training confided in interviews that they have to struggle against these very real disincentives" (Enright et al. 1996, 205, 215).

do workers change jobs frequently; they also move among completely different kinds of jobs. Among Chilean workers who changed jobs in the late 1990s, about half moved from industry, commerce, construction, or services into one of the other three sectors (Sehnbruch 2006, 128). In short, workers had little reason to expect that training in one job would be useful for the next. With little or no unemployment compensation in most countries of the region, laid-off workers have to take the next job opportunity that comes along, regardless of the sector or match with workers' existing skills (IDB 2003, 65).

Short job tenure also complicates union organizing, especially on the shop floor. If the median, and expected, job tenure is three years, workers have little incentive to spend time and money to get organized. More generally, a range of comparative evidence finds a positive relationship between higher tenure and greater organization. In the United Kingdom, for example, long tenure is strongly associated with union membership (Gottfried 1992, 108). In Brazil, the autoworker strikes in the late 1970s were initiated by toolmakers who had longer average times of employment (Humphrey 1982, 161). More generally, in Latin America, workers in the public sector have disproportionally high unionization rates and much higher job stability and tenure.

High turnover rates are also positively associated with the size of the informal economy. Without unemployment benefits, workers cannot afford to remain unemployed during extended periods of job search and turn often to the informal sector. As a consequence, the informal labor market serves as a highly flexible buffer. In Argentina, more than 8 out of 10 unemployed workers who find work start working an informal job; in Mexico, the equivalent number is 6 out of 10 (IBD 2003, pp. 73f). High turnover and economic insecurity thus make the informal sector an important temporary source of employment for Latin American workers and contribute to its large size.

Returning again to the broader complementarities of firms and labor markets, firms with strategies premised on capacities to respond to market or macro volatility have incentives to maintain a steady flow of temporary workers, so managers can lay off workers quickly at low cost in response to sudden market downturns and can hire them back quickly and without training when demand revives. Portfolio business groups, especially in volatile commodity sectors, as well as MNCs and subcontractors in rapidly shifting global production networks will be especially keen on overall flexibility and rapid turnover (Locke 2013).

*Labor Market Regulation.* Most economists agree that highly regulated labor markets promote larger informal economies (IDB 2003, 208; World Bank 2004b, 136, 148; Gonzaga 2003). The logic of this complementarity is simple: as labor regulations increase, the "opportunity costs" of formal employment (compared to informal employment) rise. In a context of weak enforcement, the costs for firms to remain completely or partially informal may be much lower than the costs of formal compliance. A World Bank study concluded that "cross-country studies show that a reduction of the employment regulation

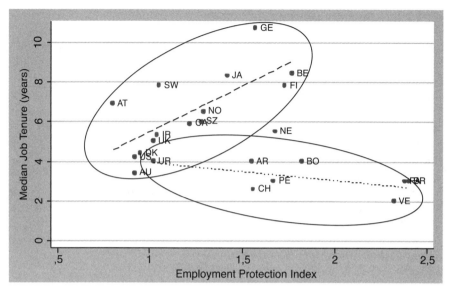

FIGURE 5.6. Job Tenure and Employment Protection

index by a third is associated with a 14-percentage-point decline in informal employment and a 6.7-percentage-point fall in output produced in the informal economy" (2004a, 37). The lack of effective social and unemployment insurance further contributes to the informalization of employment, because the informal economy becomes a means of subsistence for many.

Labor market institutions in coordinated capitalism promote employment stability and thus foster the investment in specific skills by both firms and workers. As Figure 5.6 shows, there is indeed a positive relationship between employment regulation and job tenure in developed countries. However, the correlation in Latin America runs the opposite way: employment regulation actually has a negative relationship with median job tenure.

High levels of labor regulation can lower job tenure in the formal sector in several ways. Dismissed workers are entitled in most countries to severance payments (Cook 2007, 48). As severance payments generally increase with length of service (IDB 2003, 58), employers have incentives to keep average tenure short. According to an overview of the Venezuelan labor market in the 1990s, severance provisions "make it costlier to keep workers on payroll for extended periods than to dismiss them and hire new workers. For more firms, it is cheaper to fire workers and to replace them than to promote them, since each increase in salary inflates the final payment to be made on their leaving the firm" (Enright et al. 1996, 205). Workers may also seek to get fired in order to gain access to severance pay (Gonzaga 2003, 176–77). In Brazil, workers have individual accounts (FGTS, Fundo de Garantia por Tempo de Serviço) into which employers pay about a month's salary per year. Workers cannot access their FGTS accounts if they quit but can if fired, in which case the firm pays an additional 40 percent of the FGTS balance. Often, workers will informally negotiate these claims down in order to get firms to fire them. In one survey, 62 percent of workers who said they quit their jobs also said they received their FGTS balance. Because voluntary quits do not legally entitle workers to their FGTS balance, these were "fake" or negotiated dismissals (Gonzaga 2003, 177).[13]

*Low Skills.* Low skill levels should, in principle, also facilitate (or reduce the cost to employers of) rapid turnover, because unskilled workers are easier to replace than are skilled workers. The median time to fill an unskilled vacancy in Latin America is just more than one week, compared to just less than three weeks to fill a vacancy for a skilled position (Pagés et al. 2009, 106). Surveys of workers in the 1990s showed that unskilled workers in Mexico were twice as likely as skilled workers, and in Argentina, more than 50 percent more likely, to transition from employment to unemployment or inactivity (IDB 2003, 76).[14] And, the connection between low skills and turnover is not just among small and medium firms; in Camargo Corrêa, one of the largest business groups in Brazil, more than half the workers have only a primary education or less, and median tenure is only about two years (*Relatorio Anual* 2004, p. 4).

The goal of this section was to illustrate the wide range of complementarities among the five core components where institutionalized patterns of behavior in one realm of the labor market affect the incentives of employers and workers in other realms. The intensity of these complementarities is variable as are the precise mechanisms that link the realms together, but the overall conclusion is that it makes little sense to analyze these components in isolation. Moreover, additional complementarities are mediated by politics.

## IV. Politics and Complementarities with Other Institutions

In Latin America, political systems and states structure incentives in ways that form an important part of the complementary interactions of economic

---

[13] In Brazil, regulations over the FGTS can sour labor relations overall. Workers who want access to their FGTS accounts want firms to fire them and can try to behave in ways that will get themselves fired. Similarly, employers who want workers to leave want them to do so voluntarily (so employers do not have to pay the additional 40 percent fine) and may try to make the jobs unpleasant (Mizala 2003, 217–18). Of course, knowing these incentives, workers and employers can also look for ways to negotiate informal agreements.

[14] Other surveys of workers in Argentina and Brazil show a more mixed picture (Berg et al. 2006, 39). In Argentina, skilled workers in 1992 had somewhat shorter tenure; however, by 2001, they had slightly longer tenure than did unskilled workers. In Brazil, in contrast, skilled workers had longer tenure in 1992 but roughly the same as unskilled workers by 1999.

institutions. Two institutions may not only be complementary because they reinforce each other's economic performance, but also if their joint existence reinforces their political resiliency. A complementary relationship is "political" if it is intermediated by the state or political system (e.g., union pressure for labor regulation) or if it affects the incentives for, or ability of, actors to mobilize for political goals (e.g., the difficulties a large informal economy poses for union organization).

*Labor Unions.* Unions have the strongest and best-documented effect on continuities in labor market regulation (IDB 2003, 219). These effects largely conform to expectations of approaches that emphasize feedback loops, path dependence, and insider/outsider cleavages (Carnes 2009). Lacking leverage in direct negotiations with employers, unions invested heavily in ties to states and political parties (Buchanan 1995). Extensive protective labor codes in most Latin American countries date back to the 1930s or 1940s, and unions have recently campaigned less to obtain new rights and more to safeguard old benefits, especially collective rights. This political focus was often effective even during periods of extensive liberalization of other parts of the economy (Murillo and Schrank 2005; Cook 2007).

The absence of well-organized unions in many workplaces contributes to another political or state-mediated complementarity.[15] Without strong unions, labor inspections are less likely to occur, and enforcement is less likely to be effective, thereby increasing informality; "active and well-informed labor unions are one of the best mechanisms to ensure vigilance of labor standards at the workplace" (Anner 2008, 43). Without the support of engaged and well organized involved labor unions, inspectors can only cover a small fraction of labor law infractions (Amengual 2010).[16]

*Informality.* Latin America's large informal sectors pose a major challenge for labor unions, because informal workers are almost impossible to organize. Large informal sectors of Latin American economies thus reinforce the small size of unions and encourage them to focus on the narrow "insider" interests of workers in the formal sector. Although the frequent movement of workers between the formal and informal sectors attenuates the insider/outsider cleavage, the segmentation of the labor market nonetheless restricts the scope of union organizing and the range of interests unions might represent. The incentives in this political complementarity are straightforward: the existence

---

[15] See Piore and Schrank (2008) and Schrank (2009) on the overall politics of labor law enforcement.

[16] In addition, historical and comparative analyses provide grounds for expecting that low skill levels contribute to union weakness, especially on the shop floor. In early industrializers, skilled workers were at the vanguard of early union organizing. Even today, low-skill workers (defined as those without an upper secondary education) are less likely to be union members in almost all countries (Schnabel and Wagner 2007). The same pattern holds in Latin America, where workers without a high school diploma are less likely to be unionized (IDB 2003, 231).

of a large informal sector reduces the returns for labor leaders from investing in extensive and solidaristic organizing.

The possibility of using flexible, informal employment also mutes business opposition to high levels of regulation, especially in contexts where business fears a highly charged political backlash (interview with an ex-president of the American Chamber of Commerce, Santiago, Chile, March 2007). Although business people generally favor reducing regulation (especially in interviews and surveys World Bank 2004b, 136; IDB 2001, 113,), the options for less-regulated, informal employment, both within the firm and through subcontractors, reduces the total cost of regulation and thereby the incentives for open political mobilization by employers to push reform (Cook 2007, 9, 46). According to Pagés et al. (2009, 2), "firms in the region seldom cite labor market regulations as a major concern, even though those regulations are relatively rigid from an international perspective." Moreover, lax enforcement often means that workers in the formal sector do not receive the benefits regulations entitle them to (Bensusán 2006). The considerable political discretion in enforcement means that governments can adjust enforcement efforts to economic circumstances. When, for example, the Chilean construction sector, for example, suffered from the economic crisis between 1998 and 2004, inspections became less frequent and were usually announced beforehand (Bensusán 2006, 274).

Generally, MNCs are more heavily regulated or are more likely to comply with regulations than are domestic firms, especially smaller firms (World Bank 2004b, 100; Sehnbruch 2006, 7). This disparity further reinforces the status quo politically and weakens a potential deregulation coalition between MNCs and domestic firms. First, MNCs usually shy away from high-visibility engagement in domestic politics, especially on high-voltage issues like labor rights (see Chapter 4). Second, domestic firms that compete with MNCs and that pay less than the full cost of regulation have few incentives to press for deregulation that could level the playing field and reduce their competitive advantages.

*Short Job Tenure.* Rapid worker turnover works in a similar way to reduce the costs of regulation and thereby the motivation for employers to invest in campaigning politically to reform them. Worker benefits accumulate with time, so employers can lower average dismissal costs by laying workers off after a few years. Moreover, workers who cycle quickly through many jobs are less likely to press past employers for benefits delayed or denied. In Chile, employers frequently deny severance benefits to employees, and workers face long delays, high costs, and uncertain judgments if they opt to take their cases to the labor tribunals (Sehnbruch 2006, 138). A survey in 1992 of labor leaders in 302 firms in Chile revealed that in two-thirds of potentially actionable infractions on severance pay, no case was taken to the labor courts (Haagh 2002, 105).

*High Regulation.* Although rarely noted, informality may also contribute to, or increase incentives for, high regulation, especially regarding unemployment protection and severance pay, because large informal sectors make it difficult to shift to alternative unemployment systems. Severance pay is costly in Latin America and constitutes the bulk of income protection for laid-off workers. Countries outside Latin America rely primarily on state-administered unemployment insurance (which reduces the cost of dismissals to employers). However, where governments cannot be sure that unemployment benefits are going to people who really do not have jobs, then policy makers have incentives to tie benefits to jobs and thereby maintain costly regulations. Were governments to provide unemployment insurance, then workers would have incentives to get fired from formal jobs in order to collect unemployment benefits and work simultaneously in the informal sector (Chahad 2000, 135). Brazil is one of the few countries in Latin America with modest (3–5 months) unemployment insurance. In a study from the late 1990s, unemployment insurance accounted for an average of only 39 percent of the income of those receiving benefits, and, of all beneficiaries, only 20 percent were unemployed and actively looking for work (Paes de Barros, Corseuil, and Foguel 2000, 11). In another survey, only 28 percent of beneficiaries were actively looking for work, while half were working (two-thirds of these in informal jobs but the other third surprisingly in formal jobs; Chahad 2009, 116).

In sum, this brief review of political incentives for major protagonists in labor markets – workers, union leaders, and employers – yields another layer of political complementarities that generally reinforce continuities in the economic complementarities analyzed in Section III. Beyond the straightforward interests of unions in bolstering labor regulation, the other political complementarities work in the direction of reducing or constraining impulses for change by actors who would gain from reform. So, for example, union leaders might seek to expand membership, but they cannot organize workers in the huge informal sector. Employers might gain from deregulation, but informal employment and high turnover reduce the costs of regulation and attenuate reform impulses. Thus, the absence of stronger incentives for employers and the absence for unions of new groups to organize favor the status quo, especially in political systems that are susceptible to pressure from organized or wealthy groups (as analyzed in Chapter 7).[17]

Governments over the last several decades have attempted numerous reforms; however, their ultimate impact has usually been muted. The Chilean case is illustrative. Despite radical liberalizing reforms during the military dictatorship and subsequent reforms after the return to democracy in 1990

[17] Other groups also lack powerful incentives to push for labor reform. Non-unionized workers in the informal and high turnover segments may also not be motivated as outsiders to press for labor reforms and inclusion because, as noted earlier, they may move voluntarily between formal and informal employment, especially over a working career, and hence not view themselves as permanent outsiders (or insiders).

to enhance enforcement and especially training, labor markets are not transformed nor far from the median for the region on the core dimensions such as extensive regulation, rapid turnover, low vocational skills, and sparse union representation (see Chapter 8). Government efforts to improve worker training have been especially disappointing, largely due to the lack of demand by both workers and employers, as well as the absence of dialogue between them.

## V. Conclusion

The complementarities and compatibilities that reinforce continuity help to explain the slow pace of significant improvement in labor markets in recent decades. Throughout much of the late twentieth century, labor markets in Latin America were characterized by pervasive informal sectors, low skills, politicized unions (that were weak on the shop floor and in collective bargaining), extensive regulation, and short job tenure. Previous studies have offered explanations for persistence in each of these areas; however, the argument here is that individual continuities cannot be fully understood without factoring in the multiple economic and political complementarities that reinforce continuity and raise obstacles to change.

The analysis of interactions and complementarities has several practical implications, especially for the design and implementation of common policies intended to raise skills or reduce informality. For example, efforts to crack down on informality are more likely to prosper if accompanied by compensatory policies intended to redress problems in regulation that provided incentives to go off the books in the first place (for example, by shifting from severance pay to unemployment insurance, see Pagés et al. 2009, chap. 6). On skills, proposals to improve education and vocational training focus mostly on the supply side: expand secondary education, improve educational quality, pay students to stay in school, increase funding for vocational training, and so on. However, the benefits of such efforts are not likely to be fully realized in the absence of complementary policies to improve the demand side – expansion of opportunities for long-term employment in skilled jobs. As discussed further in the next chapter, if workers expect that they will work much of their career in the informal sector or have only short-tenure jobs in a variety of different formal sector jobs, then they have few reasons to invest in skills, regardless of how good the supply of educational alternatives becomes.

Although the economic and political complementarities impede change, the result is no one's preferred outcome. Unions may enjoy protections and regulation, but they would benefit from less informality, slower turnover, and higher skills. Employers may have found ways to accommodate high regulation and turnover, but most would prefer some combination of more flexible regulation, less turnover, and better skills. Dissatisfaction among unions and employers, as well as those of the many workers shut out of the formal sector, means that proposals and pressure for reform will keep coming, and latent coalitions for reform are potentially compelling on a number of dimensions.

This chapter has focused largely on labor markets and complementarities within them. The next chapter takes the next step to connect labor markets with the strategies and structures of MNCs and business groups analyzed in Chapters 3 and 4.

# 6

# Education, Training, and the Low-Skill Trap

## I. Introduction[1]

The previous chapter analyzed some of the complementarities – such as those with the large informal sectors and short tenure – that discouraged investment in skills. This chapter elaborates on these institutional complementarities and adds in others to analyze the dynamics of a low-skill equilibrium. A sustained examination of skills is essential theoretically to establish the links and complementarities between the firm strategies analyzed in Chapters 3 and 4 and labor market dynamics. Close analysis of skills is also indispensable in practical and policy terms as skills and human capital set the parameters for possible development strategies as well as for the longer-term potential for more equitable development.

For some years, it has been a matter of settled consensus that investment in education and human capital is essential for economic development.[2] However, on the issue of how to increase human capital, research and policy recommendations focus almost exclusively on the supply side. It is, of course, important to increase funding, improve instruction, modernize curricula, and revitalize schools and educational administration, but these efforts are not likely to meet with intense student demand for education if good jobs that require their skills are not waiting at the other end. As a report from the Inter-American Development Bank put it, "policies aimed only at improving the supply of educational services will likely fail to improve young individuals' school attainment"

---

[1] This chapter draws heavily on joint work with David Soskice (Schneider and Soskice 2011). Extensive discussions with David – before, during, and after work on that paper – as well as David's earlier work on skills were fundamental in developing the general arguments in this chapter.

[2] See Hanushek and Kimko (2000), Perry et al. (2005), and de Ferranti et al. (2003). For a dissenting view, see Easterly (2001).

(Duryea, Edwards, and Ureta 2003, 18). Alice Amsden (2010) goes further and deems the overemphasis on investing in human capital a mistaken application of Say's Law (that supply creates its own demand) and a sort of "job dementia" in its neglect of complementary policies to create jobs for newly educated entrants into the labor market.

Focusing on the demand side helps illuminate a number of puzzles in Latin America. Why, for example, if business in Latin America is now exposed to international competition from firms with more educated workforces, are business people not clamoring for better education and training? Why do researchers find that in Latin America "large increases in expenditure in public education in the last decades were not matched by a corresponding increase in coverage or quality" (de Ferranti et al. 2003, 9), or, put differently, why are there "severe inefficiencies in the process of investment in human capital" (Rodríguez 2006, 106)? Why, if returns to education are high, are individuals and families not doubling down on education? And, why, if education is a perennial priority in political debate, have reform efforts not been more effective? In Brazil, for example, "there is an interesting paradox. Politicians, intellectuals, and journalists with different ideological views never tire of saying that educational policy is a maximum priority. However, the area does not advance with the required speed. Furthermore, the coalitions linked to the educational issue are politically weaker than those in other areas . . . " (Abrucio 2007, 52, my translation).

As examined in Chapter 5, education levels are comparatively low and, save some few sectors and brief periods, Latin America has historically suffered from a common low-skill equilibrium.[3] The main theoretical idea is that labor markets have two equilibria, one at low skill levels and one at high skill levels. At the low equilibrium, individuals do not invest in skills because firms offer few skilled jobs. Firms in turn do not invest in production requiring skilled workers because they do not think they can find them in the labor market. Moreover, information and search costs are high in labor markets and further impede spontaneous, gradual movement to a higher-skill equilibrium. To get out of a low-skill equilibrium either lots of vacancies for high-skilled jobs have to open up to convince workers to invest in skills or many skilled workers have to be available in order to attract high-skilled businesses. In the absence of such big shifts, skill levels tend to the lower equilibrium.

Skills and skilled labor are often broad and ill-defined concepts. Among skilled workers, it is important to distinguish between *technicians* (workers with secondary education and substantial subsequent specialized training) and *university-trained* workers (those with at least some years of university study) and between specific skills that are hard to transfer out of particular firms

---

[3] For earlier work on low-skill equilibria, see Booth and Snower (1996) and Acemoglu (1996, 1997). Snower (1994) provides a more elaborated model. See also Schneider and Soskice (2011) and Rodrik (2007, 101).

or sectors and general skills that are portable from firm to firm. Bringing technicians in gets beyond limitations of most recent studies that define high-skill exclusively in terms of university training (see IDB 2003). This is too narrow a definition of skilled labor because it will apply to less than a fifth of the workforce in Latin America for the foreseeable future. Skilled technicians are likely to be a larger segment of the labor force and an important target of policies designed to promote equality and social mobility.[4] For training technicians with specific skills, the demand and coordination problems of a low-skill trap are critical.

Much recent headline news on education in Latin America has been good: returns to education are high, more students are in school and university than ever before, and increasing education is helping to raise incomes and reduce inequality (López-Calva and Lustig 2010). Yet, it would be precipitous to declare that the skill challenge on its way to resolution. Other indicators show chronic problems persist, especially in the quality of education and overall economic productivity (see Chapters 1 and 5). Moreover, returns to education in Latin America are falling (World Bank 2011). A number of possible factors may be behind this trend, but at a minimum it recommends a closer examination of demand for skills and labor market dynamics overall. In general, the recent expansion in enrollments is significant, but in historical and comparative perspective, it is late and inefficient (in terms of attainment).

Comparisons with countries that have reached higher-skill equilibria may help illustrate the breadth of the gap and the grounds for skepticism that market incentives alone will be able to bridge it in the not too distant future. Table 6.1 offers some contrasts between Latin America and some reference countries that have been held up as potential models of successful development in the late twentieth century (Gereffi and Wyman 1990; de Ferranti et al. 2002; Foxley 2009). The table not only reveals the large gap between Latin America and these reference countries but also provides some indicators showing that these reference countries achieved a much-higher-skill equilibrium with high supply and demand for skilled workers. These reference countries are rarely portrayed as simple market successes, especially in education and technology where the state and public policy were crucial protagonists.

Section II examines the comparatively lackluster business demand, especially by leading business groups and MNCs, for higher-skilled workers, both technicians and university graduates. Section III looks at the other side of the labor market at factors that reduced incentives for individuals to invest more in education. Section IV turns to politics and the obstacles to building coalitions to promote better public investment in education. The analysis is intended to be generally applicable to most of Latin America. The empirical examples though draw heavily on Brazil and Chile in part because of their recent growth and

---

[4] In Germany, for example, technicians accounted for around two-thirds of the workforce in manufacturing in 1987 (Oulton 1996, 204, 208).

TABLE 6.1. *Education, R&D, and Researchers in Latin America and Selected Reference Countries*

|  | Average Years of Education | R&D (percentage of GDP) | Researchers (per thousand) |
|---|---|---|---|
| Korea | 10.5 | 3.0 | 3.8 |
| Taiwan | 8.5 | 2.5 | 8.9 |
| Finland | 10.1 | 3.5 | 7.6 |
| Ireland | 9.0 | 1.3 | 2.8 |
| New Zealand | 11.5 | 1.2 | 4.2 |
| Costa Rica | 6.0 | .4 | .1 |
| Argentina | 8.5 | .5 | .8 |
| Chile | 7.9 | .7 | .8 |
| Latin America | 5.9 | .3 | .3 |

*Sources*: World Bank Development Indicators, National Science Council of Taiwan, and Barro and Lee (2000).

success and in part because skill scarcity has become a more serious constraint on growth in these countries than in the rest of the region (Agosin, Fernández-Arias, and Jaramillo 2009). Section V concludes and considers several possible escape routes from the low skill trap.

## II. Constraints on Business Demand for Skills

This section examines business demand for skills from four main vantage points: (1) overall shifts in employment in the wake of market reforms, especially from manufacturing to services and commodity production; (2) weak demand for skilled labor by MNCs; (3) peculiarities of labor regulation and training programs sponsored by governments that favor in-house training; and (4) trends in return to education. Each perspective highlights limits on business demand for skills, especially compared to other countries and to past trends.[5]

Since the 1980s, the major shifts in employment in Latin America were from manufacturing to services, from the public to the private sector, from rural to urban areas, and from formal to informal employment (Stallings and Peres 2000; IDB 2003; Palma 2005; Lora 2008). Some of these were longer-term secular trends, others responses to policy shifts. Trade openings forced uncompetitive manufacturers to close and many competitive ones to down size to improve productivity. Employment fell in manufacturing, and many technicians and engineers lost their jobs. Industrial employment held steady in

[5] The general comparative benchmark would be higher technology manufacturing in Asia, especially Taiwan and Korea. See Kosack (2009, 2012) for an extended comparison of business demands for skills in Brazil, Taiwan, and Ghana.

Mexico, whereas it dropped throughout most of the rest of the region (Berg et al. 2006, 19).

In the 1990s, the greatest employment growth came in the service sector, which accounted for "more than 95 percent of new net job creation" in most of the large countries (Stallings and Peres 2000, 198). Privatization, FDI, deregulation, and suppressed demand fueled booms in telecommunications, finance, insurance, and public utilities like electricity, but these sectors accounted for only about a quarter of new jobs. Other lower-technology, low-wage sectors like "commerce, restaurants and hotels, together with social, communal, and personal services, accounted for 74 percent of all jobs created in the region" (Stallings and Peres 2000, 198). The last major, overlapping area of growth was the informal sector, which accounted for nearly 60 percent of new jobs, predominantly unskilled, in the 1990s (in one study of seven countries; Stallings and Peres 2000, 119). Service employment continued to grow into the 2000s, though by the end of the decade, informality started to decrease in some countries, notably Brazil (Berg 2010).

The commodity boom of the 2000s buoyed growth rates but did not boost overall demand for skilled labor (exceptional demand in Brazil is considered later). After 2000, international demand boomed for raw materials and semiprocessed commodities such as pulp and paper, minerals, metals (steel and aluminum), oil and gas, basic agricultural goods, and agro-industrial products like fish, meat, ethanol, wine, and vegetable oil, sectors that generally had low demand for skilled workers (Kaufman and Nelson 2004, 251). Capital-intensive sectors such as mining and metals employ skilled workers but not many.[6] In Chile, for example, the copper sector accounted for some 15 percent of GDP but employed less than two percent of the labor force (Sehnbruch 2006, 92). Moreover, commodity production rarely entails an expansion of collateral high-skilled areas such as sales, marketing, research and development, or technical support. Overall, an econometric study from the World Bank found that the commodity boom increased demand for unskilled labor and depressed returns to tertiary education (though there was considerable heterogeneity across countries; Gasparini et al. 2011, 3, 20).

Even before the commodity boom, Brazil's export sector was a drag on demand for skills. By the late 1990s, over seven million workers (12 percent of all workers) were employed in producing exports. Of these workers, 69 percent had only some primary education (0–7 years of schooling), 25 percent had some secondary (8–11 years), and only 5 percent had 12 or more years of education (Castilho 2005, 158–59). The growth of exports was thus reducing the demand

---

[6] McMillan and Rodrik (2011, 3) argue that, "the larger the share of natural resources in exports, the smaller the scope of productivity-enhancing structural change. The key here is that minerals and natural resources do not generate much employment, unlike manufacturing industries and related services. Even though these 'enclave' sectors typically operate at very high productivity, they cannot absorb the surplus labor from agriculture."

TABLE 6.2. *Percentages of Employees of Selected Business Groups in Brazil with Primary, Secondary, and Tertiary Education, 2005–06*

| Type of Business and Firm | Sector | Primary Education | Secondary Education | Tertiary Education |
|---|---|---|---|---|
| **Labor-intensive** | | | | |
| Camargo Corrêa | Diversified | 58 | 33 | 9 |
| Andrade Gutierrez | Diversified | 62 | 24 | 14 |
| Sadia | Meatpacking | 58 | 36 | 6 |
| Perdigão | Meatpacking | 47 | 42 | 11 |
| **Capital intensive** | | | | |
| Gerdau | Steel | 12 | 68 | 19 |
| Votorantim (only cellulose) | Pulp and paper | 10 | 54 | 36 |
| **Services** | | | | |
| Unibanco | Banking | 2 | 50 | 48 |
| Bradesco | Banking | – | 17 | 82 |
| Itausa | Banking | – | 53 | 46 |
| Telemar | Telecommunications | – | 25 | 72 |

*Source*: Schneider (2009a).

for skills in the labor force where by 2002, across all workers, 56 percent had some or complete primary education, 31 percent had some or complete secondary education, and 13 percent had some post secondary schooling (IDB database, http://www.iadb.organization/sociometro/index.html). Similarly, in Chile, the rapid expansion in employment (by more than a third from 1988 to 1995) in four sectors that were leading growth in higher-technology processing of natural resources (fruit and vegetable processing, seafood processing, industrial wood products, and pulp and paper) resulted not in an increase in the relative demand for skilled workers but rather a slight de-skilling of the workforce: skilled workers fell from 17 to 16 percent of workers in these sectors (Schurman 2001, 19; see also Berg 2006).

Table 6.2 provides another more micro perspective on demand from big business for skills. The firms listed are the 10 firms (out of the largest 20 private domestic firms in Brazil) that provided information on the skill profile of their employees (Schneider 2009a). As noted above, large service firms expanded employment for university-educated workers, but the larger commodity producers had much lower demand, especially in booming sectors like meat. This difference is illustrative of a broader division in employment among capital-intensive commodity producers (steel, mining, and some mechanized agriculture, for example) that employ small numbers of skilled workers, and labor-intensive producers, mostly in agriculture, that employ larger numbers of unskilled workers. This distinction is in flux, as some agricultural sectors have mechanized rapidly, shifting quickly from labor to capital-intensive sectors.

Soy production in Brazil went through an incredible transformation. From 1985 to 2004, production nearly tripled, but over the same two decades employment plummeted by 80 percent (Pérez, Schlesinger, and Wise 2008, 12). Labor productivity rose nearly 15-fold from 11 tons to 149 tons per worker of annual output. Sugar cane production in Brazil has also mechanized rapidly with similar consequences for diminished employment. Mechanized agriculture requires more educated and skilled workers but not many of them.

As analyzed in Chapter 3, the private sector historically spent very little in R&D, and the expansion of the largest business groups into commodity production is unlikely to promote much more investment. Total R&D in Latin America averaged less than .5 percent of GDP (mostly public) compared to more than 2 percent for developed countries and much of developing Asia. Table 6.1 showed the association of higher R&D expenditure with higher levels of employment for researchers. Even at 2 percent of GDP, R&D does not generate much direct demand in the overall labor market. However, it can have a larger multiplier effect in increasing demand for skilled workers among suppliers, contractors, and workers in other parts of the firm. In any event, the low levels of R&D in Latin America, especially in business, reduces demand for this very-high-skilled employment.

FDI boomed after 1990, especially in the larger countries of Latin America, but it had a relatively muted impact on the overall labor market and did less than expected, given the magnitude of incoming investment, to boost demand for skilled labor (see Chapter 4).[7] First, much of the incoming investment was in acquisitions and therefore did not create many new jobs (Berg et al. 2006). Compared with the rest of the world, Latin America attracted only about 5 percent of new investment projects by MNCs (ECLAC 2005, 16).

Second, the expansion of outsourcing and global commodity chains along the U.S. periphery (Mexico, Central America, and the Caribbean) created mostly low-skill jobs, though this growth plateaued after the 2001 recession and the shift in low-wage assembly to China. Export manufacturing in Mexico employed workers – even in higher-technology sectors like electronics – with lower education levels than workers in nonexport manufacturing. Perversely, the arrival of new job opportunities in export firms caused students to leave school earlier than students in areas or periods without new export jobs (Atkin 2009). A study of 36 new or expanding maquila firms in the mid-2000s found they were hiring workers with nine or fewer years of education (Sargent and Matthews 2008).

Third, outside Brazil, MNCs did not bring R&D operations to Latin America, and even reduced some previous operations (in the auto sector in Argentina, for example), so their demand for engineers and scientists was low, and lower than for their investment projects elsewhere (ECLAC 2005, 17).

---

[7] Hanson (2008) provides an extended analysis of the absence in Mexico of a positive MNC effect on R&D, training, and education.

MNCs tended to keep most R&D at home, and when they did move some operations offshore, they tended to opt for Asia or East Europe. Fourth, much FDI in Latin America continues to be resource seeking (as in mining) or market seeking (especially in larger countries; Berg et al. 2006, 112; Gallagher and Zarsky 2007, 17–18). For resource- and market-seeking MNCs, labor market conditions are secondary concerns (as opposed to efficiency-seeking MNCs where the cost, quality, and availability of labor are primary criteria for investing in a country). These MNCs do employ technicians and university-trained workers, but they rely heavily on in-house training, especially for technicians rather, than trying to hire skilled workers on the open market (therefore with a dampening effect on demand in labor markets, as discussed later).[8]

Fifth, skilled workers were often a small part of MNC workforces and for unskilled workers, MNCs (and large domestic firms) greatly increased the number of outsourced or agency employees (*tercerizados*) who work in their plants and offices. In one extreme case, in the high tech IT sector in Guadalajara that relied primarily on unskilled workers, "the majority of workers (72 percent) are hired and paid by the more than 25 employment firms in the region. Sixty-eight percent of the subcontracted workers receive all their training at the employment firm, not from the high tech firm itself" (Gallagher and Zarsky 2007, 147). And about two-thirds of these subcontracted workers had employment contracts of three months or fewer.[9]

Another clear empirical indicator of weak business demand for skills comes from training programs in Chile. Chile is a crucial case in labor market trends because Chile has been at the forefront of market reform and of integration into the global economy, and is viewed by many as a harbinger of changes to come in other countries. Chile is also a revealing case because it has a voluntary training program that makes it possible to gauge employer interest (most other countries have compulsory programs). Firms that choose to train can deduct the cost from their income taxes (up to an amount equal to 1 percent of payroll). However, by the mid-1990s, "only a quarter of the available tax credit was being used" (Sehnbruch 2006, 180). Among the firms that did pay for training, most of the training went to already better-paid and educated workers. Moreover, the training was concentrated in areas of general skills like administration, language instruction (mostly English), and computing. By 2010, the total cost of this program was only $226 million (or less than

---

[8]  A number of interviews with personnel managers in Argentina, Chile, and Brazil confirmed that MNCs have low expectations of workers coming out of the educational system and expect to spend a lot on training workers once hired (and pay them higher salaries to keep them from leaving once trained). See Vargas and Bassi (2010). Turnover in resource and market-seeking MNCs is quite low (on Brazil, see *Folha de São Paulo*, 8 May 2011, Radiobrás e-mail summary; on Mexican auto MNCs, see Carrillo and Montiel 1998).

[9]  Sectors that are considered high tech in terms of products such as IT and electronics can be very low tech (and rely on unskilled workers) in much of the manufacturing process, especially for simple assembly of components.

.09 percent of GDP) and 70 percent of the training courses funded by this program lasted fewer than 17 hours (Pumarino 2011).

The shortcomings of Chile's apprenticeship program provide another indication of the lack of employer interest in training. Initiated in 1988, with German technical assistance, the program was expected to attract some 10,000 apprentices. The government program allowed firms to hire apprentices at below minimum wage for up to two years and to deduct 60 percent of the first year's wages from their taxes. However, only 532 apprentices were initially engaged, and in one survey, more than 80 percent claimed to have received no training in the previous year (Sehnbruch 2006, 194, 200), which would seem to confirm union fears that firms would use the program just to hire temporary workers at lower wages (interview with José Luis Sepúlveda, 16 March 2007).

Although overall and on average firms invest little in in-house training, some of the largest, more capital-intensive, and foreign-owned companies invest a great deal in some workers. Among MNCs, as noted earlier, market- and resource-seeking investors are less concerned about existing skills in labor markets and willing to invest in training workers and pay more to keep them (Atkin 2009). Turnover in large firms tends to be lower, so workers and employers have expectations of longer-term relations (Menezes-Filho and Muendler 2007, 21). As an individual solution to the lack of a pool of skilled workers, firm investment in in-house training makes sense, but in aggregate, it reduces the "apparent" demand for skills in the labor market by shifting the demand curve left. That is, if firms expect to build skills rather than buy them, then they will not go into the labor market looking for technicians.[10] This is borne out in surveys where large firms in Brazil were less likely than small firms to view scarcity of skilled workers as an obstacle to growth, presumably because large firms are better able to train workers in-house (Blyde et al. 2009, 127). Overall, in São Paulo, returns to experience are much higher (though only for men, not for women) than in France and the United States which conforms to a build-rather-than-buy approach to skills (Menezes-Filho, Muendler, and Ramey 2008, 328). Among laid-off workers, those with longer tenure and higher skills suffered the most income loss, which suggests both that these workers had more firm-specific skills provided through in-house training and that other firms do not hire skilled workers but prefer to train their own (Pagés et al. 2009, 337).

Several other peculiarities of labor market regulation in Latin America increase incentives for large firms to invest in in-house training. Labor legislation in most countries of the region (Chile excepted) require firms to pay

---

[10] A study of workers in manufacturing in Brazil in the 1990s found that "workers in occupations of intermediate skill intensity experience significantly fewer separations, and workers are significantly less likely to be hired into high-skill intensive manufacturing occupations (with a monotonic drop in accession odds as an occupation's skill intensity increases)" (Menezes-Filho and Muendler 2007, 23).

an annual tax, often 1 to 2 percent of their payroll, to the government for training. However, firms can request to keep the funds for in-house training at a cost at least equal to what they would have paid to the government fund. These requests are subject to government approval (rarely denied), and most large firms would prefer to train their own employees rather than to contribute to a general fund. In the state of São Paulo, for example, about 20 percent of the compulsory tax was spent in-house (interview with an advisor to Senai, 17 June 2009).

Severance costs in Latin America are among the highest in the world (see Chapter 5). Although not intended as a means to promote in-house training, severance costs shift incentives in this direction. In a broader quantitative study, stricter labor codes (including high dismissal costs) were correlated with more training (Almeida and Aterido 2008). The high cost of firing employees has a silver lining for companies that invest in the skills of their longer-term workers, because – if they move – these workers lose their rights to seniority-based severance pay.[11] For example, workers in, say, their sixth year at a firm would usually receive six or more months of salary if fired. These workers, usually part of a small core workforce, can thus feel more secure knowing that employers are less likely to fire them and have fewer incentives to accept other job offers, even at higher wages, because their seniority clocks would reset to zero, making them vulnerable to layoffs and without the insurance of a large severance payment.[12]

Some trends in returns to education and increasing university enrollments are positive. From one vantage point, a virtuous market dynamic seems to be at work: high returns to education (on average 6 percent for every additional year of school; Barro and Lee 2010, 43) are encouraging ever more students to stay in school and go on to university. In manufacturing in the state of São Paulo, for example, employees with college degrees receive wages 150 percent higher than workers with some high school education. The comparable skill premium is 70 percent in the United States and 40 percent in France (Menezes-Filho et al. 2008, 325).[13] In services, especially high-end services like finance, real estate, and communications, demand for college-educated workers expanded rapidly (Berg et al. 2006, 20). In the service sector in the state of São Paulo, workers with some college education grew from 9.4 percent of workers in 1990 to

---

[11] Acemoglu and Pischke (1998, 1999) analyze various ways that labor market imperfections, information asymmetries, and wage compression give firms greater monopsony power and hence less concern about poaching and greater incentives to invest in training. Severance pay in Latin America operates in similar fashion.

[12] Interviews with Jaime Campos, 12 December 2008, and human resource directors at Hewlett Packard Brazil, 3M Chile, Cargill Argentina, and other firms. See Appendix A.

[13] Median hourly wages (the real and dollar were close to parity) in 1996 were 9.2 for workers with some college, 3.6 for workers with 9 to 11 years of school, 2.3 for workers with 6 to 8 years, and 1.8 for workers with 4 to 5 years (Menezes-Filho, Fernandes, and Picchetti 2006, 409).

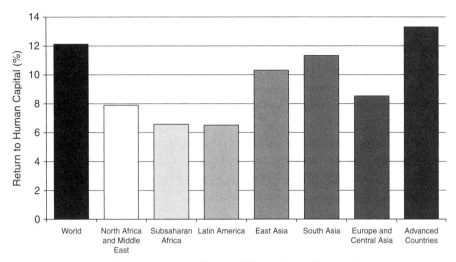

FIGURE 6.1. Rates of Return to an Additional Year of Schooling, by Region

11.3 percent in 1997 while the proportion in manufacturing fell (calculated from Menezes-Filho et al. 2008, 327).

By the end of the 2000s, an IDB report identified skills as a main, binding constraint on growth in three countries of Latin America, Brazil, Chile, and Guatemala (Agosin, Fernández-Arias et al. 2009, 36).[14] Brazil and Guatemala ranked first and second in a sample of 12 developing and transition economies in terms of the percentage of business respondents that viewed skills as a major constraint (Artana et al. 2009, 259). Returns to education were also quite high in these countries. However, current scarcity in the context of resumed growth in the 2000s is a reflection of low previous investment in skills. Moreover, even though countries like Brazil rank high in international comparisons of how many firms see skills as a constraint, firms did not rank skills highly compared to other constraints: skills ranked only 13th of 21 different obstacles (Blyde et al. 2009, 127).

Although good returns to education signal business demand for skills and a willingness to pay for them, several other trends belie an overly optimistic hope for a spontaneous, market solution to the low-skill trap. The first is comparative. Returns to education in Latin America, though positive and significant, remain the lowest of all world regions and just more than half of the world average (Figure 6.1). If returns to education depend in large part on business demand, then business in Latin America has comparatively little demand. And, the lower returns in Latin America are not due to higher supply than in other

[14] In Mexico, in contrast, many college graduates were un- or underemployed (as discussed in the next section), and 8 percent of Mexican professionals were working in the United States (Elizondo 2011, 199).

regions; average years of education and proportion with college education in the adult population are at or below what would be expected from average income levels (see Chapter 5).

The second troublesome trend is that rates of return to education started to fall in the late 2000s even as growth in GDP ticked up (World Bank 2011). Several factors may contribute to this decline. The rapid expansion of tertiary education, for example, some of it of low quality may mean that students are getting low-quality training or that their skills do not match market demand. In addition, lower-income students who started staying in school and going on to university may be running into class barriers to well-paid jobs. Although a number of factors may be pushing returns down, a key component is presumably business demand for skills, which, on average then, is not keeping up with supply. A recent World Bank study of declining returns to secondary and tertiary education in Latin America concluded that "Supply-side factors seem to have limited explanatory power relative to demand-side factors" (Gasparini et al. 2011, 3). Because the decline in returns to education is happening at a time of high economic growth and low levels of overall education, it provides a good indirect indicator of a low-skill equilibrium.

In sum, a number of factors limited business demand for skills, both historically and in recent decades. Since the 1990s, employment dropped in manufacturing and expanded in services, but in barbell fashion with high demand at the low and high ends. The following surge in commodity exports increased demand for unskilled workers relative to technicians and university-trained workers. Moreover, the institutional incentives of labor market regulations on training and severance pay encouraged firms to train in-house, raising returns to strategies to build rather than buy skills, and thereby reducing market demand for skills.

## III. Limits on Individual Demand for Education

Good returns to education would seem to augur well for a market solution to enhancing human capital. Given positive returns, rational families and individuals should strive to invest more in education, and recent increases in secondary and tertiary enrollments suggest this may be happening. However, it is important to put these returns in comparative and historical perspective. As noted in the previous section, returns to education are lower in Latin America than other regions and returns have been falling in recent years after what may have been a transitory spike in skill-biased technological change in the wake of market reforms of the 1990s (López-Calva and Lustig 2010). Both these factors mean economic incentives for students are comparatively and historically low. Moreover, a disaggregated examination shows a more complex picture, especially considering the quality of education provided and the uneven distribution of returns across social classes. Of course, many more students in Latin America are staying in school than ever before; however, a number of factors limit incentives for deep individual investment in high-quality education.

The main questions are when and why do students decide to end their formal education. The economic hypothesis is that students drop out when the opportunity costs (including broader calculations of family welfare) exceed the perceived gains from marginal investment in education. For any individual, a myriad of factors – their own talents and aptitudes, family resources and structure, macro and local economic conditions, and migration opportunities, among others – go into the decision process. For Latin America, it is important to add that many, in some instances most, students are not faced with an either/or decision, as large numbers of students in secondary and tertiary education combine work and school. Public secondary schools typically run two four- to five-hour shifts, so students can go to school and work nearly full-time jobs. Among 16- to 18-year-olds attending school, about a third of poor students in Brazil (and nearly a quarter of wealthy students) and about one-half of poor students in Bolivia were working at the same time (World Bank 2006b, 86). In tertiary education, most of the recent expansion in enrollments has come in night and weekend courses (Nunes 2012). Unlike more structured career systems, as in Germany, where students have essentially one chance to get on the technician or university track, students in Latin America are usually making ongoing decisions on investment in education and simultaneous decisions about not only the kinds of education that will get them to the ultimate jobs they want but also the kinds of jobs that will allow them to get the education they want.

One of the most thorough studies of adolescent behavior throughout the region noted that students were more likely to work full- or part-time if their parents had little education, if they had many younger brothers and sisters at home, if the family income was low, and if youth unemployment was high (Menezes-Filho 2003).[15] This study, however, focused almost exclusively on the constraints that kept students from investing in education and concluded that "Thus, in order to increase schooling levels in Latin America, it will be necessary to disseminate information on the economic returns to education, as well as find alternative forms of care for young children so that older siblings do not have to drop out of school" (Menezes-Filho 2003, 143).

Presumably, most teenagers form initial expectations about career options from watching and listening to family and friends already in the labor market (and most people in Latin America rely on family networks to find jobs; Pagé et al. 2009, 379). The majority of teenagers in Latin America would thus be hearing stories about short job tenure, frequent job changes, and wide movement across sectors, and back and forth between formal and informal employment (see Chapter 5). For some economists, the high movement of

---

[15] Additionally, students are more likely to leave school to work if one of their parents loses a job (Duryea, Lam, and Levison 2007).

workers among jobs is often taken as a positive indicator, especially in the wake of market reforms of the 1990s, of flexibility and rapid adjustment to new opportunities. This may well be part of the story, but the effect on new entrants into the labor market is to make their futures look more uncertain and therefore likely to discourage investment in skills. In these fluid circumstances, job opportunities may drive education decisions more than vice versa – students may move among temporary jobs, making marginal investment in education along the way, until they land one of the few lasting positions in the third segment of the labor elite, usually in the public sector, MNCs, or large domestic firms. Turnover in these firms is often much lower than the mean, and, where internal career ladders exist, stable employees have more reason to invest in education and training.

Younger students are probably also watching how those immediately ahead of them are faring. Although returns to education are good on average, investment in human capital carries significant risks. In Mexico in 2002, 22 percent of 15- to 29-year-olds with 10 to 12 years of school and 9 percent of students with some college were in low productivity jobs in the informal sector. Unemployment rates for these two groups in 2002 were 6 and 10 percent, respectively (Heredia 2010, 14). In other words, 19 percent of workers with some college were out of work or were getting by in the informal sector (up from 11 percent in 1989).[16] Given these risks in investing in education, it is not surprising that 70 percent of the 20–24-year-old cohort left school without completing secondary education (Heredia 2010, 15).

Many students do drop out of secondary school, which makes sense given the opportunity costs of staying in school and the lower rates of return to secondary schooling.[17] However, many students also stay on to complete traditional secondary school. Given that the quality of secondary education is generally low and does not provide most students with skills directly relevant to the labor market, why do students stay on?[18] Presumably, many students complete secondary school not for any intrinsic value it may impart but because it is required to start in tertiary education (IDB 2001, 125). Although the

---

[16] In addition, there is evidence that higher skilled workers are working in jobs below their skill levels, as in engineers filling jobs previously done by technicians (interview with Gerardo de la Peña Hernández, 17 February 2011). The *Washington Post* reported that "while the number of graduates in engineering has soared during the Calderon presidency, the number of Mexicans employed as engineers has grown only slightly, from 1.1 million in 2006 to 1.3 million in 2012" (Booth 2012). See Estrada (2011) for a full recent report.

[17] Kaufman and Nelson conclude that, among the poor, "the expectation of limited return to skills did much to account for high dropout rates at the primary school level" (2004, 251).

[18] One indication of the mismatch of secondary education and labor market demands is the low level of vocational schooling in Latin America. For European Union countries, 48 percent of upper secondary enrollments are in vocational programs. The proportions for Brazil and Mexico, with about half the students in Latin America, are, respectively, 12 and 9 percent (the share in the United States is zero). Some smaller countries like Chile have larger proportions (34 percent; Assumpção-Rodrigues 2012, 22).

monetary returns to secondary education are low, a secondary degree may be important for employment in the formal sector that carries other important nonsalary benefits such as inclusion in the pension and health care systems and legal protections.

Moreover, many firms establish high minimum credentials for jobs (whether or not the jobs require any school skills). Interviews with several employers confirmed the expansion of "credentialing" (when firms require diplomas even when the job does not require that particular level of education). Employers with good jobs to offer get so many applicants that they can afford to set education requirements higher than necessary and may do so in part to screen for middle-class background and social skills. So, for example, a small metalworking shop in Argentina requires entry-level employees to have a high school degree, and a U.S. MNC in São Paulo requires receptionists to have college degrees (interviews with managers, 5 September 2007 and 14 September 2007). In both cases, the employers had little or no expectation of the skills acquired in school and had planned long-term investments in on-the-job training of new employees.[19] A broader survey of employers found a similarly dim view of the value of what students actually learn in school and concluded that firms "hire for attitude, train for skills" (Vargas and Bassi 2010).

The quality of tertiary education is also very heterogeneous. A minority of top students go to a handful of the most selective universities (often, public and free) and get the best jobs when they graduate. The majority of students, however, go on to low-quality universities and often study at night after working during the day (Nunes, Martignoni, and Carvalho 2003). The quality of many of these programs is so low that they may do little more than fill in holes in what students missed in secondary school and signal to prospective employers that the candidates are willing to work extra to invest in skills.[20] And, low-quality education does not require much exertion on the part of students, which suggests a note of caution when interpreting data on the increase in postsecondary enrollments. If enrollment figures could be adjusted for the actual time and efforts students put into their studies, the increases in tertiary education might be less striking.

[19] The expansion of credentialing offers hypotheses for explaining two puzzles in Latin America. The first is the high rates of grade repetition by secondary students. Why, if there is an opportunity cost to staying in school, do students repeat grades, even when schools are not providing adequate support to pass to the next grade? Presumably, the calculus is that a low-intensity investment in secondary education may ultimately yield a useful credential. A second puzzle is that despite large, sustained increases in public investment in secondary education, test scores remain low. Again, the credentialing hypothesis is that students are not motivated to work in school and to study to acquire skills but rather go through the motions to get the credential.

[20] Mexico and Korea offer stark contrasts in post-secondary technical education for technicians. Both countries have two-year technical colleges: enrollment in Mexico is 60,000 compared with 900,000 in Korea (a country with less the half of Mexico's population). And, while most of Mexico's technical colleges are public, 96 percent of Korea's colleges are private, demonstrating very high demand by families willing to pay tuition (Hanson 2008, 96).

Many initial hiring decisions screen on other nonskill criteria such as appearance, social skills, cultural capital, and networks, all of which favor students from middle-class backgrounds and help explain the sometimes large differences for returns to education for rich and poor students (Perry et al. 2005).[21] The contrast with Asia on this dimension is stark; in seven of eight Asian countries, returns to education were higher in lower-income quintiles, whereas in seven of eight countries of Latin America, returns to education were higher for wealthier quintiles, almost double in Bolivia, Brazil, and Chile (Di Gropello 2006, 76–77). Differential returns according to background also increase risks: "poor people may face more labor market risk, or may be less able to hedge against it, and thus find returns to investing in human capital adjusted for risk to be less attractive" (Perry et al. 2005, 6). Thus, perversely, incentives for investing in education among the poor and disadvantaged ethnic groups are likely to be especially depressed.

Many of the skills valued in the service sector such as communication and social skills depend on prior socialization and cultural capital not imparted in school or training courses. Ethnic and class screening is even more likely for high-end service jobs – the most rapidly expanding high-skill sectors – where employers are looking for additional social, communication, and team skills. Having the right manners, accent, appearance, and name can be indispensable to advancement in high-end service jobs and therefore necessary to realize the full return on investment in training. According to a recent IDB study, employers look first to hire people with nontechnical skills such as strong motivation, good attitude toward work, problem-solving ability, and teamwork and communication skills (Vargas and Bassi 2010). Job ads often list "good appearance" among the main qualities sought in applicants, and it is generally perceived as a means for screening applicants for appropriate class, ethnicity, and race.

Low cultural capital starts with parents without much education and working in low wage jobs. Cultural capital is used as a generic term that could also include various linguistic, racial, and cultural barriers, especially in countries with large indigenous or black populations. Extensive household surveys find that parental education has the greatest impact on decisions to stay in school (Menezes-Filho 2003, 112, 141). One interpretation is that parents without much education value it less and therefore push their children less to stay on in school (and provide them less help in studying). Another complementary interpretation is that parents with low education cannot impart sufficient cultural capital for their children to be able to realize the returns to higher education in well paying jobs that require extensive social and cultural skills.

---

[21] The salary premium among university graduates in services may contain a large class component, as much as 25 to 35 percent, according to one study in Chile (Núñez and Gutiérrez 2004).

The importance noted earlier of family networks in securing employment further limits the ability of poor families to help their children get into high-end service jobs. Evidence that returns to education in Latin America are generally lower for lower-income families fits with this argument. And, of course, casual observation in Latin America reveals very few people from ethnic minorities in high-end service jobs. It may in fact be the case that social mobility through education was easier in manufacturing, which did not require many social and communication skills or contact with middle-class customers.[22]

In sum, declining returns that were already low by international standards dilute individual incentives to invest in education. And, given comparatively low returns, low exertion in poor-quality programs makes sense. Lastly, the barriers to social mobility and lower returns to education for poorer students further diminish individual incentives and demands. It is important to keep this conclusion in comparative context. In Latin America, more students than ever before are going on to secondary and tertiary education, but compared to students in other regions, their opportunities and incentives are limited.

## IV. Weak Political Demands for Education

A supply-side exit route from the low-skill equilibrium might come from governments promoting "over" investment in education to the point where firms recognize that they are headed toward a high-skill equilibrium and shift investments to take advantage of the large pool of skilled workers (see Chapter 7 on Chile). To understand the absence in Latin America of such a "big push" from politics requires an examination of the various groups that might join an education coalition.

The middle class is pivotal in structuring both the market for education and political demands for public provision. In the social pyramid in Latin America, the "middle" class was historically small in terms of income and occupation and actually closer to the top than the middle of the distribution. Over the course of the twentieth century, much of this middle class exited public education, especially at the secondary level. By the 2000s, private schools in Latin America accounted for 10 to 25 percent of enrollments of 17-year-olds, and more in poorer countries of Central America. In the wealthiest quintile, around half of students went to private schools (IDB Sociometro n.d.). As the middle class moved into the private sector, its political self-interest adjusted to favor subsidies for private schools over more government spending on public schools and, more generally, "highly skewed distributions of income increased the inclination of upper-income families to resist taxes for public education"

---

[22] Educational mobility has fallen in Mexico. The odds of getting a tertiary education, for children whose parents did not, fell from .62 for children born in the 1940s to .23 for children born in the 1970s (Heredia 2010, 18).

(Kaufman and Nelson 2004, 250–51). These preferences made the middle class less available as a potential partner for a coalition with poorer groups, a coalition that could, in principle, be sufficient to alter government policies on education.[23] In terms of existing spending, middle-class families favored more subsidies to higher rather than to basic education, because after completing secondary education in private schools, many of the best students went on to study in public universities. And public spending on education in Latin America is quite skewed to tertiary education (Rodríguez 2006, 109).[24]

Even if the middle class lacks motivation to push for more public investment in basic education, the poor should. However, the poor were politically excluded for much of twentieth century through authoritarian rule or through co-optation and clientelism in more democratic interludes (see Kurtz 2004). Democratization in late twentieth century did increase political pressure, and governments devoted more resources to education (Brown and Hunter 2004), but the shifts were not dramatic, and education levels remained, on average, below what would be expected at their income levels (Wolff and Castro 2003; Kosack 2009). Overall, governments in Latin America redistributed very little (Goñi, López, and Servén 2008; Schneider and Soskice 2009), and under investment in education for the poor conforms to this pattern.

In principle, business everywhere should have a preference for a large pool of well-educated job applicants and especially where skills have emerged as binding constraints on growth, as in Brazil and Chile. There are some indications of a growing concern among business in Latin America with education, and in some countries, "associations of industrialists are now taking a stand on education and training issues" (Wolff and Castro 2005, 22).[25] However, effective, sustained political action has been rare. A comparative study of educational reform in Latin America found that, despite the pressures of international competition, there was "little evidence that business groups actually lobbied for" upgrading skills (Kaufman and Nelson 2004, 267; see also Grindle 2004, 198). Among developing countries, Brazil ranked quite high in terms of

---

[23] As two education experts at the IDB put it, "for the most part, the children of the politically influential people attend private primary and secondary schools. Thus they do not directly feel the deficiencies of the public school system... This reduces the sense of urgency that might otherwise lead influential parents to press decision makers to make tough policy choices, and makes it harder to put together a political coalition willing to pay the high political costs that come with making basic changes in public schools" (Wolff and Castro 2003, 205).

[24] See Fernandez and Rogerson (1995) for a general model that predicts education spending to be skewed to higher education and wealthy families, especially in more unequal societies. Private tertiary education has ballooned in recent years, so the dependence of the middle class on public universities is fading. In Brazil, by the 2000s, private universities enrolled more than two-thirds of students. However, many private universities depend on public subsidies, so middle-class families may still favor shifting more public resources from basic to tertiary education.

[25] In the 2000s, business backed the creation of several visible associations pushing for education, especially Mexicanos Primero (interview with David Calderón, director of Mexicanos Primero, 16 February 2011) and Todos pela Educação (Brazil; Simielli 2008).

the percentage of firms that reported that the skills and education of available workers were serious constraints on growth (World Bank 2004b, 136). Yet, despite these concerns, business in Brazil was not a major supporter of educational reforms in the early 2000s.[26] In his comparative study, Stephen Kosack (2009) finds that business in Ghana and Brazil was never politically mobilized to demand education the way it was in Taiwan from the 1960s to the 1980s.

Several factors weaken the impulse by business to push for education (Schneider 2010a). First, education policy is not an area conducive to political engagement by business. This policy bears fruit only over the long term and requires sustained monitoring and nagging for effective implementation. Such engagement in turns depends on well-organized business associations, which were rare in Latin America. Education is also an area in which business preferences are heterogeneous which impedes consensus building on policy priorities. Last, education is a broad, encompassing policy area where temptations to free ride in political activity are stronger.

Second, for many firms, low levels of skills and education may not be a problem, especially compared to other areas of government policy such as taxes, infrastructure, and macroeconomic policies that may have a more immediate impact on profits. As noted in the previous section, many of the commodity and service sectors that expanded after 1990 created jobs that did not require much education. In some cases, employers went so far as to oppose investment in education. Textile manufacturers in northeastern Brazil hired mostly workers with low educational levels at low wages. These manufacturers feared that more-educated workers would either demand higher wages (which would undermine their competitiveness in global production networks) or move south in search of better jobs (Tendler 2002). Third, many of the largest, most sophisticated firms, whose participation is essential to any broad business push for education, often find workable private, firm-level solutions to their skill needs. One option is poaching; MNCs and larger domestic firms can afford to pay higher wages to hire workers away from smaller domestic firms. As noted earlier, large firms also invest a lot in in-house training; some large firms even have well-established internal educational divisions or subsidiaries (interview with Juliana Bonomo, 17 November 2008). Such private solutions obviate the need for public action on education.

Fourth, among big businesses, MNCs are especially hard to mobilize into coalitions for education. MNCs generally shy away from visible engagement in broad, and potentially contentious, policies like education reform (see Chapter 4). Moreover, most MNC strategies do not depend on large pools of skilled workers. Market and resource seeking MNCs are often capital intensive,

---

[26] Interviews with Maria Helena Castro, 8 December 2005 and Horacio Lafer Piva, 14 September 2007. Business in Chile was also not active in education policy (interview with José Pablo Arellano, 9 January 2012).

employ relatively few workers, and devise private, in-house solutions for their skill needs. The situation is different for efficiency seeking MNCs for whom the cost and availability of labor determines profits in intensely competitive international markets such as textiles. In these competitive, low margin sectors, in-house training would add too much to costs, so these firms might, in principle, have an interest in joining coalitions for education reform. However, these international markets can change so quickly that firms are more likely to use exit rather than voice, as the many labor-intensive maquiladoras did when, in the 2000s, they moved from Mexico to China.

Another example from the state of São Paulo illustrates the weakness of both market and political demand for skills. The state-level training body Senai is funded by a 1 percent tax on payrolls. A body dominated by business then decides how this fund should be used to provide training. Until recently, the goal was to train workers in skills for which short-term demand was easy to verify (as one Senai official put it, "we do not train people for unemployment," interview 17 June 2009), even if this meant turning away potential students (Horacio Lafer Piva, 14 September 2007). In essence, Senai was explicitly targeting a low-skill equilibrium. In the 2000s, the minister of education intervened to require Senai to open its doors and to provide training to more applicants, and such training beyond existing demand in the labor market grew to account for about a third of total Senai training (interview with Senai advisor, 17 June 2009).

Beyond particular social groups, overall opinion surveys show little preoccupation with improving education. Respondents in Latin America are more satisfied with the quality of education than counterparts in other regions, and especially with respect to actual performance on tests (Lora 2008, chap. 6). And respondents with low education were more satisfied than were those with higher education. In another survey in 2006 on crucial problems facing Brazil, education came in seventh place (Abrucio 2007, 52).

It also bears noting the historical absence of sundry political movements and ideologies that spurred mass education elsewhere, most of which, however, sought to prevent or correct undesirable behaviors and upbringing rather than to impart skills that businesses needed. For example, religious and civic reformers in early-nineteenth-century United States pushed universal education to stem moral decay. Governments in nineteenth-century Europe, and later elsewhere, imposed universal education in order to spread dominant languages and new national identities (Anderson 2006). Although similar movements emerged in some periods or areas of Latin America, they lacked sustained force and scope to push governments to full universal education (Sokoloff and Engerman 2000). This sort of movement was the hope expressed in a World Bank report: "an important element of a deeper education strategy could be the introduction of a civic drive, involving both the public and the business sector, to achieve a significant jump in both coverage and quality across the public school system . . . " (de Ferranti et al. 2004, 7).

## VI. Conclusions and Possible Escape Strategies

Multiple complementarities reinforced the low-skill equilibrium in hierarchical capitalism. The demand for skills was comparatively weak on all sides but especially on the part of firms, both domestic and foreign, and of individuals (or adolescents and their families) as they decided their investment strategies. Elements of atomized labor markets, especially high turnover and informality, discourage investment in skills. In a vicious cycle, low skill levels in labor markets also encouraged, or increased returns to, less skill-intensive investment by business. Weak labor market demands for skills were also reflected in the absence of a forceful political coalition to expand education historically and improve quality in the twenty-first century.

Although difficult to assess directly, lower business and individual demand for education likely affects overall education spending and its efficiency (educational achievement levels for amounts spent). Much of the discussion of efficiency of education spending focuses on sources of waste such as bureaucracy or incompetent or absent teachers. However, lack of student and family commitment may also be a source of low achievement, independent of supply side problems. This is not to blame the victim but rather to highlight that a low-skill equilibrium raises the opportunity costs of studying. Where credentialing is widespread, students know the content of instruction is not important beyond the minimum they need to know to get to the next grade level. In Mexico, controlling for socioeconomic background, students in private schools scored only marginally higher on the PISA test (17 points on average) than students in public schools (Elizondo 2011, 190). Given the relative lack of resource constraints in private schools, the test results would seem to reflect more about family and student choices (and suggest that families are willing to pay expensive tuition fees more for network benefits than for education). If getting into university is relatively easy and not based heavily on performance in secondary school, and if performance in university is less important than networks in getting jobs, then investing in more effective secondary schools and more studying is unnecessary. Overall, in broader comparative perspective, countries in Asia such as Japan and Korea, where entrance into university is extremely competitive and choice jobs go to top-ranked students at top-ranked universities, private investment, much of it in extra tutoring, signals greater student and family commitment.

Short of an economy-wide push to a high-skill equilibrium, several countries in Latin America have had partial success in particular industries or with policies on either the demand side or the supply side. In Brazil, historically, two sectoral examples stand out of cutting-edge technological development and high-level skills, education, and training. In an unlikely story, the world's third-largest manufacturer of aircraft is the Brazilian firm Embraer (Goldstein 2002). After thriving in the 1990s in the small regional jet market, Embraer expanded successfully into a broader range of smaller and larger aircraft. Also in Brazil, the state oil firm Petrobras has become a world leader in deep-water exploration. In both cases, the state, and within it the military, pushed long-term investment in engineering and training programs, beginning in the 1950s and 1960s, and promised jobs to those who invested in skills. In the early years, the military even assigned active officers to undertake university training in engineering, though even civilians had few doubts on the likely career payoff of investing in education in petroleum or aeronautical engineering. However, these exceptions prove the general rule in Brazil – in the absence of exceptional state investment in skills and employment, the low-skill equilibrium was the default outcome.

Countries such as Korea and Taiwan that escaped the low-skill equilibrium in the span of only a few decades in the late twentieth century did so with massive shocks on both the demand and supply sides (Kosack 2012). Cases of positive shocks in Latin America in recent decades have been more one sided: strong on the demand side in Brazil and on the supply side in Chile. In Brazil in the 2000s, demand for skills rapidly increased to the point in the post-2009 recovery that skill shortages were widespread. This demand-side shock was partly the result of commodity-led growth (especially in more capital- and skill-intensive commodities), but also the result of renewed industrial policy and a sustained increase in investment in science, technology, and R&D (see Chapter 8). But, whereas some high-tech segments of the economy are booming, demand for skills may have difficulty filtering through the rest of the economy (and hence shifting the education decisions of masses of young people) where low-skill jobs still predominate.

In another case of demand-side shock, Costa Rica used the winning of an Intel chip factory in the late 1990s as a cornerstone of a high-tech export strategy. Although still playing to mixed reviews, Costa Rica transformed its export mix and drew many more students into informatics (Paus 2005; World Bank 2006a). Although the Intel plant has not generated a lot of spin-off firms or local suppliers, Costa Rica has become a preferred location for IT-related investments by MNCs. In essence, small countries can agree on something like a multi-agent contract in which governments and large firms make long-term commitments to increase and coordinate the medium-term supply of, and demand for, higher skills.

Chile, in contrast, pushed harder on the supply side with massive and sustained investments in education. By 2005, 64 percent of 25- to 34-year-olds had at least a secondary degree, more than the 38 percent in Brazil, 24 percent in Mexico, 36 percent in Turkey, 43 percent in Portugal, and equal to the 64 percent in Spain (but less than the 97 percent in Korea; Heredia 2010, 5). College-age enrollment in tertiary education in Chile boomed in the 2000s to about 50 percent. Where the Chilean strategy was initially lacking was in promoting the expansion of technical education and policies to expand higher-technology growth and hence the demand side for skills. The commodity boom did boost growth, but did not, as in Brazil, have a significant multiplier effect in other higher-technology sectors. The Chilean strategy was premised more on the theory that if skills were built, the jobs would come.

Brazil and Chile are promising exceptions, but they also are rare and show how large an exogenous shock is needed to shift, even partially, the low-skill equilibrium. Chapter 8 returns to the demand shock in Brazil and the supply shock in Chile.

PART III

POLITICS, POLICY, AND DEVELOPMENT STRATEGY

# 7

# Business-Group Politics

## *Institutional Bias and Business Preferences*

## I. Introduction

Beyond economic complementarities, the main focus of Part II, politics and political institutions are decisive in the evolution of all varieties of capitalism. Various forms of state intervention that establish the foundations for the economic institutions – from training programs to competition agencies – depend on active, continuing support from political coalitions (Thelen 2001). In the case of hierarchical capitalism, business groups and labor unions used their political advantages to press for policies and institutions that reinforced institutional complementarities and favored insiders. At the same time, the politics and strategies of these insiders depend on their preferences that, in turn, are fundamentally shaped – in hierarchical and other types of capitalism – by the complementarities they face in the economic sphere. This chapter analyzes the politics and institutions that favor insiders and continuity. However, reformers and outsiders have cause to continue to use politics to challenge the negative complementarities examined in previous chapters. Chapter 8 considers the politics of these challenges and some efforts to escape from the negative complementarities of hierarchical capitalism.

A number of perspectives – crony capitalism, entrenchment, and rent seeking, not to mention Marxist arguments (instrumental and structural) – would expect big business to dominate policy making – especially economic and social policy. In the entrenchment (Morck, Wolfenzon, and Yeung 2005) and crony capitalism views, business groups in developing countries maintain their privileged positions and favorable regulations by virtue of close ties to sympathetic political leaders. Among other things, weak institutions, the huge size of business groups, and venal politicians favor entrenchment. The rent-seeking view, more theoretically elaborated by Olson (1982) and followers, reaches fairly similar conclusions; however, business-group dominance depends more on the organization of special-interest groups and less on the venality of politicians.

Although useful points of departure, these approaches suffer from three main shortcomings. First, they neglect institutions and pay insufficient attention to particular institutional configurations across different political contexts that privilege or block the access of business and other insider groups. Second, they do not problematize business preferences and mostly assume that business will seek available rents rather than exploring how different kinds of businesses prefer some policies over others. Third, in their stronger formulations, entrenchment and rent-seeking theories offer few possibilities for escape or resisting business pressures. In fact, business groups in Latin America often lose in politics, both particular battles and overall, so theories need to build in greater contingency and account for business defeats as well.

In contrast, this chapter shows how distinctive features of the political system favor business interests and how the different strategies and preferences of business groups in Latin America shape what they pursue in politics. Formal institutional features, such as the common combination in Latin America of majoritarian presidentialism with proportional representation legislatures (MP/PRL) and informal practices like appointive bureaucracies, favored business groups and other insider groups in distinctive ways. The interests pursued are not generic but can be traced back directly to the distinctive corporate structures and strategies analyzed in Chapter 3. Closer attention to the sources of preferences helps explain coalitions that did form, as well as those that did not. This last point is important to understand why business, if its preferences often prevail, did not try to block market reform, promote education, or generally push development strategies along different economic and social tracks. Asking counterfactual questions such as why did countries of Latin America not follow development strategies like those in East Asia requires close consideration of business preferences, politics, and coalitional possibilities (Doner, Ritchie, and Slater 2005; Kosack 2008).

Democratization in Latin America in the last decades of the twentieth century broke up many cozy backroom relations between business groups and authoritarian governments. However, business groups in democratizing polities learned quickly to avail themselves of new venues such as parties, elections, courts, and the media (Schneider 2010b). These democratic means were more costly, complex, and indirect, but when they worked to further business preferences, they could be more reliable and enduring than ad hoc relations with authoritarian leaders.

Last, injecting more politics into the analysis helps to shift explanations of institutional continuity from a functionalist equilibrium based on immediate economic complementarities to an exogenous and more politically contingent set of historical and political factors. Because many economic complementarities were negative and many social groups benefited little from hierarchical capitalism, politics tend to be more contentious than in other more inclusive varieties of capitalism. This political contingency is important to understanding divergences among countries in the region, and Chapter 8 examines the possibly transformative changes underway in the 2000s in Brazil and Chile.

The chapter proceeds as follows: Section II examines the features of political systems, formal and informal, that give dominant stakeholders, especially business groups, privileged access to policy making. Section III analyzes some of the policy consequences of this access by looking more closely at business group preferences. Section IV further disaggregates business to examine variation within countries among business groups that are more and less engaged in politics.

## II. Political Institutions and Privileged Access for Insiders

In other varieties of capitalism, political systems reinforce core economic institutions. CMEs and LMEs are associated with, and sustained by, different electoral systems (Hall and Soskice 2001, 49–50; Cusack, Iversen, and Soskice 2007). Majoritarian political systems in liberal capitalism have wider policy swings from election to election, and therefore encourage firms to maintain flexibility (through market relations) in order to adjust to shifts in policy (Gourevitch and Shinn 2005). In contrast, political systems based on proportional representation (PR) and parliamentary government generate more coalition governments in which business and other stakeholders usually get minority, veto representation, which in turn promotes the policy stability that ensures the long-term relational investing that sustains coordinated capitalism. In the case of coordinated economies, business in fact favored constitutional reforms to change to parliamentary systems in the early twentieth century to facilitate their ongoing representation, even though parliamentary systems favor the left and greater redistribution (Iversen and Soskice 2009). In Latin America, there is little evidence that business groups had a strong hand in designing electoral systems (though they often did in bringing them down), but business groups and organized labor have managed to exert influence through their political systems to reinforce core institutions and organizations of hierarchical capitalism.

Formal political systems in Latin America stand out in their combination of (1) majoritarian presidentialism and (2) elections based on proportional representation for the legislature. In 164 legislative elections in Latin America (excluding the Caribbean) from 1946 to 2000, 77 percent were proportional, the second-highest regional proportion in the world after Europe. Of the remainder, both multitier (14 percent) and mixed (5 percent) elections often had proportional components. Only 4 percent were straight-up majoritarian elections (Golder 2005, 115). In Latin American MP/PRL systems, the presidency is endowed with strong constitutional powers, but legislatures have a growing importance especially when, as is usually the case, the president's party is in a minority. Across 12 countries of Latin America from 1982 to 2003, presidents' parties were in majority in the legislature only 34 percent of the time (compared with 51 percent for presidential regimes worldwide), and presidents in five countries, including Brazil and Chile, never had a majority (Martínez-Gallardo 2010, 127).[1] Although there are many other differences across the political systems of Latin America (party discipline, decentralization, number of legislative chambers, and so on), the MP/PRL model is a good starting point, especially because this combination is ubiquitous in Latin America and rare elsewhere.[2] MP/PRL politics combine core elements of political systems in LMEs (majoritarian presidentialism) and CMEs (proportional representation), but the resulting mix has distinctive dynamics.

In developed countries, majoritarian systems historically generated more right-wing (non-redistributive) governments compared to more left-wing, redistributive governments in PR systems (Iversen and Soskice 2006). In Latin America, MP/PRL systems have not yet shown a definitive tendency left or right. For democratic periods from 1970 to 2000, the average ideological "center of gravity" for legislatures was on the right in 9 of 13 countries in Latin America (Huber et al. 2006, 956). And, through the early 2000s, governments in Latin America redistributed almost nothing, and roughly 70 percent of public transfers flowed to the richest 40 percent of the population (Goñi et al. 2008, 19; this is also the legacy, of course, of the many authoritarian regimes in the twentieth century). This rightward tendency conforms to the theoretical logic of majoritarian systems in which winning the presidency requires the median vote of those voting programmatically. At higher income levels, voters fear redistribution toward the poor financed by them, so the median voter tends right. In Latin America, beyond the logic of majoritarian system, the poor also faced obstacles to voting programmatically, thus further raising the income level of the median voter who had even less interest in redistribution.[3]

The 2000s, however, showed a marked shift in the region to the left and more redistribution by governments through taxes and especially spending (Levitsky and Roberts 2011; Huber and Stephens 2012). Some of this shift may be related to the commodity boom that could keep MP/PRL systems from listing to the right (see Weyland 2009). When government revenues depend more on rents from commodity exports than on taxes from voters, then median voters have less to fear from leftist candidates and parties that promise more social spending on the poor. Similarly, poor voters may be less inclined to sell their votes and prefer instead to risk voting for candidates who might shift significant public

---

[1] Across all political systems, and not distinguishing between proportional and majoritarian electoral systems, minority governments occur 51 percent of the time in presidential systems, 49 percent in parliamentary systems, and 67 percent in mixed systems. In these minority governments, coalitions emerge 87 percent of the time in mixed systems, 77 percent in parliamentary systems, and 62 percent in presidential systems (Cheibub 2007, 79).

[2] Parts of this section draw on Schneider and Soskice (2009), which offers a more extended discussion of the MP/PRL model.

[3] Poverty and inequality facilitate vote buying, either literally or via clientelistic relations, including jobs or other public sector resources (Faughnan and Zechmeister 2011).

spending to the poor, especially during commodity booms. This logic helps explain the recent success of left candidates in Venezuela, Bolivia, and Ecuador, part of the leftward shift in the region in the 2000s. But even outside these petro states, the left, though more moderate, and redistribution have prospered.[4] However, while the trend is redistributive, absolute levels of inequality remain among the highest in the world.

The PR legislature is well suited for representing sectoral interests and organized groups. The general weakness of unions in the economic sphere, while at the same time unions have favorable labor regulations to defend, makes it rational for them to invest in the political system (see Chapter 5). And this is encouraged by a PR legislature and, in turn, reinforces an insider/outsider cleavage in labor markets and consequently overall inequality. In the wave of market-oriented reforms, individual labor rights were somewhat reduced and union membership declined. However, unions managed to shore up collective or union rights and regulations (Murillo 2005).

Domestic business has even stronger incentives to invest in legislators. With a PR legislature and a majoritarian presidency, presidents normally have to make deals with parties and, when party discipline does not hold, with individual politicians as well. From 1982 to 2003, governments in 12 countries of Latin America had coalition governments (with more than one party in the cabinet) 52 percent of the time (and this proportion has probably increased in the 2000s). The distribution is fairly bimodal, with six countries having coalitions 80 percent or more of the time, and four countries having coalitions 22 percent or less of the time (Martínez-Gallardo 2010, 127). When parties lack leverage over legislators, the executive often has to negotiate individually with politicians not only over pork spending but also over measures favorable to core campaign contributors like business groups. Open-list PR, as in Brazil, further weakens parties and enhances the power and independence of individual politicians. In open-list PR, with large electoral districts, candidates can build very targeted constituencies among particular regions or cities, social groups (labor, ethnic, or religious groups), or with particular businesses.[5]

In Brazil, the Partido da República (Party of the Republic), formed in 2006 out of two smaller parties, illustrates how parties specialize in coalition governments. The Partido da República (or its predecessors) has long been a member of the governing coalition in Congress in exchange for a ministerial appointment,

---

[4] Fragmented electoral systems with more parties – common in MP/LPR systems – can generate some centrist, clientelist parties that do not seek the presidency but are willing to join coalitions with whichever party does (Brazil is the best example; Amorim Neto 2002). When minority presidents on the left try to draw centrist parties into coalitions, they likely diminish overall redistribution.

[5] It is usually difficult to gauge business preferences on different kinds of political systems. However, in the run-up to a referendum on whether Brazil should have a presidential or parliamentary system, two-thirds of business respondents said they preferred the latter (IDESP study cited in *Veja*, 29 July 1992, p. 28).

and after 2003 in exchange for the Ministry of Transportation. This specialization in turn helps parties pinpoint fund raising among businesses affected by the ministry and allows businesses to target their campaign contributions. In the 2010 elections, the main contributors to the Partido da República all had contracts with the Ministry of Transportation (*Brazil Focus*, 2–8 July 2011, p. 8).

Moreover, legislation has to go through committees, so committee chairs and members have the ability to slow down and amend legislation, and hence the derived ability to intervene with ministries and agencies on questions not directly related to ongoing legislation. In other words, small parties and individual legislators have multiple ways of holding up the executive, so the executive has incentives to accede to particularistic demands from legislators on policy implementation in exchange for votes on other issues.[6] So, the best way for business and other groups to lobby the executive can be indirectly through the legislature. Investment in individual legislators as well as in parties thus has potentially high rates of return for businesses whose profitability depends in part on government regulations.

By way of contrast, a political system on the far, nonporous end of the continuum would be a majoritarian two-party system with closed lists and financial contributions prohibited or restricted to parties, and consequently strong parties focused on the median voter. In this sort of system, business has fewer points of access to press individual interests. In practice, Britain's polity is on the less porous end of the continuum. In Latin America, as discussed later, Chile's political system is one of the least porous. India, with a majoritarian electoral system and stronger parties offers a stark contrast with fragmented parties and PR in Brazil. When asked where they preferred to lobby, 52 percent of Indian business people responded party leaders (versus 11 percent in Brazil) whereas 52 percent of Brazil business respondents preferred to lobby individual legislators (versus 3 percent in India; Yadav 2011, table 4–10, 96–101). The basic point is that a fragmented party system in a PR legislature is well designed to give individual politicians and small parties power independent of the presidency, and this is what big business and interest groups can exploit.

Beyond the general MP/PRL model, some countries have peculiar institutional features that further enhance business access. Mexico has a mixed electoral system with only partial PR, and never had coalition government under the PRI or since the transition to democracy in 2000, but it has other features

---

[6] In Brazil, the informal group of legislators backed by Protestant churches, the *bancada evangélica*, provides a good, non-business example. In May 2011, the Ministry of Education was preparing to send out a kit of materials to schools intended to help with training against homophobia. The bancada evangélica opposed this distribution, but Congress had no formal jurisdiction on the issue. However, the government wanted to stop Congress from opening an inquiry into a top minister, Antônio Palocci, so President Roussef ordered the Ministry of Education to suspend the homophobia initiative in exchange for support in Congress from the bancada evangélica in stopping the inquiry (*O Globo*, 26 May 2011, Radiobrás e-mail summary).

favorable to business influence. The constitutional provision against immediate reelection means that legislators have little need to pay attention to voters who elected them, especially compared to the need they have for resources for their next electoral campaign (in some other jurisdiction; see Elizondo 2011). Moreover, after the PRI lost its majority in Congress in 1997, the party system evolved into an unwieldy three way split, where each of the three main parties had opportunities and ambitions to win the presidency. The two losing parties in each presidential election since 2000 ended up with an opposition majority in Congress that had few incentives to cooperate with the president.[7] Government bills that countered strong business interests (as in antitrust laws), often made little headway in Congress, especially in years prior to major elections because business lobbyists found ready allies among opposition legislators (examples follow later and in Chapter 8).

The judiciary branch in some countries has also given business groups another political recourse though again in a negative sense of blocking adverse policies. As the judiciary gained in powers and independence in democratizing polities, business adjusted to take advantage of these new powers. Mexico again provides the clearest example. The Mexican Constitution allows citizens to sue for injunctions (*amparos*) to stop the implementation of government measures that infringe on fundamental individual rights. Although intended to protect individual liberties, firms have been successful getting amparos to stop rulings from anti-trust and other regulatory bodies (Elizondo 2011; interviews in consulting firms that help business groups file amparos, February 2011). Courts may also be directly vulnerable to lobbying and pressure politics. In 2004, the Supreme Court of El Salvador acceded, in a high-profile ruling, to a petition from major bankers not to grant access to the bank accounts of several top politicians and business people (Segovia 2005, 29).

In addition to formal institutions, other informal practices also enhance business influence. Bureaucracies in Latin America are porous and staffed at the top by political appointees. Appointees in top economic positions are sometimes suggested or vetted by business groups (and sometimes are ex-employees) and most consult regularly with business groups (Schneider 2004). In many cases, presidents appoint business people directly to the cabinet. The practice varies over time and across countries (Table 7.1). Over nine presidential terms in Venezuela (1959–99), 20 percent of all cabinet posts and 51 percent of all economic cabinet posts went to business people. The comparable figure for Mexico over seven presidents (1958–99) was 12 percent of all cabinet posts

[7] Looking across all presidential and parliamentary systems since the mid-twentieth century, Cheibub finds that "an increase in the share of seats held by the largest party (i.e., a decrease in legislative fragmentation) is associated with a decrease in the likelihood that a coalition government will emerge; an increase in the effective number of political parties (i.e., an increase in legislative fragmentation) is associated with an increase in the likelihood that a coalition government will emerge" (2007, 82).

TABLE 7.1. *Business Appointees in Recent Government Cabinets*

|          | President                | Number of Business Appointees | Percent of Business Appointees |
|----------|--------------------------|-------------------------------|--------------------------------|
| Argentina | Kirchner (2003–05)      | 0                             | 0                              |
|          | Duhalde (2002–03)        | 1                             | 8                              |
|          | De la Rua (1999–2002)    | 1                             | 9                              |
| Brazil   | Rouseff (2011)           | 0                             | 0                              |
| Chile    | Lagos (2002–05)          | 0                             | 0                              |
|          | Piñera (2010)            | 10                            | 47                             |
| Colombia | Uribe (2002–05)          | 7                             | 54                             |
| Mexico   | Zedillo (1994–99)        | 0                             | 0                              |
|          | Fox (2000–05)            | 5                             | 25                             |
|          | Calderón (2006)          | 3                             | 16                             |
| Peru     | Toledo                   | 7                             | 27                             |
|          | Humala (2011)            | 5                             | 31                             |

*Note*: Compiled from government, periodical, and other Internet sources.

(Gates 2010, table 4.4).[8] But even countries where the practice was historically uncommon – Chile under Concertación governments (1990–2010) and Mexico under the PRI (1930s–2000) – had recent governments with many business people in the cabinet. Partisanship, of course, matters in these appointments, and populist left governments in Argentina, Bolivia, Venezuela, and Ecuador had few cabinet members from business. Center left governments like those of Lula and Humala may, however, use business appointees to signal financial markets on conservative policy intentions. Leftist governments though are more likely to appoint labor leaders to top positions in government agencies.

The recent expansion of business groups abroad, largely through acquisitions of large existing firms, vastly increased the size of some firms, and as a consequence, their total investment budgets, both of which augment their political leverage and the interests of politicians and government officials in hearing their views and plans. The relative absence of MNCs from politics, discussed in Chapter 4, also magnifies the power of the largest domestic groups. MNCs make public pronouncements about narrow issues affecting their sectors, lobby officials for favorable regulation (especially on specific issues such as intellectual property and copyright protection), and push (and sometimes bribe) for contracts. But they shy away from commenting on broader, more controversial issues; do not invest much in associations or think tanks; and are usually prohibited from investing in electoral campaigns. Across Latin America,

[8] At least three of Fujimori's top economic ministers in the early 1990s were business people (Wise 2003, 208). In Mexico, "under President Fox the Minister [of Communications] was himself an ex-employee of the principal firm in the sector, Telmex. While there is nothing illegal in this, it raises concerns over the extent of independence from the industry that it is supposed to regulate" (World Bank 2007, 40).

13 of 18 countries prohibit contributions by foreign entities or individuals (Griner and Zovatto 2005, 31). Political passivity by MNCs, especially in elections, thus opens up more political space for the largest domestic businesses and reduces the range of potentially divergent views among the largest firms.

When business associations mediate access to policy makers, formally and informally, they provide domestic business groups another point of privileged access. Among the large countries of the region, business associations in Mexico, Chile, and Colombia are well organized and well connected to government. Through various internal mechanisms and specialized entities, these associations also favor the preferences of business groups (Schneider 2004). MNCs are largely excluded from associations representing big business, save for Argentina where the AEA (and CEA before), an elite club of several dozen CEOs of the largest firms, invited executives from MNCs to join.

Think tanks grew up in the late twentieth century and often provided business groups with additional avenues to participate in shaping policy debates. Think tanks have long been influential in Colombia (e.g., Fedesarrollo) and more recently in Argentina, especially in the 1990s (FIEL, Fundación Mediterránea), Chile (Cieplan, CEP, and Libertad y Desarrollo), and Mexico (IMCO; on Chile, see Cociña and Toro 2009). Brazil, surprisingly, has fewer general-purpose think tanks, though business supports single-issue nongovernmental organizations (NGOs) on topics like corporate governance (Instituto Brasileiro de Governança Corporativa) and education (Todos pela Educação). In characteristically dispersed fashion, opinion leaders in Brazil are more likely to work on their own or in small consulting firms supported largely by big business. Elsewhere, most think tanks, save some social democratic (Cieplan) or union supported ones, are largely dependent on funding from multiple business supporters and offer business sympathetic positions on policy. In a few cases, the think tanks are closely associated with particular business groups, especially CEP with the Matte Group in Chile and Fundación Mediterránea with Arcor in Argentina. Think tanks are useful to big business in shaping public debate but also in serving as a springboard for appointments to top positions in government, as the heads of think tanks are often called to public service as ministers or other top officials.[9]

Last, the media, especially television, were sometimes bought up by business groups or were mostly aligned with them on major policy issues. Some major television channels grew into important groups in their own right as in Televisa in Mexico and Globo in Brazil. In other cases, business groups

---

[9] Domingo Cavallo's move from Fundación Mediterránea to become Menem's long-standing minister of finance is a prime example. Cavallo is best known as the architect of radical neoliberal reform including sweeping trade liberalization. However, when his ministry issued a decree imposing a 10 percent tariff on imported candy and doubled tax incentives for exporting candy, many suspected that the measures were not unrelated to Cavallo's previous close relationship with Arcor through Fundación Mediterránea (see Finchelstein 2010a, 20).

have bought into television and radio (especially in Central America; Segovia 2005, 31).[10] Overall, corporate concentration is high across all media (print, radio, and television) and communication services: on average, the largest four operators control 82 percent of the market, ranging from about two-thirds in radio and print media to more than 90 percent in television (Becerra and Mastrini 2009, 213). These media outlets allowed business groups to shape public debate on major policy decisions. When owned by business groups, these media also gave business groups more direct influence over politicians who always stand to benefit from favorable media coverage. Media control thus gives business groups another potential currency in exchanges with politicians.

In sum, political systems and practices in Latin America are remarkably accommodating for business interests, especially narrow or individual interests of big business. Large business groups also have general advantages over others in politics, starting with more money. Steady acquisitions at home and abroad augmented the size advantage and added to their structural leverage. As with traditional MNCs, more internationalized business groups can also now threaten governments that they will shift investment abroad.

Business-owning families have additional advantages in politics. Families have several trusted members they can send into politics (and sometimes some members develop specialized political skills) to engage on behalf of the whole family.[11] Most important, families can make longer-term commitments to support politicians and can bear an extended and consequential grudge if crossed.[12] CEOs and other salaried managers tend to rotate through firms, especially in MNCs, and so lack comparable long-term credibility. As Morck et al. put it, "the CEOs of widely held firms in the United States serve an average seven year term – an eye blink compared to the permanence of the old money families controlling pyramidal groups in many countries" (2005, 696).

Beyond big business, MP/PRL systems are susceptible to pressure by other well-endowed and well-organized groups such as landowners, professional associations, and labor unions. As discussed in Chapter 5, labor unions have strong incentives to invest in politics, and PR electoral systems provide better returns to that investment. In the context of market reforms, unions in many countries were able to block extensive labor law reform, especially in the area of union or collective rights (Murillo and Schrank 2005). A broad cross-national study found that "countries with proportional representation

---

[10] Other business groups with major media operations include Ardilla Lülle and Santo Domingo in Colombia, and Cisneros in Venezuela, earlier in the twentieth century, when print media mattered more, business groups occasionally also owned newspapers, as in the case of *El Mercurio* and the Edwards group in Chile.

[11] For example, two members of the Agnelli family, owners of Italy's largest industrial group, served in parliament (Morck et al. 2005, 697).

[12] See Shleifer and Summers (1988) generally on the advantages of family business in maintaining credibility in implicit long-term contracts.

have more protective employment and collective relations laws... " (Botero et al. 2004, 1370).[13]

In developed countries, positive complementarities generate positive sum politics among those who benefit from the complementarities. So, cross-class coalitions among skilled workers and firms that depend on those skills sustain institutions of coordinated capitalism. In hierarchical capitalism, politics are more zero sum with smaller groups of insiders pressing to maintain core institutions and the negative complementarities among them. However, because hierarchical capitalism is exclusionary and does not automatically lead to a high road to development, it also generates political contention and pressures for change, for "incentive-incompatible" policies to undo negative complementarities. So, although political institutions and practices favor insiders and continuity, politics are not in any comfortable equilibrium.

### III. What Do Business Groups Want?

Rents and rent seeking by business groups have been pervasive in Latin America. Although systematic data do not exist, levels of rent seeking in Latin America do not seem to sharply differentiate them from other parts of the world or from one another (save for Mexico and Chile, on opposite ends of the continuum in the 2000s). However, rents and generally supportive governments do not confirm a strict entrenchment argument, largely because of the high levels of turnover among business groups. Put differently, business groups have benefited from a range of favorable policies – sometimes targeted, sometimes general – but these policies have not always been the result of lobbying by business groups, nor have governments made open-ended guarantees or always stepped in to bail out firms in trouble.

In this more complex and contingent view of business-government relations, understanding likely policy consequences of business lobbying requires an analysis of both how business groups engage in politics (as considered in the previous section) and what it is that business groups want from policy. As Pepper Culpepper (2011) argues with respect to corporate governance in developed countries, policies vary across countries not in terms of business influence (big business usually gets what it wants) but rather in business preferences. To understand what policies business groups will push and oppose requires a brief reconsideration of their overall strategies and sources of competitive advantage (see Chapter 3). As discussed in earlier chapters, many business groups have strengths in commodity and other production that involves the organization of large numbers of unskilled and semiskilled workers. Business groups are diversified but also have many core assets in naturally low-risk sectors where they have inherent advantages in international markets (natural resources), sectors

---

[13] See Chang et al. (2010) for a general argument that PR systems favor producer groups over consumers.

where they are shielded from international competition (as in nontradable service sectors), or oligopolistic or favorably regulated sectors that provide them with a reliable cash flow. Almost none of the largest business groups have most of their assets in highly competitive manufacturing activities.

Another great source of competitive advantage comes from the ability of business groups, because of their large size, to mobilize capital both from their many subsidiaries and from domestic and, more recently, international financial markets. A last advantage is in flexibility and speed. Business groups (similar to many private equity firms) are flexible externally in their ability to buy and sell subsidiaries because they have access to sufficient cash and because managerial control is so highly centralized (Grosse 2007). Business groups have internal flexibility because they can hire and fire workers easily largely because skill levels are, on average, low and because firms circumvent costly labor regulations through subcontracting or keeping worker tenure (and hence accumulated benefits) short.

A first policy implication of this set of competitive strategies helps to explain the surprising lack of opposition to trade liberalization, and market-oriented reform overall, in the 1990s (Naim 1993; Kingstone 1999). Because they are diversified, business groups are not composed of inherently protectionist or export-oriented firms; they usually have some mix. Diversification reduces the intensity of business-group preferences on trade protection and makes them amenable to a range of policies.[14] If anything, diversified business groups are uniquely suited to adapting to abrupt changes in overall development strategy. In addition, privatization programs opened up attractive new opportunities to business groups that were exiting manufacturing in the wake of trade liberalization. Similarly, diversified business groups are fairly well insulated from, or hedged against, exchange rate fluctuations. Although exporters prefer undervaluation, most commodity producers in the 2000s had costs well below world prices and could thus more easily absorb the costs of currency appreciation. Business groups in services are largely shielded from international competition (they rarely export) and so are less affected by exchange rates (see Steinberg 2010).

Less surprising but still puzzling is the absence of business groups in coalitions pushing to reform education and labor regulation. In principle, reforms in these areas could benefit business groups significantly, and business groups in Asia did push education (Kosack 2009). However, as discussed in Chapters 5 and 6, the complementarities in Latin America reduce incentives for business groups to invest in the costly, protracted politics of education reform. To summarize the analysis in previous chapters, business-group strategies tend to rely on a combination of firms employing lots of low-skill labor and

---

[14] Smaller, more specialized, import-competing firms, of course, had more to lose and sometimes opposed trade liberalization (Shadlen 2004). Governments also adopted compensatory policies to ease adjustment and weaken political opposition (Etchemendy 2011).

capital-intensive ventures employing smaller numbers of skilled workers. For the latter, firms can find private solutions in training the workers themselves, and labor regulations help protect that investment. These private solutions reduced incentives for firms to invest in pushing public education reform.

A final puzzling nonissue for business groups is foreign investment. In principle, domestic business might be expected to press governments to restrict the entry of foreign firms, as domestic incumbents have often done around the world. However, business groups in Latin America have rarely voiced opposition to MNC entry.[15] Following on complementarities discussed in Chapters 3 and 4, three plausible motives stand out. First, MNCs have long been in Latin America, and business groups grew up around MNCs in sectors like cement or beer where FDI was rare. Initially, MNC lack of interest in these sectors provided natural protection for business groups. Second, MNCs expanded markets for business-group services and products and sometimes bought business-group subsidiaries, thereby buoying corporate asset prices. Last, and more abstractly, MNCs shored up property rights by raising the costs to governments of arbitrary intervention in the private sector.

Where business groups have stronger interests is in what Culpepper (2011) calls the "quiet politics" of maintaining the regulatory environment that gives them competitive advantages over local start-ups and potential MNC entrants. Many business groups sought out regulated sectors in the wake of market reforms in the 1990s. As cited in Chapter 1, a top financial executive at the Grupo Matte in Chile said the group strategy was to be big in four or five regulated sectors that were therefore "low risk and capital intensive" (*Qué Pasa*, 5 November 2005, p. 22). Many regulations are technically complex and low visibility, and politicians and voters lack the expertise and interest to engage them. Such areas of low-salience politics give big business an advantage in pressing their preferences into policy (Culpepper 2011).

Stock markets are one area where business groups want to maintain favorable regulation. Historically, stock markets in Latin America rarely functioned as expected: they did not create markets for corporate control (listed companies all had controlling owners), did not provide significant opportunities for smaller, newer firms to raise capital, and rarely developed into a reliable alternative for retail investors. However, stock markets did grant business groups access to additional capital and sophisticated means for extending business-group control over more corporate assets especially through mechanisms like pyramids and nonvoting shares. In Brazil, for example, firms could issue two-thirds of their shares as nonvoting, so business groups could control 50 percent of voting shares with only 17 percent of the firm's total capital (Coutinho and Rabelo 2003, 44). Through the 2000s, stock markets grew (after a drop

---

[15] In one surprising case, from the late 1990s, Mexican banks owned mostly by business groups, did not oppose the opening of the sector to the entry of foreign banks, and MNCs then proceeded to buy up most domestic banks (Martinez-Diaz 2009, 62–63).

in the 1990s), measured in terms of total capitalization as a percentage of GDP, but turnover – the actual trading of shares – remained small (Stallings 2006). And, in some cases, listed firms organized to keep stock markets from expanding beyond the limited functions useful to business groups. For example, Abrasca (Asociação Brasileira de Companhias Abertas) mounted effective opposition to a bill in 2001 designed to strengthen minority shareholder protections (Coutinho and Rabelo 2003, 49).[16]

Business groups share an abiding interest in weak and passive antitrust regulators, largely because many of them have market power in some segments of their operations that allows them to generate the steady cash flow needed to expand and sustain other firms in the group (see Chapter 3). Mexico provides the clearest examples. With its near-monopoly of fixed line telephony, Telmex, the flagship of Carlos Slim's Grupo Carso, charged some of the highest rates in Latin America. Telmex's interconnection rates were 44 percent above the OECD average that raised steep barriers to entry by potential competitors (*Economist*, 17 March 2011; see also World Bank 2007, 39–40). In essence, Mexican consumers helped finance Grupo Carso's massive expansion into telecommunications markets throughout Latin America. In cement, as noted earlier, Cemex controls around two-thirds of the Mexican market, and Mexican consumers pay double what U.S. customers pay, in large part due to "Mexico's deliberately flaccid antitrust regime" (Schrank 2005, 109).

Overall, "regulatory agencies in Mexico are weak and lack autonomous power" (World Bank 2007, 40). The antitrust legislation and agency Comisión Federal de Competencia (CFC) has greater independence, but is still ineffectual because it depends on the judiciary and other branches of government to enforce decisions (World Bank 2007, 41). Governments in the 2000s made several attempts to strengthen the CFC, successfully though partially in 2006, and unsuccessfully in 2010. In early 2010, the Chamber of Deputies passed, nearly unanimously, a strengthened competition law. However, once it got to the Senate, the opposition PRI party derailed it as would be expected given the incentives described earlier for the PRI to favor big business over their rivals in the presidency (Pardinas 2010).

Business groups in television and media initially had more impressive success in the legislature. In March 2006, the Chamber of Deputies unanimously passed, in seven minutes, a law extending television concessions and raising barriers to entry, a law subsequently known as the Televisa Law. The bill was reportedly drafted by Televisa lawyers and was passed without amendment (against the recommendations of the CFC; World Bank 2007, 41). The timing was auspicious for Televisa because campaigning was heating up for the elections in July 2006. Santiago Creel, secretary of the Interior

---

[16] In a study of 41 developed and developing countries, higher proportions of family firms were negatively correlated with various measures of financial development (Fogel 2006). See Chapter 3 on more recent, and successful, reforms in the Chilean and Brazilian stock markets.

(Gobernación, 2000–05) and later a senator, said the law was passed under the pressure of the elections in which all parties needed television coverage (Becerril 2007). The Supreme Court later ruled some provisions unconstitutional. The episode though provides a clear window on incentives in Congress and the ability of business groups to exploit them for favorable regulations.[17]

A last area in which business groups have interests is in the continuation of various policies intended to promote domestic business or national champions. These preferences are not as strong as those over other kinds of regulation, and business in fact lost many subsidies and protections in the 1990s often without putting up much of a fight. However, as other policies emerged, including privatizations favoring national buyers, business groups stood ready to take advantage of them (see Chapter 3). The largest, by far, program of business promotion is directed by the BNDES, the development bank in Brazil, which survived the state retrenchment of the 1990s and more than tripled its lending the 2000s. Although this growth did not apparently result from business pressures, business groups were undoubtedly the major beneficiaries (Almeida 2009).[18] As Eike Batista, founder of EBX (a new business group in mining and logistics) and one of the wealthiest men in Brazil, put it: the BNDES is "the best bank in the world" (*Economist*, 5 August 2010). The innovation policies in Brazil and Chile in the 2000s (discussed in the next chapter) devoted major new resources and subsidies to technological development. However, the sectors targeted were often related to natural resources where the main players were existing business groups.

In sum, it is incomplete and misleading merely to establish that business groups have power and conclude that they will use it to seek rents. The specific rents and benefits business groups seek depend on their core capabilities and strategies. So most business groups in Latin America are less intensely interested in trade, exchange rate, and foreign investment policies and rarely invest their political energies in pushing major reforms in education or labor law. Where their interests are strong is in the "quiet politics" of various forms of regulation in financial and product markets that shore up their privileged market positions and raise barriers to entry. The institutional and informal forms of access discussed in Section II are well suited to permit big business to influence these less publicly visible regulations.

---

[17] Ironically, sufficient political impetus for breaking up the near monopolies in television and telecommunications may, in the end, come from the incumbents themselves. As bundled telecommunication and television services became the norm, Telmex and Televisa wanted to enter the other's markets to offer bundled services and waged a battle in the press in 2011 attacking the other's regulatory protections (*Economist*, 17 March 2011, *América Economia*, April 2011, www.americaeconomia.com/guerra-de-monopolios, accessed 27 April 2011).

[18] BNDES's president Luciano Coutinho (2007– ) had been close to business and his appointment to BNDES may not have been unrelated to business support. There is some evidence (Musacchio and Lazzarini forthcoming) that political contributions help with BNDES loan disbursements.

## IV. Degrees of Political Intimacy

All business groups have advantages in politics, but some are active and politicized while others steer clear.[19] A well-known example is the distinction between Suharto and non-Suharto groups in Indonesia (Hanani 2006). Although such distinctions are less black and white in other regions, most countries manifest clear cases on each end of the continuum of intimacy. The concept of political intimacy is not restricted narrowly to crony capitalism as found under Suharto, Marcos, or Putin, but also comprises business groups that most thoroughly "buy into" the government's major policies, be they developmentalist as in Brazil or Korea in the 1970s or neoliberal as in Argentina or India in the 1990s. A major external indicator of a group's level of intimacy would be periods of rapid expansion in group activities that cannot be explained by normal economic factors, as in the expansion of the chaebol in Korea in the 1970s, the meteoric rise of the Cruzat-Larrain business group in Chile in the same period, or the rapid growth of many business groups through privatization in the 1990s. Cronyism characterized relations in many cases, but it was also combined with official industrial policies or market reforms that granted business groups preferential access to subsidies, protection, or state assets.

Business groups on the more intimate end of the spectrum generally have more volatile fortunes, rising quickly when they are close to political patrons and falling dramatically, Icarus-like, once the incumbents or policies change or the business group falls out of favor. However, some adept groups use their close connections, like a gravitational slingshot, to launch them into longer-term expansion even after their government patrons have decamped. However, on the end of greater political intimacy, Icarus groups seem to outnumber slingshot groups. These differences are best illustrated by contrasting the longer-term trajectories of some emblematic groups.

In Mexico, business groups in the northern city of Monterrey historically stood apart from those in Mexico City in cultural, familial, and political terms (Camp 1989). Monterrey groups were largely independent (at least through the 1980s) and generally opposed central governments in the twentieth century, and sometimes countermobilized through new parties and associations. The Banamex and Carso groups represent the other end of the spectrum, however, with very different endings. Banamex was the largest bank and the core of one of the largest business groups throughout much of the twentieth century. Banamex retained close, harmonious relations with a series of presidents and developed a dense network of ties through major business associations. In addition, Banamex responded enthusiastically to a series of development policies in the second half of the twentieth century designed to promote particular sectors and regulate the entry of MNCs (Hoshino 2010). In particular, MNCs in many

[19] This section draws on Schneider (2010c).

sectors could only enter Mexico in joint ventures, and Banamex offered itself as a well-connected partner (interview Agustín Legorreta, 23 June 2004). Even before the government dismantled these policies, it nationalized Banamex in 1982, and although compensated, the owners were unable to reconfigure a major new group. Carlos Slim, owner of the Grupo Carso, in contrast, cultivated close ties to President Carlos Salinas (1988–94), bought into privatization in a big way and went on, after Salinas went into exile in 1994, to construct the largest business group in Latin America. Slim may have benefited from the fact that his closest political intimacy was relatively short, which may have helped him leverage this brief gravitational boost on to a less dependent trajectory (though Carso's flagship telephone monopoly, Telmex, continued to benefit from favorable government regulation long after 1994).

Chile in the 1970s and 1980s offers one of the most spectacular examples of Icarus groups. In the mid-1970s, the Pinochet dictatorship embarked on radical neoliberal reform that included a fire sale of government-owned firms as well as an overnight opening of product and capital markets. Two business groups, Cruzat-Larraín and BHC, had especially close relations with the Pinochet government, maintained in part by a handful of economists who circulated through top positions in government as well as top jobs in these groups. Both business groups leaped at new opportunities and used international loans to buy dozens of firms the government was auctioning off to become, in the span of a few years, the dominant companies in Chile. Cruzat-Larraín grew from 11 companies in 1974 to 85 companies just three years later, while BHC grew from 18 to 62 companies in the same period. By 1978, these two groups controlled more than 37 percent of the assets of the 250 largest firms in Chile and 40 percent of private-sector bank assets (Silva 1997, 160–61). The next two largest groups, Matte and Luksic, controlled only 12 percent of the assets of the 250 largest firms. But, when the debt crisis hit Chile with devastating impact in 1982, Cruzat-Larraín and BHC collapsed, and the government took over most of their assets. The Matte and Luksic groups survived to become two of the largest groups in the 2000s.[20]

In other countries, the reversals of fortune have been less extreme. In Brazil, turnover on the list of largest groups has been high, though politics is not the only cause. Two business groups, Votorantim and Villares, illustrate well the range of political strategies over the late twentieth century. Votorantim earned a reputation in the 1970s for refusing to follow government direction, and subsidy, into new sectors, preferring instead to stick with its own more gradual and focused strategy of growth and diversification.[21] Villares, in contrast, grew

---

[20] In a longer-term calculation of high turnover in Chile, only three of the largest groups in the 2000s were among the large groups in the 1960s (Lefort 2010). By the 1990s, Matte and Claro were more engaged in politics and Angelini and Luksic less so (interview with Edgardo Boeninger, 22 March 2006).

[21] Evans (1979) provides an early comparison of these two groups and highlights the fact that Votorantim was the only business group in Brazil that resisted policy and other inducements to

very rapidly in the 1970s, and responded to several government initiatives to expand sectors such as capital goods, metals, and even computing. In one instance, Paulo Villares planned, with government support, to invest in capital goods. By coincidence, he met with then president Ernesto Geisel who asked him how much Villares was planning to invest. When Villares responded, Geisel immediately said, 'double it, and we'll make sure it works out.' Villares doubled the investment, but by 1982, the government was in the midst of an economic crisis, and Geisel was no longer in office (interview, 2 August 2006). By the late 1980s, Villares was selling off subsidiaries, and by the 1990s, in part due to debilitating family infighting, the group was a marginal operation compared to its standing in the 1970s. Votorantim, in contrast, came into the 1990s in much stronger shape and continued to thrive into the 2000s.[22]

In Argentina, several Icarus groups soared in the early 1990s only to crash and burn by the 2000s. Among the groups that endorsed Menem's stabilization polices and participated in broad privatization policies were Macri, Fortabat (Loma Negra), Pérez Companc, Soldati, and Techint. Most of these groups went into debt to buy privatized firms in new sectors, and most of them came out poorly (Fracchia, Mesquita, and Quiroga 2010). Fortabat and Pérez Companc ended up selling out to Brazilian firms, while Macri and Soldati sold off many subsidiaries and came through the decade in much leaner form (Finchelstein 2004; interview with Santiago Soldati, 18 September 2007). More of a slingshot case, Techint was, among the intimate groups, one that came through well, in part because its acquisitions were more closely related to its core steel business and because it relied more on exports than did other business groups. One of the groups that chose to maintain its distance was Arcor, a group with core activities in candies and diversified subsidiaries in related industries (sugar, packaging, and other food products).

In sum, business groups differ in their propensity to invest in politics, to seek rents, to follow government policies, and to prosper through politics. The consequences also differ. Some politicized groups rise and fall quickly, often through acquisitions and then spin-offs, in an Icarus syndrome. Other initially politicized business groups leverage their political gains into long-term growth, in a sort of gravitational slingshot. The nonpoliticized firms experience neither the policy-induced booms nor the subsequent busts, but grow more slowly, often through greenfield investments rather than large-scale, leap-frogging acquisitions.

The collapse of politically connected firms raises two further, related questions: Why do governments withdraw support for previously favored firms,

---

enter into joint ventures with MNCs in the 1960s and 1970s. For a complete history of both groups, see Reiss (1980).

[22] Over a longer period in Brazil, less than one-quarter of the 500 largest firms in 1973 were still among the top 500 by 2006 (*Valor Online*, 25 September 2006).

and why, more generally, do turnover rates among top business groups vary cross nationally? Although these questions cannot be answered here, it is worth noting a few hypotheses. On the first question, Khanna and Yafeh propose a possible life cycle of relations: "from government protégés to a strong lobby with often captured regulators...Or to a sector that loses favor with the authorities because of its excessive influence" (2007, 359). Although systematic data are lacking, some prominent cases seem to fit this life-cycle hypothesis. For example, excessive influence seems an apparent motive, among others, in the intervention by the Putin government in Yukos (see Guriev and Rachinsky 2005). Similarly, firms that do not show active enough enthusiasm for government patrons may fall out of favor, as was reportedly part of the reason for the Korean government's withdrawal of support for the Kukje chaebol in the 1980s (Kang 2002).

Government turnover, especially from one end of the political spectrum to the other (e.g., from left to right or from democratic to authoritarian), can turn previously cozy relations into liabilities. What looks like normal, close relations between business groups and one government may seem like "excessive influence" to the next. So, when he took office in 1998, Kim Dae Jung presumably had few incentives (beyond avoiding the collapse of the financial system) to come to the rescue of chaebol he had so long publicly reviled. Similarly, the de la Rua government in Argentina might not have worried overly about the business groups that had strongly supported, and at least initially benefited from, the previous Peronist government of Carlos Menem. More generally, incoming governments with strong commitments to new development strategies may view existing business groups as part of the discredited old order. This disdain may have informed some of the actions, or rather inactions, in favor of existing business groups on the part of radical neoliberal reformers like Salinas in Mexico and Fernando Collor in Brazil in the early 1990s. Collor in fact openly castigated what he considered retrograde, rent-seeking businesses. His government did not last long enough to do more than initiate a process of trade liberalization, but the opening did, in the end, have mortal consequences for parts of several large business groups.

## V. Conclusions

Few will be shocked by the idea that big business and well-organized social groups have disproportionate political influence. However, it certainly bears repeating because so few studies of democracy in Latin America even consider it.[23] It makes little sense to focus exclusively on political inputs like public

---

[23] General studies of democracy in Latin America make virtually no reference to business (Hagopian and Mainwaring 2005; Munck 2007; Mainwaring and Scully 2010; Oxhorn and Postero 2010; Levine and Molina 2011).

opinion, voting, parties, and the institutions that shape them if in fact policy outputs depend on other actors like business that distort these inputs or twist later stages of policy making and implementation. What is more interesting than the argument that business has influence is the particular ways this influence is channeled. Business in coordinated capitalism, for example, has enormous influence on some issues that is facilitated by PR legislatures (Iversen and Soskice 2009). However, that influence is quite different because it comes through encompassing associations and goes into institutionalized parties, in contrast to the sorts of direct, personalized links between individual business people (or business families) and individual politicians that are more characteristic of hierarchical capitalism in Latin America.

Although the general economic features of hierarchical capitalism exist in other middle-income countries outside Latin America, the political dynamics are more region and country specific. The particular political factors reinforcing hierarchical capitalism in Latin America were institutional (MP/LPR and judiciary), structural (huge firms facing few countervailing economic forces and media dominance), and informal (appointive bureaucracies and privileged consultation). Similar features may favor incumbents elsewhere, but the specific combination is particular to Latin America, as are peculiar additional rules in specific polities such as no reelection in Mexico.[24]

Comparisons of Latin America with other regions, especially developing Asia, raise intriguing what-if and why-not questions. Why did Latin American governments and businesses welcome MNCs? Why did business groups invest so little in R&D? Why did pro-education coalitions not form? Answers to these questions require close attention to the positions, strategies, and political influence of large domestic firms. The examination reveals that business group strategies in most commodity and service sectors was not threatened by MNC entry, did not require R&D to remain competitive, and did not require large pools of skilled workers. The general theoretical implication of this chapter is that comparative research is likely to be better advanced by focusing on how business engages in politics rather than on how much influence it has. In terms of practical implications, reform efforts may be better focused on specific aspects of the political system (parties, campaign finance, consultative councils, and so forth) that grant business groups undue political advantage rather than on trying to change business-group behavior directly.

This chapter focused primarily on institutional continuities and path dependence and on the institutions and practices that favor powerful incumbents

---

[24] A number of suggestive studies correlate various measures of dominance by family firms or business groups to a range of negative outcomes in growth, inequality, and social welfare (Fogel 2006; Morck et al. 2005). However, given the opacity of business politics and the wide range of intervening political and institutional variables between business groups and social and economic outcomes, nailing down the causal mechanisms will be elusive.

and allow them to push for continuity in the policies and institutions that benefit them. However, as noted earlier, negative complementarities and the exclusion of many groups in hierarchical capitalism create political tensions and occasionally opportunities to break out of vicious cycles. The next chapter considers further the politics of change.

# 8

## Twenty-First-Century Variations

*Divergence and Possible Escape Trajectories*

### I. Introduction

While pushing the notion of a single ideal type of hierarchical capitalism for Latin America, previous chapters also noted exceptions and deviations. This chapter takes the analysis of variation a step further by examining recent trends in four countries. Mexico (Colombia could be included as well) offers a benchmark of continuity on all four dimensions of hierarchical capitalism: business groups, MNCs, segmented and atomized labor markets, and a low-skill equilibrium. Argentina, in contrast, starts to move away from the ideal type in the 1990s (with the demise of many business groups), and in the 2000s, the Kirschners' heterodox economic policies and support for labor unions furthered the trend. Brazil and Chile appeared by the 2000s to have the greatest potential for escaping the middle-income trap in part by using technology and education policy to counter the negative complementarities of hierarchical capitalism.

Sources of intraregional variation are many, ranging from colonial legacies (Mahoney 2010), to geography (Engerman and Sokoloff 2012), to contemporary economic and political trends, the focus of this chapter. At the start of the twenty-first century, two major trends – the boom in natural resources and the leftward shift in politics – buffeted the region, although variably across countries. For example, by the late 2000s, international demand for exports was putting countries of the region on two separate tracks. Stagnation in the United States depressed exports and growth in Mexico, Central America, and the Caribbean, while booming Asian demand for food and minerals fueled higher growth across most of South America (Izquierdo and Talvi 2011).

After a period in the 1990s of remarkable policy convergence among countries of the region around a neoliberal development strategy, similar in extent to the earlier convergence in the 1960s around a statist model of ISI, the 2000s brought marked divergence. Simplifying, three main development strategies emerged: continued neoliberalism (Mexico and Chile), nationalist developmentalism (Brazil and Argentina), and left populism (Venezuela and Bolivia).[1] Yet, setting aside the more radical left cases, governments throughout the region maintained core items on the agenda of the Washington Consensus including mostly free trade, fiscal prudence, openness to foreign investment, and few state-owned enterprises. Beyond development strategies, countries also diverged in how much they attempted to redistribute income and opportunities and to redirect government spending toward health and education, though most made significant improvements.

On the political dimension, the major source of divergence in the region was the rise of radical left populism in the petro states of Bolivia, Ecuador, and Venezuela. These radical left, personalist governments do not receive much attention in this book nor in this chapter. This neglect is due partly to the small weight of these three countries in total output and population in the region: less than a tenth on both dimensions. The radical left countries have also pushed state intervention and political control of the economy so far that, as argued in Chapter 2, these countries are better considered as cases of statist or political capitalism, rather than as cases of hierarchical capitalism. Signal policies have been nationalizations and policies hostile to MNCs. So on the corporate side, the space and size of the remaining private sector is much smaller, and analytically then, it makes more sense to approach the study of these political economies from the state. Nonetheless, the large private firms that remained were mostly MNCs and large domestic, family-owned, diversified business groups. And, on the side of labor and skills, these countries are still onliers, with low educational attainment, short job tenure, high regulation, and high informality.

This list of variations goes on. However, the focus in this chapter is on particular dimensions of variation and change that have the potential to disequilibrate the complementarities of hierarchical capitalism. Such variations are especially relevant in corporate governance (such as the shrinkage of business groups in Argentina and the expansion of financial markets in Brazil and Chile) and in skills (such as the expansion of education and R&D in Chile and Brazil). Despite these significant departures, few policies or economic trends in the region fundamentally altered the institutional foundations of labor markets and corporate governance, so talk of transformation or transition to another variety of capitalism is premature. Consequently, understanding future potential and challenges for development, requires a continued focus on the strategies

---

[1] One illustrative dimension of variation across the three strategies is the treatment of big domestic businesses and MNCs. The neoliberal model takes a hands-off approach and treats all firms equally. In the nationalist strategy, governments often discriminate against MNCs and in favor of domestic firms through regulation, procurement, financing, and trade protections. More leftist strategies discriminate against both MNCs and domestic firms through nationalizations and other restrictions. See also Bizberg (2012).

and capabilities of business groups and MNCs and on the impediments (such as precarious job tenure, informality, and overregulation) to high-road employment.

Section II starts with Mexico as a case of continuity and continued close approximation to the ideal type of hierarchical capitalism. Section III examines Argentina to highlight its recent shifts and divergence from hierarchical capitalism on some dimensions, especially in the resurgence of organized labor and the partial eclipse of domestic business groups. Following sections consider two cases of possible escape from negative complementarities. The important challenges to hierarchical capitalism in Brazil (Section IV) and Chile (Section V) result from their respective mixes of good fortune (commodity prices), good policies (especially technology and education), and stable politics (Section VI).

## II. Mexico: Continuities and Gridlock

Despite the epochal transformations of NAFTA and democratization, indicators of continuity in Mexican capitalism are legion. The twin shocks of the commodity boom and left politics mostly skipped over Mexico, and few domestic policies shifted complementarities and the behavior of firms and labor markets. Moreover, as noted in the previous chapter, political dynamics in the 2000s favored insiders (especially business groups and organized labor) and allowed them to defend and extend their regulatory rents.

The decision in the early 1990s by the Salinas government to pursue integration with the U.S. economy through NAFTA set Mexico on a trajectory distinct from the countries of South America (Izquierdo and Talvi 2011). In South America, market reforms and trade liberalization contributed to precocious de-industrialization, but in Mexico, maquila investments kept industrial production and employment up (Palma 2005). During the 1990s, Mexican exports shifted almost completely to the United States and into manufactured goods (Stallings and Peres 2000). Mexico still exported commodities like oil, minerals, and agricultural products, but they shrank to a small proportion of total exports. So, the commodity boom of the 2000s did little to boost Mexican exports and growth.

Politically, Mexico also trended against currents prevailing in South America. As countries in the south shifted left, Mexico moved right. In 2000, many of those who voted for the PAN did so less out of conservative conviction and more so to evict the PRI. With the PRI out of contention, the 2006 elections were a clearer contest between left and right, and the conservative PAN won again, though by a hair. The PAN had long preached economic liberalism, and so once in power, it had little reason to deviate from the neoliberal development strategy inherited from the PRI or, as was increasingly common in South America, revive state intervention in the economy. But, the PAN could not have changed much even had it wanted to.

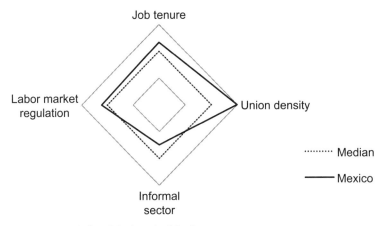

FIGURE 8.1. Labor Markets in Mexico

More significant for inertia and continuity was the post-1997 gridlock in Congress, which stymied efforts at regulatory reform and policy innovation. As discussed in Chapter 7, gridlock and other channels of influence favored insiders and entrenched groups. Business groups used access to legislators and courts to defend regulatory benefits and maintain oligopolies and monopolies. Unions were politically more successful in the public sector (especially teachers and Pemex workers; Elizondo 2011). After the privatization wave of the early 1990s, the top business groups internationalized, as elsewhere, but otherwise changed little. Some specialized (most sold off the banks they had bought during privatization), but most of the larger business groups remained diversified, and dominant family owners retained firm control (while local equity and credit markets languished).[2] After NAFTA, MNCs expanded their presence in manufacturing. MNCs also took over most of the banking system and moved into other services (Martinez-Diaz 2009). As noted in Chapter 6, MNC manufacturing relies heavily, even in high-tech sectors like electronics, on unskilled labor. Compared to Brazil, R&D spending by MNCs was minimal.[3]

Labor markets in Mexico show onlier scores on most dimensions: slightly longer median job tenure (3.5 years), higher union density (22 percent), and marginally higher labor market regulation (Figure 8.1; Schneider and Karcher 2010). In terms of the three main segments of the labor market, (1) the informal sector is smaller (30 percent) relative to regional averages; (2) the formal, high-turnover, and low-skill segment larger (probably around half because

[2] Consumer credit and mortgage loans grew, but long-term credit to firms did not. As noted in Chapter 3, by 2006, just 3 percent of Mexican firms were using banks to finance investment, compared with 7 percent of firms in Argentina, 29 percent in Chile, and 48 percent in Brazil.

[3] Total R&D spending averaged around .5 percent of GDP in the 2000s, and more than half was public (OECD 2008, 138). In the 1990s, U.S. MNCs were investing in R&D in Mexico only one-quarter of what they were investing in Brazil (Hill 2000, 5).

most maquila employment fits in this segment); and (3) a somewhat smaller long-tenure, skilled segment (as in the large auto sector) of 10 to 20 percent (19 percent of workers had ten or more years of tenure in the 2000s compared to the regional median of 22 percent; see Table 5.2).

On education and skills, PISA scores in Mexico were somewhat above the regional average: the mean reading score was 425 in 2009 compared to the median for Latin America of 413. However, the percentage of boys scoring below level 2 on the PISA test (the minimum deemed necessary to be able to continue with higher education or training) was 46 percent (though still below the median for Latin America of 54 percent; see Table 5.7 in Chapter 5). Nonetheless, many more students are going on to universities, and private universities, as elsewhere in the region, have expanded briskly. However, as noted in Chapter 6, nearly a fifth of graduates were unemployed or in the informal sector, and many others had emigrated. Education indicators are trending gradually in the right direction but do not yet signal an immanent exit from the low-skill equilibrium.

In sum, Mexico approximates well the ideal type of an HME, and the dysfunctions of the political system have impeded political and policy possibilities for countering negative complementarities. The other large country of Latin America that also closely approximates central tendencies in hierarchical capitalism is Colombia. Its labor market and education scores are on or very close to the median for Latin America, save for an astonishingly short median job tenure of 1.9 years. On the side of corporate governance, big private business is divided among stable, diversified family-controlled business groups and MNCs. In fact, in terms of the top business groups, continuity has been the greatest in Colombia, where the top four in the early 1990s were still the top four two decades later.[4]

### III. Argentina: Left Populism and the Eclipse of Business Groups

As with many comparative frameworks, Argentina is a hard case to classify (see Etchemendy and Garay 2011). In the 2000s, Argentina benefited from a classic commodity boom, especially in soy, that helped lift the economy out of the collapse in the early 2000s. It was in politics and development strategy, however, that Argentina most differed from other large countries of the region, especially in maintaining through the mid-2000s an undervalued exchange rate that boosted manufacturing. Other policy measures combined an ad hoc set of taxes, price controls, subsidies, trade protections, exchange controls, and micro-level interventions (sometimes down to the level of ministers calling up individual firms). Although state intervention was pervasive, nationalizations (as in Venezuela) were less common and, by the late 2000s, had not pushed

---

[4] Although some had new names: GEA (Grupo Empresarial Antioqueño) formerly Sindicato Antioqueño), Sarmiento Angulo, OAL (Organización Ardila Lülle), and Santo Domingo.

the political economy into the realm of state capitalism because production remained predominantly in private hands.

By the 2000s, the small size of business groups represented a potentially significant departure from hierarchical capitalism.[5] Throughout the second half of the twentieth century, Argentina's political economy was (in)famously dominated by a small number of huge business groups, the so-called captains of industry or the "group of 12" (Ostiguy 1990). These were also some of the most sprawling business empires – Bunge y Born, for example, had scores of firms spread throughout the economy. The early 1990s appeared to bring further consolidation as the Menem government sold off many state-owned enterprises to established business groups. However, this apparent consolidation was short-lived (see Fracchia et al. 2010). Through the 1990s, various business groups divested subsidiaries, sold out, collapsed, or left Argentina.

By the 2000s, only a few of the traditional family business groups survived among the behemoths, and these survivors were somewhat more specialized (and diversified mostly through vertical integration). Techint (steel, oil, and construction) and Arcor (food and agribusiness) were among the largest and most internationalized of the survivors (Finchelstein 2010b). The handful of other business groups with sales around $1 billion included AGD (Aceitera General Deheza) and Pérez Companc in agribusiness and Bulgheroni in oil and gas.[6] As noted in Chapter 4, by the 2000s, more than 80 percent of the sales of the largest firms in Argentina were by MNCs. In this dominance of MNCs, and with the historically high levels of education, Argentina came to resemble much of Eastern Europe, and the model there of "dependent market economies" (DMEs; see Chapter 2 and Nölke and Vliegenthart 2009).

Yet, by the late 2000s. new local, family controlled business groups were emerging, though initially they were fairly specialized (as most business groups are when they start out; Cabot 2009). The commodity boom in Argentina was heavily concentrated in soy, and so did not initially inflate large firms the way it did elsewhere in mining (Vale and Luksic), cellulose (Votorantim and Angelini), or other commodities with greater scale economies and capital intensity. Nonetheless, some large firms did start to emerge in soy, such as los Grobo (the Grobocopatel family). By 2010, Los Grobo was the largest grain producer in Latin America, though with revenues of around half a billion dollars, Los Grobo was still small compared to the largest business groups in the region. Los Grobo started in grain production, but has increasingly diversified along the production chain to offer inputs, storage, and milling (Bell and Scott 2010).

In addition, other new business groups emerged or gained significant scale through government concessions and contracts in infrastructure (the Eurnekian

[5] Many traditional business groups in Peru also struggled or went under (Miller 2010, 656).
[6] Another 20 or so smaller business groups had revenues in the hundreds of millions of dollars (Fracchia et al. 2010, 327).

group for example) and became known as the "empresarios K" (Stok 2006).[7] These business groups are good examples of the policy-induced type introduced in Chapter 3. In the same years that these business groups were growing, Kirschner policies (and at times targeted harassment) encouraged MNCs to scale back or decamp, leaving more room for local groups to grow into the ranks of the largest firms. In sum, it seems premature to declare business groups extinct in Argentina. In Chile and Brazil turnover among business groups was high in recent decades, with new groups emerging to take the place of fading groups. The same process may be underway in Argentina, though with a lag.

On the labor front, unions made a comeback in the 2000s, buoyed by government backing and then in addition by tightening labor markets in the late 2000s (Etchemendy and Collier 2007). Such a dramatic comeback was rare in Latin America and distances Argentina from both HMEs and DMEs. However, the union revival is not pushing Argentina in the direction of CME-style bargaining and coordination because unions were strong outside the firm on narrow issues of wages yet mostly absent on the shop floor. Unions in Argentina derive more of their bargaining leverage from political support and more of their organizational strength from state concessions of major social benefits (here there are some parallels to Scandinavia), especially health insurance provided through union-controlled social funds (*obras sociales*). These social funds provide both strong reasons for workers to join unions and resources to support union activities. What is missing though is the CME-type union presence on the shop floor to coordinate with management on core nonwage issues of training, work organization, layoffs, working time, and the introduction of new technologies that are crucial to productivity increases in CMEs. On other labor market indicators, Argentina has longer median job tenure, a smaller informal sector, and slightly less regulation than regional medians (Figure 8.2). The long tenure (10-plus years), labor elite segment accounts for 25 percent of workers, slightly above the regional median (Table 5.2).

On education and skills, Argentina led the region through much of the twentieth century (Engerman and Sokoloff 2012). However, although still near the top of the rankings for average years of schooling, Argentina's PISA rankings for 2009 were surprisingly low and even below the regional median (see Table 5.1). On the mean reading score, Argentina ranked sixth out of eight countries in the region, below Brazil and Colombia, and 59 percent of boys in Argentina scored below level 2, considered the minimum necessary for going on to tertiary education and advanced vocational training. On the plus side, technical education at the secondary level remains strong, and tertiary education is expanding.

---

[7] In the late 1990s, the Eurnekian group won concessions to run several dozen airports. In the 2000s, the Eurnekian group diversified rapidly into various infrastructure areas (rail, highways, hydroelectricity) and other sectors like biofuels, banking, and pharmacies, as well as airport concessions in other countries, mostly in Latin America (see eduardoeurnekian.com).

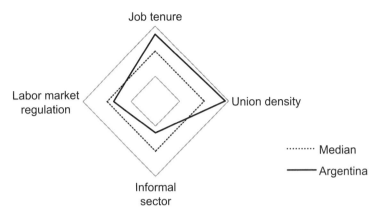

FIGURE 8.2. Labor Markets in Argentina

Moreover, several high-tech sectors such as software and business services are thriving, and recent governments expanded support for R&D. However, the low quality of education reflected in the PISA performance will limit how far the positive trends can extend, and suggest that getting out of the low-skill trap will also be a major challenge in Argentina.

Beyond booming commodities, several isolated manufacturing and service sectors were competitive internationally and resembled CME-type configurations in some sectoral pockets. Wine is the best-known success story. The rapid move from insignificant to major player in international markets was a classic story of coordinated cospecific investment among many stakeholders in skills, R&D, educational programs, logistics, innovation, and marketing, instigated and backed by the provincial government of Mendonza (McDermott 2007). Provincial governments have also promoted and helped coordinate key software clusters (López and Ramos 2008). However, software firms rely more on LME-type strategies: small flexible firms, short job tenure, high mobility among firms, and strong general skills acquired in high quality educational institutions. Two other success sectors, or rather niches, are steel tubes and candy, both driven by single business groups, Techint and Arcor, respectively (Catalano 2004; Ghemawat, Rukstad, and Illes 2005). These stories, like the handful of other successful business groups in manufacturing, are sui generis, and each managed training, skills, labor relations, and tenure differently from patterns common in their general environment of hierarchical capitalism (Friel 2011). Yet these are still isolated cases and exceptions more than the rule.

In sum, Argentina in the 2000s looked different from standard hierarchical capitalism on the core dimensions of lacking many large business groups and having strong unions. However, these anomalies were in part the result of policies over recent decades, policies that could – in a country not known for policy stability – be reversed.

## IV. Brazil: Industrial Policy and Demand Shock

Brazil and Chile came out of the 2000s well poised to move on from the middle-income trap. In both countries, the 2000s saw sustained growth, improvements in social welfare, and increasing investment overall and in technology and innovation specifically. Their progress resulted from a fortuitous intersection of luck, legacy, and policy. Good fortune came largely in the form of very high prices of the commodities exported by Brazil and Chile. The legacy benefits were visible in various longer-term sectoral, technology, and education policies initiated in the late twentieth century that continued to bear fruit into the 2000s. A famous example is Brazil's heavy investment in ethanol beginning in the 1970s that helped it become the world's second-largest producer by the 2000s. Last, more contemporary policies made crucial contributions to investment and upgrading. This section focuses on good fortune and effective policy as the proximate factors in mitigating some of the negative complementarities in hierarchical capitalism, before turning to the macro-political factors that reinforced stability and good policy.

On the fortune side, the boom in commodity prices was a boon for most countries of Latin America, but commodity prices were especially frothy in iron ore and soy (Brazil's main exports) and copper (which accounted for more than half of Chile's exports) which rebounded quickly after 2009 to pre crisis levels. From 2002 to 2007, iron ore prices increased 185 percent (the same as oil) and copper prices went up 357 percent. Metal prices went up much more than agriculture commodities, as China entered a "metal-intensive" phase of development (Jenkins 2011, 75). Commodity rents, and a general international "tailwind," fueled overall growth and eased major macro constraints on investment, government spending, and balance of payments. In the early phase of the boom (2002–06), the terms of trade increased by almost 50 percent and along with other favorable international factors such as capital inflows and low interest rates explain more than half of the variance in growth in the seven largest economies of the region. By a different estimation, the external tailwind from 2002 to 2006 raised annual GDP growth by almost two percentage points from a projected 3.8 percent to the actual 5.6 percent (Izquierdo, Romero, and Talvi 2008, 7, 11, 15).[8]

The commodity boom strengthened business groups (and to a lesser extent MNCs) and consolidated their dominance among domestic firms. By the late 2000s, Brazil had shifted back to exporting mostly primary products, and its largest nonfinancial firms were in mining (Vale, EBX), semiprocessed natural resources (steel [Gerdau], aluminum and pulp and paper [Votorantim]), and

---

[8] Izquierdo et al. (2008, 19–20) also forecast that a modest reduction in terms of trade coupled with higher costs for external financing could easily tilt Latin America into recession. Using different calculations, Österholm and Zettelmeyer (2008, 614) estimate that a 20 percent drop in commodity prices would take nearly 2 percent off growth rates. See also Gallagher and Porzecanski (2010) and World Bank (2011).

meat processing (Brazil Foods and JBS). The only manufacturing firm was Embraer, ranked 79th among the largest firms in Latin America (Schneider 2009a).[9] Although not ranked among the few dozen giants, a sort of Brazilian Mittelstand emerged with dynamic medium-sized firms in sophisticated manufacturing and some services. Some of the better known and more internationalized include Weg and Lupatech (engines and compressors), Iochpe-Maxion and Randon (auto parts), Romi (capital goods), Natura (cosmetics), EMS (pharmaceuticals), Totvs and Bematech (information technology; Fleury and Fleury 2009; Arbix and Caseiro 2011).[10]

In Brazil, contrary to historical precedent, some commodity firms leveraged the boom into greater investment in R&D and greater consequent demand for skilled employees. In the traditional pattern, discussed in Chapter 6, commodity production generated little demand for skilled labor. Yet, several large Brazilian commodity firms broke with this pattern, partly by chance and partly by strategy (Amann 2009). For example, the emergence of the ethanol complex was driven by technological advances all along the productive chain, from biotechnology in cane production, to flex fuel engines in automobile production, to diversification into electricity (*bagasse*), biodiesel, and ethanol-based petrochemicals. By 2004, Brazil was producing one-third of the world's sugar cane, and by 2007, sugar cane accounted for 16 percent of total energy consumption in Brazil (Leite 2009, 127). Similarly, the curse of having oil in very deep offshore deposits became a developmental blessing when Petrobras decided to invest heavily in developing the technology for deep drilling. Ethanol and petroleum exploration are the best examples of legacy benefits – long-term policies that involved decades of subsidy, investment, training, and policy experimentation, and that started reaping major returns in the 2000s.[11] Other examples include steel, aircraft (Embraer), agricultural research (Embrapa), and petrochemicals; these were key sectors created by government programs, usually SOEs, in the 1960s and 1970s that were flourishing by the 2000s.

Several business groups invested commodity rents in R&D and high-tech ventures in new sectors. In the late 2000s, Vale moved beyond mining into biofuels and electricity, especially through VSE (Vale Soluções em Energia, half financed by BNDES), and created its own technology institute, ITV (Instituto

---

[9] Rankings for 2009 from www.americaeconomia.com/rankings, accessed 27 April 2011. Steel firms like Gerdau and CSN were larger than Embraer, but they produced commodity steel (though Gerdau was moving more into manufacturing in the 2000s).

[10] The emergence of these dynamic middle-sized firms is related in part to the expansion of credit and equity markets. Brazil and Chile are regional leaders in financial development, according to the World Economic Forum, though Brazil ranks ninth in the world, far above Chile, in terms of IPOs (*América Economia* online, 13 December 2011, accessed 14 December 2011).

[11] The Brazilian government started an ambitious ethanol program, Pro-Álcool, in 1974 and spent $30 billion on various subsidies and investments over 20 years. By 1980, ethanol still cost about three times more than gasoline, but by 2004, it was competitive with gasoline (Goldemberg 2007, 809).

Tecnológico Vale). Vale created ITV in 2009 with three major research centers spread across the country: sustainable development in Pará, mining in Minas Gerais, and energy in São Paulo. By 2011, ITV accounted for around a third of total R&D by Vale (interview with Luiz Mello, president of ITV, 18 October 2011). By 2007, two commodity firms, Petrobras and Vale, were investing more than $1 billion in R&D, amounting to 1 and 2.3 percent, respectively, of sales (Arbix and Caseiro 2011, 598) and accounting for 4 percent of total R&D and 10 percent of private R&D (calculated from Brito Cruz and Chaimovich 2010, 104).[12]

In the early 2000s, Votorantim, one of the largest traditional business groups, created a venture capital subsidiary. Votorantim had a long tradition of entering and exiting sectors and contracted the consulting firm McKinsey to devise a more formal structure and strategy for managing diversification. McKinsey proposed establishing a subsidiary with $300 million to invest in new ventures. So, Votorantim created Votorantim Novos Negocios (VNN), which generated several dozen proposals for diversifying into existing sectors and invested venture capital into 12 new projects (interview with Fernando Reinach, one of the top executives at VNN, 5 July 2011). Eight of these twelve did not pan out; the other four took off. As noted in Chapter 4, Votorantim sold two of these, Allelyx and Canavialis, to Monsanto and the other two to other investors. But, to the surprise of many, by 2010, Votorantim closed VNN despite whopping financial returns (on the order of 60 percent) from the four successful investments. From one perspective, VNN was a failure because the investment (including public funding) did not spawn a national firm with a sustained vocation for R&D and venture capital nor establish a precedent for commodity business groups diversifying into higher-technology sectors. From another perspective, however, the fact that VNN could sell its start-ups and make a bundle for itself and the scientists who co-invested sent a clear signal to other would-be innovators that a lot of money could be made in science and engineering (and Fernando Reinach went on to create another venture capital fund with other investors).

However, this trend was far from universal, and other business groups and commodity firms, especially in food and beverages, spent little or nothing on R&D (see Table 3.2). Thus, total R&D by the private sector, especially leaving Petrobras out, remained low and less than half of total R&D. The share of private R&D in Brazil is one-third of the OECD average (Brito Cruz and Chaimovich 2010, 106). Moreover, as noted in Chapter 4, by the 2000s, MNCs started accounting for a larger share of private R&D. MNC investment was especially heavy in industry, about $2 billion in 2005, nearly half of total

---

[12] These are not though standard private commodity firms as Petrobras was state owned, and Vale strongly influenced by the government and pressured to invest in Brazil. Even though Petrobras is majority owned by the government, its investments are included in, and greatly inflate, private R&D.

private R&D in industry, and more than 20 percent of all private R&D (de Negri et al. 2010, 29).[13] Last, private R&D was heavily subsidized, mostly through tax exemptions, especially to the IT sector. Exemptions and subsidies in 2008 totaled $3.6 billion, equivalent to 37 percent of business investment in R&D (Brito Cruz and Chaimovich 2010, 108–09).

Two other areas of renewed state promotion helped big business upgrade and expand: technology and internationalization. After 2004, the Lula government started a major push in new technology policies and mobilized a range of public agencies such as IPEA, Finep, BNDES, Ministry of Development, Industry, and International Trade, and the Ministry of Science and Technology. New policies and incentives targeted technology investment by all relevant actors: universities, start-ups, large firms, and government agencies (Arbix and Martin 2010).[14] By 2008, government subsidies for R&D reached .08 percent of GDP, more than Mexico (.05) but less than France (.18), the United States (.22) and Canada (.23) (Arbix 2010, 18). In 2011, the Rousseff government launched Brasil Maior, a package of policies (tax exemptions, subsidies, protections, regulations, and preference in government purchases) to promote technology and industrial upgrading.[15] Petrobras, by itself, has a major industrial policy. As it develops the huge pre-salt oil deposits, Petrobras's procurement policies will have an outsized impact on industrial and technological development in the oil sector and related industries (Almeida, Lima-Oliveira, and Schneider 2012). Overall, by 2011, Brazil accounted for 60 percent of all R&D in Latin America (Dalmasso 2011), well above its 45 percent share of regional GDP.

Support for internationalization came largely from the BNDES, with strong backing from other top ministries. BNDES funding for international acquisitions grew after 2005 and especially after Coutinho was appointed president in 2007. Then minister Dilma Rousseff, a former student of Coutinho's, publicly supported helping Brazilian firms expand abroad and favored generally "an intimate relation, in the good sense" between government and business (*Valor Econômico*, 24 September 2007, e-mail summary from Radiobrás).[16] Through 2009, the "vast majority" of financing for international acquisitions, over $8 billion, went to meat processing firms (Arbix and Caseiro 2011, 608).

[13] By another calculation, by 2006, MNCs from the United States were investing $571 million; however, this was still only 6 percent of private R&D and 3 percent of total R&D (Brito Cruz and Chaimovich 2010, 104, 108).

[14] Other ad hoc policies also incorporated support for R&D. For example, in 2011, the Rousseff government raised taxes on imported cars and cars produced in Brazil with less than 65 percent domestic content. To avoid the tax increase, firms had to raise domestic content above the threshold, spend .5 percent of sales on R&D, and comply with a range of other measures.

[15] Brasil Maior was a revised and expanded continuation of PITCE (Política Industrial, Tecnológica, e de Comércio Exterior, 2003–07) and PDP (Política de Desenvolvimento Produtivo, 2008–10; Brazil 2011, 9). See Almeida and Schneider (2012).

[16] In the same interview, Rousseff also argued that firms need 'strong operators' and entrepreneurs rather than salaried managers, partially endorsing the model of hierarchical business groups (*Valor Econômico*, 24 September 2007, e-mail summary from Radiobrás).

BNDES financing was part of a significant, broader shift in corporate finance and governance. As discussed in Chapter 3, equity markets expanded rapidly after the 1990s, and many firms raised new capital through IPOs, diminishing the advantages of self-financing business groups. Although almost no firms sold enough shares to dilute ownership control, managers in many listed firms became, as in LMEs, more attentive to minority shareholders. The other more consequential shift in capital markets came from the state. Unlike other liberalizing governments of the 1990s, the Brazilian state devised several means to retain control or influence in state enterprises it privatized. In some companies (especially Embraer and Vale), the government retained a "golden share" allowing it to veto major changes in ownership structure and location. In other instances, the BNDES joined with other firms to buy controlling shares in privatized firms. Last, pension funds of remaining SOEs (mostly public banks and Petrobras) also invested heavily in privatized and other large firms. As the new patterns of share ownership emerged, it first appeared that government shareholders would be passive (as were new pension fund investors in Chile).

However, by the late 2000s, the picture looked quite different. For one, part of the BNDES's support for internationalization also involved active promotion for domestic concentration in key sectors through managed mergers and acquisitions. The BNDES did not create a market for corporate control but did make clear that it would not hesitate to foster radical shifts in corporate control in its drive to forge national champions (Almeida and Schneider 2012). Moreover, BNDESpar also became a major shareholder in many of the merged firms, so that by the late 2000s, BNDES held a significant share in many of the largest listed firms. By the late 2000s, it also became clear that shareholding by the BNDES and pension funds of SOEs (whose directors were appointed by political appointees in the government) was no longer passive. The most visible demonstration of activist shareholding came in the defenestration of Roger Agnelli in 2011 from the presidency of Vale by the controlling bloc of shareholders, BNDES and SOE pension funds dominant among them (interview, 14 September 2011). Although an isolated incident, it sent a clear signal to other managers that they needed to be more attentive to state shareholders.

At first glance, this novel form of state intervention – Leviathan as minority shareholder, as Musacchio and Lazzarini (forthcoming) call it – could be seen as a shift toward a more coordinated economy, a sort of state directed CME. Certainly state shareholding trumps the possible transition to more LME-type corporate governance through expanding equity markets. However, this pressure through BNDES and pension funds on firms to pursue government policy priorities is not the sort of coordination among private actors – among firms and between labor and capital – that define CMEs. Rather, Leviathan as minority shareholder is a direct hierarchical relationship between state actors and individual firms and does not involve voluntary cooperation among businesses.

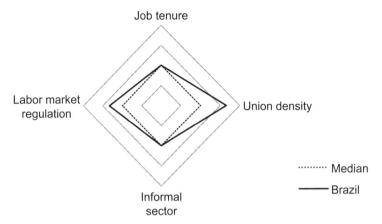

FIGURE 8.3. Labor Markets in Brazil

As such, <u>indirect state intervention in firms through the stock market adds a further element of hierarchy to hierarchical capitalism.</u>[17]

Labor market indicators in Brazil are mostly close to the median for the region, though regulation and union density are somewhat higher (Figure 8.3). However, union dues are compulsory in many sectors, so the density figures overstate the real extent of labor organization. Recent governments in Brazil <u>boosted investment in education, but enrollments at higher levels are still comparatively low</u>: 20 percent of Brazilian students make it to higher education compared with 50 percent in Chile (Gaspar 2011), and tertiary education has been expanding much more rapidly in Chile than in Brazil. An OECD study comparing older generations (55 to 64 years old) to younger generations (25 to 34 years old) found increases in the percentage with tertiary education from old to young generations of 18 percent in Chile (from 17 to 35 percent) but only 3 percent in Brazil (from 9 to 12 percent). Among the outliers, increases range from 50 percent in South Korea (from 13 to 63 percent) to zero in the United States (41 percent in both cohorts; *Brazil Focus*, p. 7, 16 September 2011). And, by one estimate, only 14 percent of Brazilian students are studying science and engineering (compared, for example, with 67 percent in India).[18]

To the extent Brazil is breaking out of a low-skill equilibrium, it is mostly demand driven. Growth in demand has been strong for skills at all levels fueled by rapid expansion in construction, middle class consumption (heavy in services), and in the R&D and higher-technology sectors noted earlier

[17] Of course, states are integral to CMEs in providing framework legislation and regulation for collective bargaining, inter firm collaboration through business associations, codetermination, and apprenticeship programs. However, this is the public framework through which private cooperation occurs, rather than direct state intervention into corporate governance.

[18] *Economist Intelligence Unit*, cited in *Brazil Focus*, 30 September 2011, p. 10.

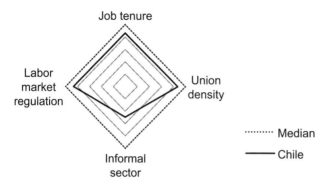

FIGURE 8.4. Labor Markets in Chile

(Blyde et al. 2009). Supply shocks have also helped. By the late 2000s, Brazil was becoming a regional hub for R&D investment by MNCs, in part because Brazil universities were graduating more than 10,000 PhD candidates a year (see Chapter 4). Yet, by the late 2000s, firms in various sectors were raising concerns about skill shortages and – signaling general shortages at the high end – executive pay and returns to university education generally were among the highest in the region. If sustained, scarcity and high demand for skills should shift longer-term incentives for families and individuals to invest more in human capital.

## V. Chile: Technology Policy and Education Supply Shock

In Chile, the push for upgrading came more from government than from business. Commodity firms followed historical tradition and did not leverage rents into higher-technology ventures. Large business groups in Chile bifurcated into two groups: the traditional diversified business groups and new more specialized firms in services. The first traditional set included stalwarts like the Matte, Luksic, and Angelini groups. The newer service firms emerged in the 1990s and 2000s and were Chile's leading outward investors: LAN (airlines), Cencosud and Falabella (retail), and Claro (shipping and logistics). Neither group of firms contributes much to R&D, the first set because it is concentrated in natural resources and simple manufacturing (e.g., beverages) and the second because it is in services. However, the service firms are acknowledged innovation leaders even though their innovations do not show up in R&D expenditures.

Labor market indicators in Chile are mostly close to the regional median, save on informality, which is lower (Figure 8.4). The share of workers with long tenure, 21 percent, is right at the regional median (22 percent; see Table 5.2). Given Chile's fame as a liberal reformer, it is surprising that its score on labor regulation is so high (Carnes 2009). However, increasing numbers of workers in Chile have temporary contracts and are therefore not covered by many regulations or their associated benefits. Also, the union density figure does not capture the crucial dimensions of union weakness in Chile, namely, the restrictions on bargaining only at the firm level and only on wages. In all though, Chilean labor markets are pretty similar to others in the region.

Government policy in Chile played a greater role in both promoting R&D and especially in expanding the supply of education. The centerpiece of a public push into R&D came in the mid 2000s in debates over how to tax copper rents and how to use those taxes. In 2005, the Bachelet government created the CNIC (Consejo Nacional de Innovación para la Competitividad; Agosin, Larraín, and Grau 2009; CNIC 2010). The council decided to focus on promoting innovation in sectors in which Chile already had advantages in agriculture, mining, and business services. A 5 percent royalty tax on profits in copper firms provided CNIC $60 million in 2006 and $78 million in 2008 (as overall government spending on science and technology rose from $287 million in 2006 to $462 million in 2008; Paus 2011, 75). In 2008, the government introduced additional tax deductions for firms undertaking R&D. Based largely on this public push, the percentage of GDP in Chile going to R&D started to rise well above the average for Latin America.

The second main, and broader-based, government policy focused on expanding the supply of education. The enormous investment in the 1990s and 2000s, public and private, expanded the pool of general skills and helped fuel the expansion of the service sector. Total education spending, both public and private, increased steadily after 1990 and reached 7.4 percent of GDP in 2000 (4.3 percent public plus 3.1 percent private; Cox 2004, 100). Unlike most countries, the great majority (85 percent) of public spending went on pretertiary education (Cox 2004, 101). Vast increases in spending did not initially boost student performance, but by 2009, Chile's PISA scores far exceeded the regional average (see Table 5.1).[19]

At the same time, tertiary enrollments soared from 120,000 in 1981 to a million in 2011, with 40 percent of these students in technical and professional education (*El Mercurio*, 18 June 2011, accessed online 18 June 2011). By the late 2000s, 70 percent of students were the first in their families to go to university (Engel 2011). By 2009, public spending on tertiary education was .8 percent of GDP, close to the OECD average of 1 percent, and total (public and

---

[19] Costa Rica provides another example of investing heavily in human capital to break out of a low-skill equilibrium. Costa Rica had higher education levels than most of its neighbors in the Caribbean basin and spent far more on worker training (Chapter 6) and on R&D (as a percentage of GDP) than other countries in Latin America (Alcorta and Peres 1995, 28, table 7). The government touted its comparative advantage in human capital to attract manufacturing investment, and from 1985 to 2001 Costa Rica's share of world exports grew rapidly (from .07 to .12) and within this growing flow of exports the share of high-technology products mushroomed from 3 to 28 percent (ECLAC 2004, 75) propelled largely by Intel's massive investments (IDB 2001, 258).

private) spending as a percentage of GDP was among the highest in the OECD (*El Mercurio*, 17 June 2011, accessed online 18 June 2011).

And, to the extent that tertiary education is concentrated in general skills, and large service firms are employing them, it makes Chile resemble a more liberal variety of capitalism. Yet, the overall picture in services is mixed. Employment in services grew during the 2000s from 70 to 74 percent of all employment, but much of this came from low-end jobs. As a proportion of GDP, services fluctuated in the 2000s around 50 percent (below OECD and Latin American averages), and service exports were only 6 percent of GDP (Prieto, Sáez, and Goswami 2011, 312–16). On the brighter side, some of the areas where service exports were booming were clusters tied to large internationalizing business groups in transport, engineering, and especially retail. By one calculation, six of the top ten business groups were in services like retail (Falabella, Paulman, and Ibáñez), transport (Claro and LAN), and finance (Yarur, with large parts of other groups like Luksic and Matte).[20] However, overall, the expansion of service exports and high-end service jobs is still constrained by low education levels, low Internet penetration, and a low total pool of tertiary grads in science and engineering (Prieto et al. 2011, 320, 334).

For a time, this supply-side approach seemed to be working, and seemed to signify a major shock to the low-skill equilibrium. As new graduates came into the market, returns to education started to fall, indicating that skills were in more abundant supply and no longer a binding constraint.[21] However, the student demonstrations of 2011 – more than 50 of them – cast a long shadow over an optimistic view. And, disaggregating the data on returns to education showed that while the average stayed fairly high, a significant segment of grads was getting meager returns. By one calculation, of the 60 percent who make it through university (the other 40 percent drop out along the way), about half end up unemployed or with lousy salaries (*"pésima remuneración"*; Waissbluth 2011, 37). It is too early to tell whether this student upheaval was just a bump in the road or the end of the road for a supply side shock, but at a minimum, it shows that the supply-side route to a high-skill equilibrium is not always smooth.

## VI. Political Stability and Good Governance in Chile and Brazil

Although less proximate causes than commodity rents and development policies, both Brazil and Chile stand out in the region in terms of effective governance, political stability, and bureaucratic capacity. Chile has had a reputation since its transition to democracy in 1990 for centrist programmatic parties, strong government institutions, low corruption, and resilience against rent

---

[20] *Que Pasa*, reproduced online at aquevedo.wordpress.com, accessed on 23 December 2011.
[21] In interviews, human resource managers confirmed that it was easier to hire college graduates (see the Appendix; Eberhard and Engel 2008; World Bank 2011).

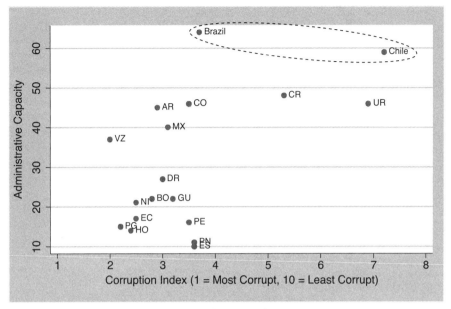

FIGURE 8.5. Administrative Capacity and Perceived Corruption. *Sources*: Transparency International and Longo (2005).

seeking and state capture. The surprise was that Brazil in the 2000s began to approximate Chile on most of these dimensions: especially the emergence of two dominant programmatic center-left parties (PT and PSDB) and the consolidation of an effective bureaucracy and regulatory agencies, though perceived corruption and business lobbying are still high (Figure 8.5).[22] On the party front, Hagopian et al. find that "there are signs that Brazilian parties are growing stronger: electoral volatility is down, and party unity in congressional voting has risen. Arguably, parties are being transformed from loose patronage machines to programmatically coherent and distinctive groupings" (2009, 361).

By a variety of governance indicators on the development of civil service, administrative capacity, perceived corruption, and policy continuity, Brazil and Chile stand apart from other countries in Latin America (Figures 8.5 and 8.6). These figures are not intended to demonstrate causal relations among these variables (though the case could be made) but rather to highlight how different Chile and Brazil are from the rest of the region. Centrist trends and associated policy stability are new in Brazil, but administrative capacity and civil service development cannot be created overnight and count among the

[22] As an indication of the scholarly surprise, as late as 2005, Weyland's (2005) overview of the progress of democracy in Brazil was titled "The Growing Sustainability of Brazil's Low-Quality Democracy."

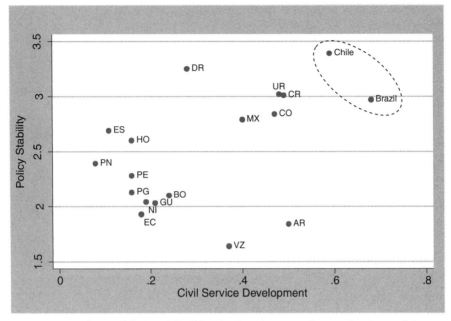

FIGURE 8.6. Policy Stability and Civil Service Development. *Source*: Pereira et al. (2011: 65) for policy stability and Stein et al. (2005: 152).

legacy benefits in both countries. Beginning in the nineteenth century in Chile and mid-twentieth century in Brazil, both countries took the lead in the region in developing comparatively strong civil services.[23]

In addition to trends in programmatic parties and better administration, business politics in Brazil and Chile did not produce as much entrenchment and damaging oligopoly. Domestic business in both countries was, as in the rest of the region, dominated by business groups, though less diversified and more internationalized business groups emerged in both countries. Although mighty, and with veto power over certain policies, business groups were less engaged in debilitating rent seeking. The benchmark comparison is with Mexico (discussed in Section II and Chapter 7), where the political system was very vulnerable to individualized rent seeking.

In Chile, business groups were collectively, publicly powerful. They funded think tanks that supported organic intellectuals and policy debates. They financed parties on the right and maintained close relations to them (Fairfield 2010). And big business actively promoted (and dominated) major encompassing associations (CPC and Sofofa especially; interview with Andrés Concha, presidente, Sofofa, 10 December 2010). This pattern of collective, organized, relatively transparent business politics – rare in Latin America – made individual rent seeking more difficult and costly, because monitoring by other business

[23] See Patricio Silva (2008) for a full history of technocracy in Chile through the twentieth century.

and political actors was easier and sanctions, especially informal, were potentially more costly (Schneider 2010b). However, crucial to maintaining collective, organized politics was the fact that the government, especially the center-left Concertación governments (1990–2010) provided much less individualized access than did most other polities. Finance ministers, for example, during the Concertación period maintained a tradition of refusing meetings with individual business people and requiring them to work through their business associations (interview with Andrés Velasco, 26 January 2012).

The party coalitions were encompassing on their respective sides of the political spectrum, and the Concertación did not owe its electoral success to business backing but rather to many outsider groups (those that do not share in the benefits of hierarchical capitalism).[24] The near complete absence of business appointees in the executive branch through 2010 also limited individualized networking and access by business groups. Blocking rent seeking did not mean though that governments could overcome business opposition in major policy battles. On the contrary, on fundamental issues like taxation, an effective business veto thwarted government reforms, and Chile came through the 2000s with very low taxes (Fairfield 2010).

Business politics in Brazil are more puzzling. The political system was clearly more fluid and porous than in Chile. The main parties may have become more programmatic, but individual deputies and smaller parties were dependent on business contributions and amenable to subsequent requests for assistance. The political appointment of business people to government continued at low levels in the Cardoso and Lula administrations though virtually ended in the Rousseff government. However, Rousseff appointed Jorge Gerdau Johannpeter to several commissions and met with him more often than some of her ministers.[25] Last, business associations were fragmented and more likely to lobby for narrower sectoral interests, and large businesses preferred to bypass them to lobby politicians and officials directly.

What mitigated the dangers of rent seeking was a mix of partisanship, institutions and institutional innovation, and markets. The size, diversity, and

---

[24] Campaigns in Chile were expensive, and all candidates relied on large donors. Until 2003, there were no regulations on campaign finance, and even after 2003 contribution limits remained "very high." This overall dependence generally favors "a proprivate sector policy orientation." However, the right benefits much more, and the Concertación had less reason to accede to individualized business lobbying derived from campaign financing (Huber, Pribble, and Stephens 2010, 81–82).

[25] By the 2000s, Gerdau, from one of the largest 20 business groups, was the doyen of the business community and frequent interlocutor with a series of governments and ministers. Lula appointed him to the CDES (and reportedly invited him to be a minister, which Gerdau declined), and Rousseff asked him in 2011 to chair a newly created Chamber for Management Policies, Performance, and Competitiveness (CGDC) composed of the four main economic ministries and four businessmen. Relations between Rousseff and Gerdau were long standing and especially close (http://www.cdes.gov.br/noticia/21555/governo-cria-camara-de-politicas-de-gestao-desempenho-e-competitividade.html; Bacoccina and Queiroz 2012).

dynamism of the Brazilian economy made markets more competitive, lowered barriers to entry, and therefore made it more difficult for firms to use politics to capture and retain rents. Recurring protectionism in autos, for example, supported by lobbying by assemblers, provided rents, but the rapid expansion of the domestic and export markets, and the entry of new producers maintained strong competitive pressures. New and fortified regulatory institutions reinforced competition in core nontradable sectors. Telecommunications in Brazil provides an illuminating contrast to Mexico because the Cardoso government took great pains, when privatizing in the late 1990s, to build in competition. One good indicator of the lack of politically abetted entrenchment was the high turnover among business groups. Among the largest 50 industrial groups in 1995, fewer than half (21) were still in the top 50 only 11 years later in 2006. Of the 29 that were no longer in the top 50, 13 dropped to lower rankings, 11 were bought, and 5 went belly up (Roland Berger Consultants 2008, 14).

Both the PSDB and the PT sought to position themselves to the left of center (though the PSDB later drifted to the right) and drew on support, the PT especially, of outsider groups (those in precarious and informal jobs), and therefore had partisan reasons to resist pressures from business. The Cardoso government had avoided close consultation with business and devised much of the postprivatization regulation and regulatory agencies to withstand lobbying by business (interview with lobbyist for Oi, July 2011; see also Prata, Beirão, and Tomioka 1999). Successor PT governments were also less open to business pressures. PSDB and PT governments steadily increased taxes and interest rates to the highest levels in Latin America against vocal protests from business. It is noteworthy that the PT's many corruption scandals, in both the Lula and Dilma governments, rarely involved big business or career civil servants. From the huge *Mensalão* scandal through the series of improprieties that brought down Dilma's ministers in 2011, the alleged crimes revolved mostly around self-enrichment of politicians and their families with public resources or various deviations of public funds to allied parties and politicians. It was politicians pilfering the public purse, rather than business bribing politicians to get rents.

One clear and major area of subsidies to business groups came through the BNDES; by the 1990s, total subsidies through loans at below-market interest rates exceeded 1 percent of GDP (Castelar 2007) that likely grew with rising BNDES lending in the late 2000s. The BNDES has always been a major lender to, and champion of, large domestic firms and, as noted in the previous sections, expanded lending in the 2000s, heavily favoring existing business groups. However, even if some of these loans were unnecessary and wasteful (with high opportunity costs in terms of other foregone public investments), and favored some firms over others, recipients in competitive markets still had incentives to use the subsidies productively. In sum, despite the fact that the Brazilian political system is vulnerable to individualized lobbying (as seen in Chapter 7) and the fact that the government distributes myriad subsidies and benefits, rents and rent seeking have not been as visibly damaging as elsewhere (Mexico, for example).

Overall, how do development policies and political capacities in Brazil and Chile relate to the institutions and complementarities of hierarchical capitalism? In essence, they work against the complementarities in "incentive incompatible" ways. In Brazil, the policy impacts, as well as the commodity boom, had the deepest effects on big business by encouraging specialization, more open corporate governance, and, most important, sustained investment in some higher-technology ventures. As such, some business groups, associated suppliers, and government agencies have become leaders in shifting expectations in high-end labor markets. In contrast, in Chile, policy interventions had less impact on business groups and MNCs but rather shifted – in noncomplementary ways – the supply curve for skilled labor.

Brazil and Chile had an excellent start to the twenty-first century and projecting out from this experience leads to rosy predictions for the next decades. Although plausible, these projections rest on a number of assumptions: that commodity prices will stay sky high, that political institutions will be able to resist the debilitating effects of the natural resource curse and Dutch disease, and that individuals, companies, and governments will sustain massive investments in education and human capital. Were any one of these assumptions not to hold, Brazil and Chile could stall. Central to escaping the middle-income trap is the steady increase in the supply of higher skill jobs, at all education levels, but especially for technicians with postsecondary training. The complementarities in hierarchical capitalism generally reinforce continuity, but that continuity is politically contingent. Favorable economic shocks and governments capable of taking long-term advantage of them, backed by coalitions that included outsiders, can upset these complementarities. The relative success of Brazil and Chile gives grounds for optimism, yet they also show how difficult it is – how many positive factors had to converge – to begin to break out of negative complementarities in hierarchical capitalism.

## VII. Conclusions

In thinking about how to interpret variations within hierarchical capitalism, it is useful to remember that differences within liberal and coordinated capitalism are wide. For instance, unionization rates in liberal Australia are close to those of coordinated Germany, and far higher than in the United States, whereas government spending and welfare benefits in liberal Britain are closer to CMEs in continental Europe than to the United States. Among CMEs, Japan has rates of union density and government spending much closer to the liberal United States than to European CMEs. The within-type variations in hierarchical capitalism considered in this chapter thus seem no greater than within-type heterogeneity in coordinated and liberal capitalism.

Despite major policy changes in Latin America in the 2000s and the over-all divergence in development strategies (liberal, nationalist, and populist), few governments attacked, head on, core features of hierarchical capitalism. Where business groups suffered reversals (Peru and Argentina), it was mostly the result of collateral damage and unintended consequences of freer trade and openness to MNCs rather than deliberate government policy to restructure big business. Elsewhere, business groups thrived, in some cases with significant government support (as in BNDES lending in Brazil). Few governments outside Argentina (after 2002) and more radical petro states imposed major restrictions on MNCs, and elsewhere, FDI maintained its upward trend (save for dips after the recessions of 2001 and 2009). Although some governments made efforts to reduce informality, the other elements of segmented and atomized labor markets – especially short tenure and high regulation – changed little. Education is probably the area that governments tried hardest to reform, though it was often more talk than action. Yet, Chile aside, educational attainment and quality remained low, especially in relation to levels of economic development, and much of the increase in investments in education was not directly tied to increasing the supply of usable high-end skills. In short, underlying features of hierarchical capitalism were affected little by policy shifts of the 1990s and 2000s.

Why did politicians and policy makers not find more to question in business groups, MNCs, and segmented labor markets? In part, of course, this is the water they swim in, so policy makers may not have perceived a need for fundamental institutional change. By contrast, governments coming out of communism had to decide actively on the shape and role of MNCs and big business because they never had them before. In addition, the pervasive ideological legacy of the Washington Consensus feeds into thinking on corporate governance. The popular backlash against neoliberalism has been largely on distributional grounds (see Silva 2009). That is, voters reject higher charges from privatized firms, reductions in subsidies, and dislocations caused by free trade. However, among policy makers, even in many leftist governments, the liberal premises remain that business in general knows best how to produce and that it makes little difference how firms are structured or whether the owners are shareholders, families, or foreign companies. In addition, a deeper issue in worldviews of policy makers and opinion leaders is a tendency to take the United States as the primary external referent and model (Katzenstein 2005). Discussion of alternative Asian models of development, and their very different treatment of MNCs and business groups, is infrequent and isolated. That other latecomers like Korea, India, and Turkey severely restricted FDI almost never comes up in policy debates in Latin America.

Overall, however, explanations for why policy makers did not attack business groups, MNCs, and segmented labor markets do not have to reach deep into unconscious Weltanschauungen of policy actors, because the political disincentives are strong and immediate, especially given the short time horizons and weak potential reform coalitions. Open confrontation with big business is universally rare, save among left populists (usually with state-controlled mineral rents and thus alternative sources of investment), when the goal is more to mobilize political opposition than to force business groups to become more innovative and productive. The costs, particularly during commodity booms, of attacking MNCs (and driving down flows of FDI) are lower, but still substantial enough that few governments in the region have followed Argentina and the more radical petro states.

The potential costs of reforming labor regulation and informality probably slow reform impulses in government. Although unions are weak in numbers and internal organization, most still have substantial disruptive potential in calling strikes in pivotal sectors such as energy and transportation, and in mobilizing street protests. Moreover, if reform proposals can be cast by unions as an overall offensive against working people, then sympathies are likely to side against government reformers. Would-be reformers would also have difficulty selling labor reforms as costly to only a few insiders and beneficial to the majority of outsiders. Even if the great majority of workers are not covered by severance benefits, most workers probably know someone, in many cases another family member, who is, or they hope one day to have a job with severance benefits (see Perry et al. [2007, 7] on how workers move through formal and informal segments over a working career). And, as noted earlier, business may not be an ardent ally in conflicts over labor regulation because regulation helps some large firms retain highly skilled workers and because other firms have found ways to evade the costs of regulation. Reducing informality with carrots and incentives may have modest impacts without provoking much political opposition, but ramped-up enforcement could put many small business and their employees out of work. This is clearly a desirable goal over the longer run – to move workers out of precarious, low-paying jobs into better ones – but the costs of forcing the transition through police action are usually enough to attenuate impulses for coercive reform (Holland 2012).

The brief comparison in this chapter of policy making in Brazil and Chile versus Mexico and Argentina highlights the centrality of politics. Politics and institutions in Argentina and Mexico impeded the sort of credible policies that would promote upgrading, competition, and investments in human capital, though in different ways. In Mexico, political institutions such as the judiciary, division of powers, and regulatory agencies were well institutionalized but in ways that favored business influence and impeded reform. In Argentina, in contrast, institutions were weak (certainly those that might constrain presidential power), and policies were often ad hoc, temporary, or arbitrary with consequently depressing effects on long-term investments. In contrast, Concertación governments promoted policy stability in Chile (with continuities in many areas from the 1980s) and sustained promotion of education after 1990. In Brazil, after the political turbulence of the lengthy transition to democracy, policy stability and renewed state promotion of education and technology set in after 1994.

Although negative complementarities of hierarchical capitalism are still strong through most of Latin America, luck (commodities), legacies (like effective bureaucracies), and policy (technology and industrial) countered these complementarities in Brazil and Chile and made them cases of hierarchical capitalism with high growth (although still moderate by Asian standards) and rising productivity (at least in some recent periods). In the medium run, shallow capital markets, dominant business groups, high labor market regulation, and large informal sectors will keep Brazil and Chile as higher performing instances of hierarchical capitalism. For a possible transition to liberal capitalism (or more statist versions of liberal economies), the crucial dimensions to watch are financial markets (and the expansion of smaller specialized firms to challenge business groups), labor regulation and informality (and the expansion of the segment of workers with formal jobs but short tenure), and skills (especially the expansion of high-end jobs in the service sector with strong consequent increases in productivity).

For many observers, moderate growth based on high commodity prices, continuing flows of FDI, and expanding domestic demand fueled by services and a growing middle class is a sufficient development strategy for the medium term, and one that involves no difficult institutional reengineering. However, longer-run development depends on diversification and new sources international competitiveness (Imbs and Wacziarg 2003). Put differently, hierarchical capitalism is compatible with competitive advantage based on natural resources and low cost, unskilled labor. To find alternative, better niches in the international economy, as Brazil and Chile seem to be doing, requires new areas of competitive advantage based on skilled labor and human capital, and leading areas of innovation.

# 9

# Conclusions

## I. Introduction

In 2006, Andrés Benitez, the rector of the Universidad Adolfo Ibáñez, wrote an op-ed column, titled "Why the Papelera is not Nokia," in the Chilean news magazine *Capital* (Benítez 2006). The column noted that Nokia, like la Papelera (the nickname for the Compañia Manufacturera de Papeles y Cartones, CMPC, of the Matte Group), had started in forestry, pulp, and paper, but that Nokia had invested heavily in R&D and shifted out of forestry. Nokia's investment in telecommunications, over many years and drawn from profits in other Nokia subsidiaries, allowed Nokia in the 1990s to lead the first boom in cellular phones (see also Sabel 2009). La Papelera, in contrast, had no strategy, according to Benitez, for using innovation and R&D to work its way out of forestry. Several weeks later, *Capital* published a response article by Bernardo Matte, one of the scions of the Matte family, that defended CMPC's investment in forestry (Matte 2006). Matte wrote that Nokia was no longer competitive in forestry and did the right thing in moving into other sectors. But, CMPC was still the lowest cost producer in the world and was investing in R&D in forestry to keep it that way, so the Matte group saw no reason to invest in other sectors.[1]

This exchange was revealing on multiple levels. Business groups have a diversified structure that makes them, in principle, ideally suited to lead diversification out of commodities and low value added activities, as Nokia and many Asian business groups have done. As noted in Chapter 3, some groups are more

---

[1] Palma (2009, 212–24) provides an overall contrast between the rapid upgrading in forestry products and machinery in Finland and Malaysia and the absence of upgrading in Brazil and Chile.

predisposed to new ventures and higher-technology activities (or states pushed them in that direction). The Matte group fits best in the category of the less specialized, less innovative portfolio-type of business group. The exchange over La Papelera also illustrates at least implicitly the effect of the commodity boom on more conservative business groups. When commodity prices are sky high, the irresistible incentive for business groups is to invest more in these commodities, thereby reinforcing their structure, strategy, and relative absence of R&D. The Votorantim group in Brazil also expanded investments in forestry at the same time it closed down its subsidiary in venture capital (see Chapter 8). In sum, business groups are responding to the commodity boom in ways that reinforce their strategy and structure. Something similar may characterize national development trajectories.

By the 2010s, politicians in Chile were talking about joining the developed world within a decade and celebrated their entry into the OECD as a signal that they were almost there (without noting that Mexico had joined in the 1990s). Per-capita income levels in richer countries of Latin America may in fact, over the next decades, come to approximate those of poorer countries of Europe. As tourists can tell, major parts of cities (and surrounding provinces) of São Paulo, Buenos Aires, Santiago, and Mexico City already feel just as wealthy, and as costly, as the developed world. Favorable commodity prices and capital flows, as well as prolonged stagnation in developed countries, would accelerate the closing of the gap. Convergence on GDP per capita will also bring convergence on other basic socioeconomic indicators such as life expectancy and years of schooling.

However, approximation in income levels does not entail a simultaneous institutional convergence. Harkening back to early debates between stage theories of W. W. Rostow (1960) (and earlier Marx) and type theories of Alexander Gerschenkron (1962), this book sides with the latter. For Rostow, and later followers, all countries passed through similar stages of development to finish at the same general end point. For Gerschenkron, in contrast, each country's path of development differed depending on when it started industrializing relative to countries that preceded it. Gershenkron's main insight was that scale economies were greater for later industrializers that therefore required new types of institutions to mobilize more capital for larger industrial undertakings. To Gerschenkron's scale economies, the twentieth century added several other factors – such as changes in transportation and communication technologies and patterns of world trade – that further altered obstacles and opportunities for late, late industrializers. Hirschman (1968) laid out clearly the main differences between late industrializers in Europe (based largely on heavy industry and capital goods) and early stages of industrialization in Latin America (mostly in light industry and consumer goods).

The general points here are several. First, Latin America did not go through the same stages of industrialization and development as earlier developers, which gives reasons to suspect that capitalism would evolve differently in

Latin America.[2] Second, the institutional consequences or sedimentation from the different development trajectories contributed to distinct institutional foundations of capitalism – corporate forms, labor regulation, skill regimes, and so forth – in early and late developers.

Last, and most generally, development options at any particular historical juncture are best conceived, in a globalized economy, as the interplay of three things: the prevailing world technological frontier in production, predominant trading patterns, and domestic economic institutions. The main relevant recent shifts in technology have been falling transportation and communication costs that in turn have facilitated the geographic fragmentation of manufacturing and burgeoning trade in previously non-tradable services. The main changes in trade for Latin America, especially after the 2008–09 financial crisis, were falling demand from developed countries especially for manufactured goods, and rising demand from Asia for natural resources. The domestic economic institutions of hierarchical capitalism are, of course, MNCs, business groups, segmented labor markets, and an undeveloped skill system. In recent decades, this interplay of technology, trade, and domestic institutions has meant for Latin America: (1) de-industrialization (save Mexico) as simple manufacturing shifted to low-wage Asia, (2) increased commodity production in response to Asian demand, (3) strengthening of business groups and MNCs in sectors without much R&D, and (4) continuing low-skill employment for the majority of workers.

Although assessing opportunities and constraints in the evolving global economy is, of course, essential in any debate on development strategy, this book has been mostly preoccupied with analyzing the domestic institutional capacity for embarking on a high-road development strategy. This conclusion extends that domestic focus backward in time to consider some institutional origins and ahead to reflect on possible institutional changes and policy shifts.

## II. Configurations and Complementarities: Implications for Policy and Theory

This book proposed using the framework of comparative capitalism and the specific type of hierarchical capitalism to analyze development challenges and alternatives in Latin America.[3] The concept of hierarchical capitalism is a first cut at conceptualizing the distinctive institutional foundations of capitalism in Latin America. The lack of much of the basic types of data that informed

---

[2] More stagelike processes characterize the process of social modernization where urbanization, and universalization of education and health care occurred more gradually and incrementally and are more tied to growth in per-capita income. These processes are affected little by development elsewhere or shifting frontiers of technology (save advances in medicine that allow later developers to achieve longer life expectancy earlier in their development process).

[3] For an overview of various approaches in comparative capitalism, including varieties of capitalism, see Jackson and Deeg (2008).

debates on liberal, coordinated, and other types in developed countries makes analysis of varieties of capitalism in developing countries necessarily preliminary. The goal here was more to gather available evidence into a general comparative capitalism framework and to start a debate rather than settle one.

As noted at the outset, this book departs from the internationalist and statist perspectives to focus instead on institutions of the domestic economy, but at some points, it draws heavily on these other perspectives. MNCs, one of the four core institutions of hierarchical capitalism, are the most tangible face of globalization. My interest, however, is less in the international forces driving MNC strategies than in the domestic impact of those strategies on other firms, workers, and overall options for development strategies. Similarly, although the state is not one of the four core components of hierarchical capitalism, the state was, and is, decisive in shaping the strategies and structures of business groups and MNCs, as well as labor relations and skill regimes.

Readers who are not convinced by my specific formulation of hierarchical capitalism, or are generally disinclined to this sort of broad theoretical exercise, would do well to try to hold on to the baby as they toss the bath water. Leaving aside the particular HME type, the general comparative capitalism approach has several fundamental conceptual innovations that deserve further consideration in research on development in Latin America. A comparative capitalism approach, of course, first assumes that capitalism is not the same everywhere. As such, it raises the question, not often asked in Latin America, of how contemporary economic institutions might differ from the rest of the world and whether, among institutions across realms of the economy, the configuration found in Latin America is somehow distinctive.[4] Other researchers may answer the question in the negative and argue that capitalism in Latin America is fundamentally similar. The important thing is to ask the question in the first place and to start the debate on what constitutes difference or similarity and what are the analytic consequences for outcomes of interest: growth, innovation, and good jobs.

The second major benefit from a comparative capitalism perspective is precisely this view of the whole. Once the analysis has looked over corporate governance, labor regulation, unions, skill regimes, and financial systems, it is then a shorter step to asking if and how they fit together in mutually reinforcing ways (Miller 2010). Thus, complementarities – or other terms that characterize linkages across realms of the economy – are crucial to understanding the dynamics of development. Complementarities or linkages help explain the

---

[4] There are numerous global surveys with comparative country indices and ranking on dimensions such as regulatory quality and costs, property rights and contract enforcement, and bureaucratic requirements for opening new businesses, as well as perceptions of corruption (see transparency.org, doingbusines.org, weforum.org). However, these offer only superficial views of comparative institutions, based largely on the perceptions of business people, and do not delve into firm structures and strategies, let alone institutional complementarities.

sources of preferences as well as institutional resilience or frailty. In addition, as noted at the outset, analyzing complementarities offers an alternative way of thinking about cross-realm connections without reducing them to simple, unidirectional causal relations.

A third general conceptual contribution of the approach of comparative capitalism, especially the "variety of capitalism" perspective, is that it directs attention to the sources of good jobs. This perspective is important to policy making in the advanced economies, but even more so in contemporary debates on development and renewed state intervention (Amsden 2010). Policy reforms in developing countries in the 1990s focused heavily on what in retrospect were fairly abstract policy goals: markets, private property, and state retraction. Many more-concrete benefits were presumed to flow from these abstract goals such as efficiency, higher productivity, and ultimately steady development. As these benefits failed to materialize quickly in many developing countries, policy attention turned to "reforming the reforms" to promote more specific goals such as better education, health care, and regulation. Yet, it was still rare for policies to target the creation of the kinds of high-skill, high-wage jobs necessary over the longer run to sustain development and reduce inequality.

The concept of hierarchical capitalism draws on the framework developed by Hall and Soskice (2001), but it also departs from it in significant ways. To start with, the state is central to understanding the evolution of all components of hierarchical capitalism. In part because the state is central, so too are the politics that orient state action, especially in economic policy. These often-contentious politics in large measure derive from the complementarities and components of hierarchical capitalism both because they encourage insiders like business groups and union leaders to defend existing institutions and complementarities and because the many outsiders have good reason to engage in politics to contest negative complementarities. And, this political contention in hierarchical capitalism makes equilibria based on economic complementarities less stable.

Identifying particular types of capitalism and their respective internal logics and complementarities helps specify which policies are "incentive compatible" (Hall and Soskice 2001). So, for example, it is not advisable to invest public resources in industry-specific vocational training for workers in LMEs (Finegold and Soskice 1988). Nor, as securities reformers discovered in countries like Chile, is it sufficient to provide legal protections to minority investors to foster the expansion of stock markets in countries where hierarchical business groups dominate (Lefort 2005). Devising more compatible policies is simpler if the complementarities are positive, and policy makers can seek out incremental policy adjustments to fine tune these complementarities or mitigate the negative impact of external shocks on them.

When, as in the low-skill trap, the complementarities are negative, policy options become more complicated. In such instances, the policy challenge may in fact be how to push a perverse complementary relationship out of equilibrium. Such anti-complementarity policies may be promising options for promoting particular development goals, but it is essential to take into consideration the interconnections with other spheres that may compromise policy effectiveness. As such, a varieties-of-capitalism perspective can help with the elusive challenges of devising a employment-based strategies of development. This perspective is important not only in emphasizing the kinds of jobs liberal, coordinated, and other varieties create, but crucially in showing how these employment patterns in turn result from interactions among firm strategies, corporate governance, interfirm coordination, education systems, and active labor market policies as well. Thus, the policy implications for governments endorsing a labor-based development strategy is not merely to adopt employment policies to promote the creation of good jobs but to tie these incentives and subsidies to a package of policies affecting firm incentives and public educational institutions.

Hall and Soskice (2001, 45) also argue that policy should focus less on inducing changes in behavior among economic agents and more on encouraging them to coordinate better among themselves. This advice may hold for developed countries, but it seems less relevant for hierarchical capitalism in developing countries. Where, as in Latin America, economies are dominated by a small number of towering hierarchies, it may be difficult (and potentially hazardous) to induce better cooperation among economic agents, and governments may therefore need to use blunter, more direct and heavy-handed policy instruments that are deliberately "incentive *in*compatible." In some ways, the revival of state intervention in Brazil in the 2000s can be read in this light. Although some policies, such as the BNDES's promotion of national champions in commodities, are incentive-compatible in hierarchical capitalism, other technology and skills policies (such as training scientists and investing in R&D), and local content restrictions on MNCs push firms hard in incentive-incompatible ways.

Among other policy implications is the caution that shifting toward a more coordinated type of capitalism involves heavy sustained investment in institutions of the sort that is beyond the capacity of most political economies. Therefore, to the extent that governments have options of pushing their capitalism in one direction or another, it is institutionally less costly to push toward liberal or hierarchical capitalism. However, as many governments in developing countries discovered, moving toward markets does not automatically create LMEs. Many of the reforms in the 1990s Washington Consensus pulled the state out of various forms of intervention and introduced more market forces and private property. However, these policies often favored MNCs and business groups and thereby reinforced hierarchy on the capital side. In labor markets, despite some apparent convergence on unions and job tenure, the continued three-way division into informal, formal but high turnover (and therefore low skill), and highly regulated, long-tenure segments continued to differentiate HME labor markets from those in liberal capitalism. Thus, market reforms of the 1990s often reinforced hierarchical capitalism rather than setting economies on a fast track to liberal capitalism.

As noted in Chapter 1, theorizing on development in the dominant Northian approach has over emphasized rules and neglected organizations, like businesses, associations, unions, and the organization of labor within firms. The alternative approach adopted here not only incorporates the general rules but also pushes the analysis to include the organization of business and labor in order to understand the consequences of organizational heterogeneity encountered among (and sometimes within) different varieties of capitalism. This fine-grained organizational examination of large firms highlighted core differences in strategy and structure between MNCs and domestic business groups as well as variations among business groups, both regional differences between Latin America and Asia and heterogeneity within Latin America. Of course, some variation in strategy and structure resulted from sectoral concentration where, for instance, firms in services and commodities spent less on R&D. However, firms in the same sectors sometimes pursued different strategies, and more important, diversification (and the ever-present option to do so) delinked business groups from the strict sectoral logics that might drive the strategies of narrowly specialized firms.

In sum, much of the analytic benefit of a focus on complementarities derives from its view of the whole political economy and multiple interactions across different realms. Even those who do not buy the whole varieties-of-capitalism package can benefit by taking some of the pieces, especially when it comes to the challenges of devising an employment-based development strategy.

## III. Institutional Origins and Change

Even before industrialization in the twentieth century, earlier path dependence in Latin America precluded movement toward either market or more coordinated capitalism. Just as cooperative roots of coordinated economies and market roots of liberal economies can be traced back to early industrialization in Europe (Iversen and Soskice 2009), so inequality, business groups, foreign capital, and comparatively low education characterized much of Latin America from the first stages of industrialization and development in the early twentieth century. In a first fundamental sense, prior centuries of extreme inequality and social hierarchy in Latin America foreclosed the early emergence of market or coordinated relations (see Mahoney 2010). To the extent that small holder farming in Anglo economies and rural cooperatives in Northern Europe in the nineteenth century contained the seeds of liberal and coordinated relations, the comparable forerunner of hierarchical capitalism was labor coercive agriculture: latifundia, landed estates, and slave plantations. Although prior centuries of labor-coercive agriculture did not cause hierarchical capitalism, they did not create propitious conditions for a transition to liberal or coordinated capitalism when Latin America began to industrialize. More generally, extremes of social, economic, and political inequality date back at least to early colonial rule. The most direct legacy for hierarchical capitalism was that inequality stalled the early expansion of education and skills, so that by the early twentieth century, literacy rates in Latin America lagged far behind those in North America (Engerman and Sokoloff 2012, 156).

State-led development strategies during much of the twentieth century also precluded coordinated and liberal alternatives to hierarchical capitalism. Extensive state intervention, of course, restricted markets in numerous ways. State intervention, as well as the introduction of compulsory corporatist modes of organization, encouraged business and labor to focus on relations with the state rather than on possibilities for coordination among themselves. More directly, state intervention fostered the formation of the first large business groups; both ISI and industrial policy encouraged firms to diversify broadly, as in the policy-induced business groups discussed in Chapter 3 (Guillén 2001). On the labor front, government regulation, dating mostly from the 1930s and 1940s, often directly impeded coordination (among unions or between unions and managers) while at the same time establishing extensive and rigid labor codes (Carnes 2012). Last, in stark contrast to counterparts in Asia, developmental states in Latin America opened their economies to foreign investment, especially after World War II, and allowed MNCs to gain dominance in many sectors before most of today's business groups started emerging in other sectors (Amsden 2009).

Thus, the roots of hierarchical capitalism are several. Some like socioeconomic inequality were centuries old; others such as segmented labor markets were more recent creations of developmental and corporatist states. This historical trajectory is path dependent in two ways (Mahoney 2000). First, in terms of historical, fork-in-the-road causes, possible movement toward coordinated or liberal capitalism was closed off at various historical junctures. Second, by segmenting and organizing labor and by fostering large business groups and MNCs in the mid-twentieth century, states created powerful groups that in turn pressed governments to continue policies favorable to them (positive feedback loops) and to sustaining the core institutions and organizations of hierarchical capitalism (as examined in Chapter 7).

Thus, in the question of origins, institutional complementarities in hierarchical capitalism derived from a historically contingent, coincidental process (Amable 2000; Streeck 2005) rather than a more spontaneous, functional equilibrium (see Aoki 2001), or a more deliberate process of elite creation. In this latter view, economic elites recognize the value of institutional complementarities in either market or coordinated form in one realm and then seek to extend them to other realms of the economy (Hall and Soskice 2001). This deliberate, business-driven pattern was not much in evidence in the historical evolution of hierarchical capitalism in Latin America.

In contrast, in the former, coincidental view, institutional complementarities emerge over time among institutions that were often created for other purposes or that emerged as unintended consequences. Much of the skills regime and labor regulation came through top-down imposition by often authoritarian governments. The goals were various but usually included efforts to control union organization and incorporate urban labor into political coalitions (Collier and Collier 1991). Benefits of labor regulation were restricted to a small labor elite, and employers were able to pass costs on to consumers in mostly closed economies. Family-owned, diversified, business groups in turn formed during early industrialization in the mid-twentieth century in more bottom-up, spontaneous manner partially in response to undeveloped financial markets. However, diversification was also partly an unintended response to ISI. As firms saturated one product market, they were not efficient enough to expand through exports, so they turned instead to other domestic sectors (Guillén 2001).

Following the coincidental, sequential view of institutional complementarities, patterns of rapid labor turnover emerged then more as responses to other institutions and circumstances. Firm strategies targeted protected domestic markets and could rely on less-skilled labor, which made workers more easily substitutable. Moreover, the accumulation of worker benefits over time, especially severance pay, encouraged employers to lay off workers. These and other trajectories of institutional formation and consolidation could be more fully fleshed out, but this brief historical summary should suffice to illustrate the wide variation in the orientations and goals of builders of institutions and organizations, the absence of coherent "intelligent design" by economic elites, and the sequential establishment of institutions that later came to cohere.

Once established, institutional complementarities knit together the core components of hierarchical capitalism. Figure 9.1, a copy of Figure 2.1, summarizes the key complementarities analyzed in previous chapters. Given the shallowness of credit and equity markets in Latin America, the analysis of corporate governance started with the large firms that mobilize investment: MNCs and business groups. A first complementarity emerged in the division of labor or sectors with MNCs dominant in manufacturing which increased returns to business groups that invested in commodities and services. Other core complementarities emerged between these large firms – both MNCs and business groups – and their relatively low demand for skilled workers. This low demand was due to several factors including low levels of R&D and a general make-rather-than-buy strategy for skills based on in-house training. In addition, both categories of business had some capital-intensive firms that employed skilled workers, but few of them, and labor-intensive operations that employed mostly semi- and unskilled workers. Thus, demand from large firms for skills was relatively low, which reduced incentives for workers to invest in human capital.

The reverse complementarity completed the low-skill equilibrium; the absence of large pools of skilled workers increased incentives for firms to engage in activities that relied on less-skilled workers. Low skill levels also

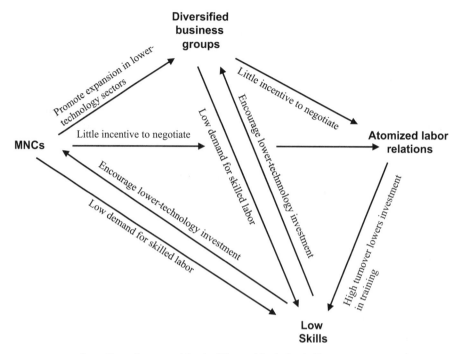

FIGURE 9.1. Core Complementarities in Hierarchical Capitalism

increased returns to firms to segmenting their formal workers into a small labor elite with longer tenure (in which firms invested in training) and a larger group of workers with short tenure and low skills (and who could therefore be more easily replaced). Short tenure in turn reduced returns for workers to invest in sector- and firm-specific skills.

These, in sum, are some of the core complementarities. Without repeating the arguments on each of the arrows, Figure 9.1 should nonetheless serve as a general reminder of the broad range of complementarities that knit together hierarchical capitalism and contribute to path dependence. However, despite negative complementarities and institutional resilience overall, change is clearly afoot in Latin America, and the start of the twenty-first century was a very dynamic period for the region. As noted in several of the thematic chapters, a complementarities perspective helps to understand the constraints on progress as well as the implications of changes that are underway. Public promotion of education, for example, cannot fully change incentives for individuals to invest in education without corresponding increases in demand for skilled labor.

The major sources of institutional change in Latin America in the last several decades have come through a combination of bottom-up market forces and top-down policy measures. On the market side, financial intermediation has steadily expanded. The dominance of business groups and MNCs is greatly abetted by advantages in accessing capital. For other firms to challenge them requires flush equity and credit markets. Both stock markets and bank finance for firms have grown, but slowly and unevenly (see Chapter 3). Where change has been most dramatic has been in credit markets in Chile and equity markets in Brazil. Within the framework of hierarchical capitalism, such shifts could facilitate the entry of new, professionally managed, specialized firms that could alter complementarities with labor markets and innovation by ramping up investment in R&D and demand for skilled workers. And, in fact, turnover among the largest business groups in both countries has been high, and many of the newcomers are more specialized, for now. Other new groups, however, immediately started diversifying, and others adopted traditional forms of family control (e.g., JBS and EBX in Brazil). Moreover, MNCs and traditional business groups are still prospering, so it is premature to talk of transformation in corporate governance and leading firms. However, the new firm entrants with different corporate governance and corporate strategies could continue to weaken traditional complementarities in hierarchical capitalism. The open question is whether challenger firms would alter the demand for skills or adapt their strategies to existing supply.

Labor markets have undergone substantial evolution including falling unemployment, greater labor force participation by women, rising wages, falling informality, and resurgence of unions in a few countries (most notably Argentina). However, these important changes, though positive and important in their own right, had little impact on the core features of segmented and atomized labor markets in hierarchical capitalism. On core dimensions such as high turnover, high regulation (for a minority), continuing high levels of informality, and an absence of plant-level intermediation, little has changed. Overall, these factors continue to limit incentives for investing in skills.

Yet, education, especially higher education, has been booming, and returns to higher education have remained positive and significant (though decreasing in the 2000s). Part of the demand for skilled workers, and occasional scarcity, in the 2000s, is a reflection of the under investment in skills in previous decades, and part of the new investment in education is going to "credentialing" (when the course of study is low quality and little use for raising productivity). And Latin America is still behind Asia in generating a reputation for labor markets with large pools of highly skilled workers. Nonetheless, incremental shifts in educational levels across the population could, if sustained over time, shift the skill profile of labor markets and possibly start attracting more investment dependent on those skills. Given the absence of coordinating CME-type institutions, if such a shift occurs, it will likely be in the direction of general skills central to LMEs.

The major top-down government reforms that countered complementarities in hierarchical capitalism were limited in scope and undertaken in only a few countries. Governments, especially in Brazil and Chile, intervened mostly in technology policy and education, but made less progress in reforming labor markets, financial markets, or corporate governance. Numerous policies affected all these areas, but none altered the fundamental patterns identified in Part II. Brazil, Chile, and Argentina increased government investment in R&D and incentives for private firms to do likewise. Although total R&D in these countries was still less than half the averages in developed countries, the trend was upward. More governments in the region made significant new investments in education, mostly to expand access to secondary and tertiary education. If sustained, and expanded to improve quality, these policies could deliver a supply shock to the low-skill trap and generate positive complementarities in some segments of labor markets characterized by a high skill equilibrium in areas like mining, petroleum exploration, mechanized agriculture, and high-end services.

Ironically, neoliberalism and market reform, as implemented in Latin America, mostly reinforced hierarchical capitalism. Privatization favored business groups and MNCs. Trade liberalization broke up some oligopolies, but business groups adjusted out of manufacturing into other semi-protected markets. Re-regulation after privatization often came up late and short in effectively promoting competition. Trade liberalization did lead at least initially to skill-biased technological change in surviving sectors, but it mostly led to de-industrialization and falling employment in industry (Palma 2005). Workers shifted instead to low productivity service jobs, reinforcing the low-skill equilibrium.

Governments that adopted interventionist policies to counter the negative complementarities in hierarchical capitalism were often first rejecting neoliberalism, at least its more extreme forms. Government support coalitions depended heavily on outsiders – groups excluded from the benefits of hierarchical capitalism. The major policy reforms often targeted the social area – pensions, conditional cash transfers, health, and education – but the opposition to neoliberalism also opened the doors for new and increased forms of micro-level state intervention in the economy through industrial policy, nationalizations, and other indirect mechanisms of leverage on private firms (as for example, through shareholder blocs and pension funds of state enterprises in Brazil; Lazzarini 2011).

Thinking theoretically about types of institutional change, recent shifts in hierarchical capitalism have been characterized less by transformation, conversion, or punctuated equilibrium, and more by drift and especially displacement (Mahoney and Thelen 2010). Where new, smaller, innovative firms have emerged, it has been alongside the old mastodons. Where higher-skilled niches have developed, it has been new segments alongside the traditional low-skill segments of labor markets. This pattern of displacement is similar to recent trends in coordinated capitalism as in Japan and Germany, where expanding service sectors and shrinking manufacturing have reduced the core areas of coordination in industry. Similarly, though potentially more transformational, some governments in CMEs (Scandinavia especially) adopted more far reaching labor deregulation to promote flexicurity, a blend of flexible LME-style labor markets combined with generous welfare benefits and heavy state support for labor mobility and training (Martin and Thelen 2007). Such transformational shifts, especially in labor markets, have not been common in Latin America and institutional displacement has been slow and partial, so it is still more analytically fruitful to view the region first through the lens of hierarchical capitalism.

# APPENDIX

# Interviews

## Argentina

Jaime Campos. Director, Asociación Empresaria Argentina, 19 September 2007 and 12 December 2008.

Daniel Funes de Rioja. President of Coordinadora de las Industrias de Productos Alimenticios (COPAL) and board member of Unión Industrial Argentina (UIA), 28 July 2010.

Marshall Gaylord. Industrias Lander, 19 September 2007.

Claudia Jacinto. Researcher at Instituto de Desarrollo Económico y Social (IDES), 23 July 2010.

Marta Novick. Ministry of Labor, 23 July 2010.

Dina Pesce. Staff member, American Chamber of Commerce, 29 July 2010.

Santiago Soldati. President of Sociedad Comercial del Plata (SCP), 18 September 2007.

Gerardo Soula. Director of human resources for Latin America, Cargill, 12 December 2008.

Enrique Zuleta Puceiros. President, Fundación de Investigaciones Económicas y Sociales, 18 September 2007.

## Brazil

Roger Agnelli. President of Vale 2001–11, 14 September 2011.

Glauco Arbix. President, Financiadora de Estudos e Projetos (Finep), 4 July 2011.

Juliana Bonomo. Head of education, Valer, Vale, 17 November 2008.

Andrea Calabi. Former secretary of planning in São Paulo and former head of Receita Federal, 4 August 2006.

Carlos Henrique Brito Cruz. Scientific Director, Fundação de Amparo à Pesquisa do Estado de São Paulo (FAPESP), 14 November 2011.

Ana Lucia Caltabiano. Director of human resources for Latin America, Hewlett Packard, 14 September 2007.

Fernando Henrique Cardoso. President of Brazil 1994–2002, former senator and finance minister, 16 August 2010.

Carlos Alberto Cidade. Diretor of regulatory policy, Oi and former head of legislative action, Confederação Nacional da Indústria (CNI), 1 July 2011.

Deisi Difune. Advisor, Serviço Nacional de Aprendizagem Industrial (Senai), 17 June 2009.

José Ermírio de Moraes Neto. Board member and heir, Votorantim, 9 December 2005.

Rodolfo Fischer. Executive vice-president, Banco Itaú, 3 August 2006.

Patricia Freitas. Head of venture capital at Financiadora de Estudos e Projetos (FINEP), 4 July 2011.

Daniel Gleizer. Head of macro analysis, Unibanco, 2 August 2006.

Francisco Gros. President of Fosfertil and former president of BNDES, 8 December 2005.

Horacio Lafer Piva. Former president, Federação das Indústrias do Estado de São Paulo (FIESP) and board member, Klabin, 14 September 2007.

Luiz Mello. President, Instituto Tecnológico Vale, 18 October 2011.

Nanci Meneghetti. Director of human resources, Itautec, 15 June 2009.

Vladson Menezes. Director of legislative affairs, Confederação Nacional da Indústria (CNI), 30 June 2011.

Alexandre Miceli. Instituto Brasileiro de Governança Corporativa (IBGC), 15 June 2009.

José Luis Osorio. Former president of Comissão de Valores Mobiliários (CVM, 2000–02), 5 December 2005.

Fernando Reinach. Former head of Votorantim Novos Negocios, 5 July 2011.

José Florencio Rodrigues. Director, Camargo Correa, 2 August 2006.

Gilson dos Santos Filho. Head of training, Ford do Brasil, 4 August 2006.

Walter Sigollo. Superintendent of human resources, Sabesp, 14 September 2007.

Walter Vicioni. Director, Serviço Nacional de Aprendizagem Industrial (Senai), São Paulo, 27 January 2010.

Paulo Villares. Former head of Grupo Villares, 2 August 2006.

## Chile

Fernando Alvaro. Executive director, CPC, 6 September 2011 and 5 January 2012.

José Pablo Arellano. Former minister of education (1996–2000), 9 January 2012.

José Miguel Benavente. Board member, CNIC, 23 March 2010.

Edgardo Boeninger. Former minister (1990–94) and senator (1998–2006), 22 March 2006.

Andrés Concha. Presidente of Sofofa. 10 December 2010.

Felipe Domínguez. Head of human resources, 3M, 22 March 2009.

William Dorat. Manager for human resources, Madeco, 9 December 2010.

Michael Grasty. Law partner and ex-president of American Chamber of Commerce (Amcham, 2004–06), 15 March 2007.

Luis Hernán González. Director of human resources, Sigdo Koppers, 23 March 2010.

Carlos Hurtado. Former minister in the 1990s, 20 March 2009.

Felipe Irarrázaval. Fiscal Nacional Económico, 7 December 2010.

Felipe Lamarca. Ex-president, Copec (Angelini group), and ex-president, Sofofa, 26 March 2006.

Adrónico Luksic. CEO, Banco de Chile and heir to Luksic group, 29 September 2010.

Peter Morse. Banco de Chile, 10 January 2012.

Ernesto Ottone. Former advisor to President Lagos, 24 March 2010.

Andrés Pumarino. Academic director, DUOC, 9 January 2012.

Gustavo Rayo. Advisor, Servicio Nacional de Capacitación y Empleo (Sence), 8 January 2010.

Andrea Repetto. Chair of tripartite commission on unemployment insurance, 9 January 2012.

Flavia Ronconi. General manager, Fundación Sofofa, 19 March 2009.

José Luis Sepúlveda Zapata. Manager of Firms and Education Area, Corporación Sofofa, 16 March 2007.

Francisco Silva. Superintendencia Valores y Seguros, 3 November 2010.

Sara Smok. President, Manpower Chile, 11 January 2010.

Piero Solari. Ex-manager and part owner of Falabella, 5 January 2012.

Andrés Velasco. Former minister of finance (2006–10), 26 January 2012.

Jorge Vergara. Director, Asociación Gremial de Industriales del Plástico (Asipla), 17 November 2009.

Pablo Vescovi Ewing. Director of human resources, Compañía de las Cervecerías Unidas (CCU, Luksic group), 9 December 2010.

Ignacio Walker. Former deputy and former minister of foreign relations (2000–06), 16 March 2007.


## Colombia

Consuelo Arbeláez Bernal. Administrative director, Consejo Gremial Nacional, 8 August 2011.

Carlos Julio Ardila. CEO of Radio Cadena Nacional and one of two heirs to the Organización Ardila Lülle group, 10 August 2011.

Simón Gaviria. President of the Chamber of Deputies, National Congress, 11 August 2011.

Roberto Junguito. Former minister of finance, minister of agriculture, and president of the Sociedad de Agricultores de Colombia, 8 August 2011.

Joaquín Moreno. Ex-manager of Shell Oil in Colombia and Venezuela, 11 August 2011.

Mabel Muñetones. Human resources manager, Bundy Refrigeration, 10 August 2011.

Angélica Peña. Technical director, Consejo Gremial Nacional, 8 August 2011.

Guillermo Perry. Former minister of finance (1994–96), 8 August 2011.

Luiz Carlos Villegas. President of Asociación Nacional de Empresarios de Colombia (ANDI), president of Consejo Gremial Nacional, 5 September 2011.

## Mexico

David Calderón. Director of Mexicanos Primero, 16 February 2011.

Gabriel Castañeda. Antitrust lawyer and top government official in early 1990s, 16 February 2011.

Genaro Guerra. Subdirector in the training division of the labor ministry, 22 June 2004.

Agustín Ibarra. Top official in the labor ministry in 1990s, 17 February 2011.

Agustín Legorreta. President of Banamex through 1982 and president of several top business associations in the 1970s and 1980s, 23 June 2004.

Juan Pardinas. Executive director, Instituto Mexicano para la Competitividad (IMCO), 15 February 2011.

Gerardo de la Peña Hernández. Director General of Capacitación e Innovación Tecnológica in the Secretaría de Economía, 17 February 2011.

## Other

Daniel Blume. Corporate Affairs Division, OECD, 4 June 2007.

Juan Chacaltana. Researcher at the International Labor Organization, Lima, Peru, 14 August 2009.

Mike Lubrano. Corporate Governance Department, International Finance Corporation, 30 August 2006.

# References

Abrucio, Fernando. 2007. "Coalizão educacional no Brasil: importância e condições de sucesso." In *O Plano de Desenvolvimento da Educação (PDE)*, ed. Mariangela Graciano. São Paulo: Ação Educativa.

Acemoglu, Daron. 1996. "Credit Constraints, Investment Externalities, and Growth." In *Acquiring Skills*, ed. Alison Booth and Dennis Snower. New York: Cambridge.

Acemoglu, Daron. 1997. "Technology, Unemployment and Efficiency." *European Economic Review* 41: 525–33.

Acemoglu, Daron, and Jörn-Steffen Pischke. 1998. "Why Do Firms Train? Theory and Evidence." *Quarterly Journal of Economics* 113(1, February): 79–119.

Acemoglu, Daron, and Jörn-Steffen Pischke. 1999. "Beyond Becker: Training in Imperfect Labour Markets." *Economic Journal* 109(453, Features, February): 112–42.

Agosin, Manuel, Eduardo Fernández-Arias, and Fidel Jaramillo, eds. 2009. *Growing Pains: Binding Constraints to Productive Investments in Latin America*. Washington, DC: Inter-American Development Bank.

Agosin, Manuel, Christian Larraín, and Nicolás Grau. 2009. "Industrial Policy in Chile." Paper prepared for a project on Productive Development Policies. Washington, DC: IDB.

Agosin, Manuel, and Roberto Machado. 2005. "Foreign Investment in Developing Countries: Does It Crowd in Domestic Investment?" *Oxford Development Studies* 33(2): 149–62.

Albornoz, Marcelo, Francisco del Río, Andrea Repetto, and Ricardo Solari. 2011. "Hacia una Nueva Legislación Laboral." Santiago: Universidad Aldolfo Ibáñez.

Alcorta, Ludovico, and Wilson Peres. 1995. "Innovation Systems and Technological Specialization in Latin America and the Caribbean." Discussion Paper Series No. 9509. Intech, United Nations University.

Alfaro, Laura. 2003. "Foreign Direct Investment and Growth: Does the Sector Matter?" Boston, MA: Harvard Business School.

Alfaro, Laura, Areendam Chanda, Sebnem Kalemli-Ozcan, and Selin Sayek. 2004. "FDI and Economic Growth: The Role of Local Financial Markets." *Journal of International Economics* 64(1, October): 89–112.

Alfaro, Laura, and Andrew Charlton. 2007. "Growth and the Quality of Foreign Direct Investment: Is All FDI Equal?" IMF Conference, Washington, DC.

Almeida, Mansueto. 2009. "Desafios da real política industrial brasileira do século XXI." Brasília: IPEA.

Almeida, Mansueto, Renato Lima-Oliveira, and Ben Ross Schneider. 2012. "Industrial Policy and State Owned Enterprises in Brazil: BNDES and Petrobras." Brasília: IPEA.

Almeida, Mansueto, and Ben Ross Schneider. 2012. "Globalization, Democratization, and the Challenges of Industrial Policy in Brazil," Paper presented at the Korean Development Institute, Seoul, South Korea.

Almeida, Rita, and Reyes Aterido. 2008. "The Incentives to Invest in Job Training: Do Strict Labor Codes Influence This Decision?" Working paper. Washington, DC: World Bank.

Amable, Bruno. 2000. "Institutional Complementarity and Diversity of Social Systems of Innovation and Production." *Review of International Political Economy* 7(4, Winter): 645–87.

Amable, Bruno. 2003. *The Diversity of Modern Capitalism*. New York: Oxford University Press.

Amable, Bruno. 2005. "Complementarity, Hierarchy, Compatibility, Coherence." *Socio – Economic Review* 3(2, May): 371–77.

Amann, Edmund. 2000. *Economic Liberalization and Industrial Performance in Brazil*. New York: Oxford University Press.

Amann, Edmund. 2009. "Technology, Public Policy, and the Emergence of Brazilian Multinationals." In *Brazil as an Emerging Economic Superpower?* ed. Lael Brainard and Leonardo Martinez-Diaz. Washington, DC: Brookings Institution.

Amengual, Matthew. 2010. "The Politics of Labor and Environmental Regulation in Argentina." PhD Dissertation. Cambridge, MA: MIT.

Amorim Neto, Octavio. 2002. "Presidential Cabinets, Electoral Cycles, and Coalition Discipline in Brazil." In *Legislative Politics in Latin America*, ed. Scott Morgenstern and Benito Nacif. New York: Cambridge University Press.

Amsden, Alice. 1989. *Asia's Next Giant: South Korea and Late Industrialization*. New York: Oxford University Press.

Amsden, Alice. 2001. *The Rise of "the Rest": Challenges to the West from Late-Industrializing Economies*. Oxford: Oxford University Press.

Amsden, Alice. 2009. "Nationality of Ownership in Developing Countries: Who Should 'Crowd Out' Whom in Imperfect Markets?" In *Industrial Policy and Development*, ed. M. Cimoli, Giovani Dosi, and Joseph Stiglitz. New York: Oxford University Press.

Amsden, Alice. 2010. "Say's Law, Poverty Persistence, and Employment Neglect." *Journal of Human Development and Capabilities* 11(1, February): 57–66.

Anderson, Benedict. 2006. *Imagined Communities: Reflections on the Origin and Spread of Nationalism*. London: Verso.

Andrade, Luis, José Barra, and Heinz-Peter Elstrodt. 2001. "All in the *Familia*." *McKinsey Quarterly* 4: 81–89.

Anner, Mark. 2008. "Meeting the Challenges of Industrial Restructuring: Labor Reform and Enforcement in Latin America." *Latin American Politics and Society* 50(2): 33–65.

Aoki, Masahiko. 2001. *Toward a Comparative Institutional Analysis*. Cambridge: MIT Press.

Arbix, Glauco. 2010. "Innovation Policy in Brazil: New Approaches in the Lula Government." Unpublished paper.

Arbix, Glauco, and Luiz Caseiro. 2011. "The Recent Internationalization of Brazilian Companies." In *Technological, Managerial and Organizational Core Competencies*, ed. Farley Nobre, David Walker, and Robert Harris. Hershey, PA: IGI Global.

Arbix, Glauco, and Scott Martin. 2010. "Beyond Developmentalism and Market Fundamentalism in Brazil: Inclusionary State Activism Without Statism." Unpublished paper.

Artana, Daniel, Sebastián Auguste, and Mario Cuevas. 2009. "Tearing Down the Walls: Growth and Inclusion in Guatemala." In *Growing Pains*, ed. Manuel Agosin, Eduardo Fernández-Arias, and Fidel Jaramillo. Washington, DC: Inter-American Development Bank.

Assumpção-Rodrigues, Marta. 2012. "Skill Formation, Governance, and Democracy in Brazil: The State of the Art of a Public Policy." Unpublished paper.

Atkin, David. 2009. "Endogenous Skill Acquisition and Export Manufacturing in Mexico." Unpublished paper, Yale University.

Ayala, Natalia. 2003. *El Consejo de Desarrollo Económico y Social de Brasil*. Observatorio de la Globalización 2. Montevideo: D3e.

Aykut, Dilek, and Andrea Goldstein. 2006. "Developing Country Multinationals: South-South Investment Comes of Age." Working Paper 257. Development Centre. Paris: OECD.

Bacoccina, Denize, and Guilherme Queiroz. 2012. "O Fator Gerdau." *Dinheiro*, 19 September.

Bair, Jeniffer, and Gary Gereffi. 2001. "Local Clusters in Global Chains: The Causes and Consequences of Export Dynamism in Torreon's Blue Jeans Industry." *World Development* 29(11): 1885–903.

Banerjee, Abhijit, and Esther Duflo. 2011. *Poor Economics: A Radical Rethinking of the Way to Fight Global Poverty*. New York: Public Affairs.

Barba Navaretti, Giorgio, and Anthony Venables. 2004. *Multinational Firms in the World Economy*. Princeton, NJ: Princeton University Press.

Barro, Robert, and Jong-Wha Lee. 2000. "International Data on Educational Attainment: Updates and Implications." NBER Working Paper 7911. Cambridge, MA: National Bureau of Economic Research. http://www.nber.organization/papers/w7911.

Barro, Robert, and Jong-Wha Lee. 2010. "A New Data Set of Educational Attainment in the World, 1950–2010." NBER Working Paper 15902. Cambridge, MA: National Bureau of Economic Research. http://www.nber.org/papers/w15902.

Batt, Rosemary, David Holman, and Ursula Holtgrewe. 2009. "The Globalization of Service Work: Comparative Institutional Perspectives on Call Centers." *Industrial and Labor Relations Review* 62(4, July): 453–88.

Beausang, Francesca. 2003. *Third World Multinationals: Engine of Competitiveness or New Form of Dependency?* New York: Palgrave.

Becerra, Martín, and Guillermo Mastrini. 2009. *Los dueños de la palabra: acceso, estructura y concentración de los medio en la América Latina del siglo XXI*. Buenos Aires: Prometeo.

Becerril, Andrea. 2007. "La Ley Televisa, una imposición previa a las elecciones de 2006 según Creel." *La Jornada*, 5 de mayo.

Bell, David, and Cintra Scott. 2010. "Los Grobo: Farming's Future?" Boston, MA: Harvard Business School.

Benítez, Andrés. 2006. "Por qué la Papelera no es Nokia." *Capital*. Posted to http://www.franciscocerda.cl/content/view/122/Por-que-la-papelera-no-es-Nokia.html#content-top.

Bensusán, Graciela, ed. 2006. *Diseño legal y desempeño real: instituciones laborales en América Latina*. Mexico, DF: Porrúa.

Berg, Janine. 2006. *Miracle for Whom? Chilean Workers Under Free Trade*. New York: Routledge.

Berg, Janine. 2010. "Laws or Luck? Understanding Rising Formality in Brazil in the 2000s." Working paper. Decent Work in Brazil Series, n.5. Brasilia: International Labour Office.

Berg, Janine, Christoph Ernst, and Peter Auer. 2006. *Meeting the Employment Challenge: Argentina, Brazil, and Mexico in the Global Economy*. Boulder, CO: Lynne Rienner.

Bisang, Roberto. 1998. "Apertura, reestructuración industrial y conglomerados económicos." *Desarrollo Económico* 38 (Otoño): 143–76.

Bizberg, Ilan. 2012. "Types of Capitalism in Latin America." Unpublished paper, Colegio de México.

Blyde, Juan, Armando Castelar, Christian Daude, and Eduardo Fernández-Arias. 2009. "What is Impeding Growth in Brazil." In *Growing Pains*, ed. Manuel Agosin, Eduardo Fernández-Arias, and Fidel Jaramillo. Washington, DC: Inter-American Development Bank.

Bohle, Dorothee, and Bela Greskovits. 2007. "The State, Internationalization, and Capitalist Diversity in Eastern Europe." *Competition & Change* 11(2, June): 89–115.

Bohle, Dorothee, and Bela Greskovits. 2012. *Capitalist Diversity on Europe's Periphery*. Ithaca, NY: Cornell University Press.

Booth, Alison, and Dennis Snower, eds. 1996. *Acquiring Skills: Market Failures, their Symptoms and Policy Responses*. New York: Cambridge University Press.

Booth, William. 2012. "Mexico Is now a Top Producer of Engineers, but Where Are the Jobs?" *Washington Post*, 28 October.

Bornschier, Volker, and Christopher Chase-Dunn. 1985. *Transnational Corporations and Underdevelopment*. New York: Praeger.

Boschi, Renato, ed. 2011. *Variedades de capitalismo, política e desenvolvimento na América Latina*. Belo Horizonte: UFMG.

Botero, Juan, Simeon Djankov, Rafael La Porta, Florencio Lopez-De-Silanes, and Andrei Shleifer. 2003. "The Regulation of Labor." NBER Working Paper 9756. Cambridge, MA: National Bureau of Economic Research.

Botero, Juan, Simeon Djankov, Rafael La Porta, Florencio Lopez-De-Silanes, and Andrei Shleifer. 2004. "The Regulation of Labor." *Quarterly Journal of Economics* 119(4, November): 1339–82.

Boyer, Robert. 2005. "How and Why Capitalisms Differ." *Economy and Society* 34(4): 509–57.

Brazil. 2011. *Brasil Maior. inovar para competir. competir para crescer. Plano 2011/2014*. Brasília: Ministério do Desenvolvimento, Indústria e Comércio Exterior.

Brito Cruz, Carlos Henrique, and Hernan Chaimovich. 2010. "Brazil." In *UNESCO Science Report*. Paris: UNESCO.

Brown, David, and Wendy Hunter. 2004. "Democracy and Human Capital Formation: Education Spending in Latin America, 1980 to 1997." *Comparative Political Studies* 37(7, September): 842–64.

Buchanan, Paul. 1995. *State, Labor, Capital*. Pittsburgh: Pittsburgh University Press.

Bucheli, Marcelo. 2010. "Multinational Corporations, Business Groups, and Economic Nationalism: Standard Oil (New Jersey), Royal Dutch-Shell, and Energy Politics in Chile 1913–2005." *Enterprise and Society* 11(2): 350–99.

Bugra, Ayse. 1994. *State and Business in Modern Turkey*. Albany: State University of New York Press.

Cabot, Diego. 2009. "El repliegue de grandes grupos empresarios." *La Nación*, 11 January.

Calderón, César, Norman Loayza, and Luis Servén. 2004. "Greenfield Foreign Direct Investment and Mergers and Acquistions: Feedback and Macroeconomic Effects." World Bank Policy Research Working Paper 3192. Washington, DC: World Bank.

Camp, Roderic. 1989. *Entrepreneurs and Politics in Twentieth-Century Mexico*. New York: Oxford University Press.

Carnes, Matthew. 2009. "Institutionalizing Inequality: The Political Origins of Labor Codes in Latin America." Working Paper # 363. Kellogg Institute, University of Notre Dame.

Carnes, Matthew. 2012. "Continuity Despite Change: The Politics of Labor Regulation in Latin America." Unpublished manuscript. Georgetown University.

Carney, Michael, Eric Gedajlovic, Pursey Heugens, Marc Essen, J. van Oosterhout. 2011. "Business Group Affiliation, Performance, Context, and Strategy: A Meta-Analysis." *Academy of Management Journal* 54(2): 437–60.

Carrillo, Jorge, and Yolanda Montiel. 1998. "Ford's Hermosillo Plant: The Trajectory of Development of a Hybrid Model." In *Between Imitation and Innovation*, ed. Robert Boyer, Elsie Charron, Ulrich Jürgens, and Steven Tolliday. New York: Oxford University Press.

Cassis, Youssef. 1997. *Big Business: The European Experience in the Twentieth Century*. Oxford: Oxford University Press.

Castelar, Armando. 2007. "Bancos públicos no Brasil: para onde ir?" In *Mercado de Capitais e Bancos Públicos*, ed. Armando Castelar and Luiz Chrysostomo. Rio de Janeiro: Contra-Capa.

Castilho, Marta. 2005. "Regional Integration and the Labour Market: The Brazilian Case." *CEPAL Review* 87 (December): 147–65.

Catalano, Charles. 2004. "Tenaris: Creating a Global Leader from an Emerging Market." Case IB-60, Stanford Graduate School of Business.

Chahad, José. 2000. "As transformações no mundo do trabalho e o futuro do seguro-desemprego no Brasil." *Economia Aplicada* 4(1): 121–55.

Chahad, José. 2009. *Flexibilidade no mercado de trabalho, proteção aos trabalhadores e treinamento vocacional de força de trabalho*. Santiago: CEPAL.

Chandler, Alfred, Franco Amatori, and Takahashi Hikino, eds. 1997. *Big Business and the Wealth of Nations*. New York: Cambridge University Press.

Chandler, Alfred, and Takashi Hikino. 1997. "The Large Industrial Enterprise and the Dynamics of Modern Economic Growth." In *Big Business and the Wealth of Nations*, ed. Alfred Chandler, Franco Amatori, and Takahashi Hikino. New York: Cambridge University Press.

Chang, Eric, Mark Kayser, Drew Linzer, and Ronald Rogowski. 2010. *Electoral Systems and the Balance of Consumer-Producer Power*. New York: Cambridge University Press.

Chang, Ha-Joon. 2003. *Globalisation, Economic Development and the Role of the State*. London: Zed Books.

Chang, Sea-Jin. 2003. *Financial Crisis and Transformation Korean Business Groups: The Rise and Fall of Chaebols*. New York: Cambridge University Press.

Chang, Sea-Jin, ed. 2006. *Business Groups in East Asia: Financial Crisis, Restructuring, and New Growth*. New York: Oxford University Press.

Cheibub, José Antonio. 2007. *Presidentialism, Parliamentarism, and Democracy*. New York: Cambridge University Press.

Cheng, Lu-Lin. 1996. "Embedded Competitiveness: Taiwan's Shifting Role in International Footwear Sourcing Networks." Phd dissertation. Duke University.

Chudnovsky, Daniel, and Andrés López. 2007. "Inversión extranjera directa y desarrollo: la experiencia del Mercosur." *Revista de la CEPAL* 92 (agosto): 7–23.

Chudnovsky, Daniel, Andrés López, and Eugenia Orlicki. 2007. "The Impact of Foreign Takeover and FDI Presence on Growth, Employment and Equity: The Argentine Experience." *Research Monitor* 3 (November): 6–7.

Chudnovsky, Daniel, Andrés López, and Gastón Rossi. 2008. "Foreign Direct Investment Spillovers and the Absorptive Capabilities of Domestic Firms in the Argentine Manufacturing Sector (1992–2001)." *Journal of Development Studies* 44(5, May): 645–77.

Chung, Chi-Nien. 2001. "Markets, Culture, and Institutions: The Emergence of Large Business Groups in Taiwan, 1950s-1970s." *Journal of Management Studies* 38(5, July): 719–45.

Chung, Chi-Nien, and Ishtiaq Mahmood. 2006. "Taiwanese Business Groups: Steady Growth in Institutional Transition." In *Business Groups in East Asia*, ed. Sea-Jin Chang. New York: Oxford University Press.

Claessens, Stijn, Daniela Klingebiel, and Mike Lubrano. 2000. "Corporate Governance Reform Issues in the Brazilian Equity Markets." Unpublished paper.

CNIC. 2010. *Evaluation Report of National Innovation Strategy for Competitiveness*. International Evaluation Panel. Santiago: Consejo Nacional de Innovatción para la Competitividad.

Coase, Ronald. 1937. "The Nature of the Firm." *Economica* 4(16): 386–405.

Coates, David. 2000. *Models of Capitalism: Growth and Stagnation in the Modern Era*. Cambridge, UK: Polity.

Cociña, Matías, and Sergio Toro. 2009. "Los Think Tanks y su rol en la arena política chilena." In *Dime a Quién Escuchas... Think Tanks y Partidos Políticos en América Latina*, ed. Enrique Mendizabal and Krisetl Sample. Lima: ODI-IDEA.

Colli, Andrea, and Mary Rose. 2003. "Family Firms in Comparative Perspective." In *Business History Around the World*, ed. Franco Amatori and Geoffrey Jones. Cambridge: Cambridge University Press.

Collier, Ruth, and David Collier. 1991. *Shaping the Political Arena: Critical Junctures, the Labor Movement, and Regime Dynamics in Latin America*. Princeton, NJ: Princeton University Press.

Collin, Sven-Olof. 1998. "Why Are These Islands of Conscious Power Found in the Ocean of Ownership? Institutional and Governance Hypotheses Explaining the Existence of Business Groups in Sweden." *Journal of Management Studies* 35(6, November): 719–46.

Colpan, Asli, Takashi Hikino, and James Lincoln, eds. 2010. *Oxford Handbook on Business Groups*. New York: Oxford University Press.

Conaghan, Catherine. 1988. *Restructuring Domination: Industrialists and the State in Ecuador*. Pittsburgh: University of Pittsburgh Press.

Cook, Maria. 1998. "Toward Flexible Industrial Relations? Neo-Liberalism, Democracy, and Labor Reform in Latin America." *Industrial Relations* 37:311–36.

Cook, Maria. 2007. *Politics of Labor Reform in Latin America: Between Flexibility and Rights*. College Park: Penn State University Press.

Coutinho, Luciano, and Flavio Marcilio Rabelo. 2003. "Brazil: Keeping It in the Family." In *Corporate Governance in Development*, ed. Charles Oman. Paris: OECD and CIPE.

Cox, Cristián. 2004. "Las políticas educacionales de Chile en las últimas dos décadas del siglo XX." In *Las Reformas Educativas en la Década de 1990*, ed. Martin M. Carnoy. Buenos Aires: Akian Gráfica.

Crouch, Colin. 2005. *Capitalist Diversity and Change: Recombinant Governance and Institutional Entrepreneurs*. Oxford: Oxford University Press.

Crouch, Colin. 2010. "Complementarity." In *Oxford Handbook of Comparative Institutional Analysis*, ed. Glenn Morgan et al. New York: Oxford University Press.

Crouch, Colin, Wolfgang Streeck, Robert Boyer, Bruno Amable, Peter Hall, and Gregory Jackson. 2005. "Dialogue on 'Institutional Complementarity and Political Economy.'" *Socio – Economic Review* 3(2, May): 359–82.

Cruz, Sebastião Velasco e. 1995. *Empresariado e Estado na transição brasileira*. São Paulo: Unicamp.

Culpepper, Pepper. 2005. "Institutional Change in Contemporary Capitalism: Coordinated Financial Systems Since 1990." *World Politics* 57(2, January): 173–99.

Culpepper, Pepper. 2011. *Quiet Politics and Business Power: Corporate Control in Europe and Japan*. New York: Cambridge University Press.

Cunningham, S. 1986. "Multinationals and Restructuring in Latin America." In *Multinational Corporations and the Third World*, ed. C. Dixon, D. Drakakis-Smith, and H. Watts. London: Croom Helm.

Cusack, Thomas, Torben Iversen, and David Soskice. 2007. "Economic Interests and the Origins of Electoral Systems." *American Political Science Review* 101(3, August): 373–91.

Dalmasso, Juan Pablo. 2011. "El ataque de los geeks latinoamericanos." *América Economia*, 21 June.

Davis, Gerald, Kristina Diekman, and Catherine Tinsley. 1994. "The Decline and Fall of the Conglomerate Firm in the 1980s: The Deinstitutionalization of an Organizational Form." *American Sociological Review* 59: 547–70.

Davis, Gerald, and Christopher Marquis. 2005. "The Globalization of Stock Markets and Convergence in Corporate Governance." In *The Economic Sociology of Capitalism*, ed. Victor Nee and Richard Swedberg. Princeton, NJ: Princeton University Press.

de Ferranti, David, Guillermo Perry, Francisco Ferreira, and Michael Walton. 2004. *Inequality in Latin America: Breaking With History?* Washington, DC: World Bank.

de Ferranti, David, Guillermo Perry, Indermit Gill, J. Luis Guasch, William Maloney, Carolina Sánchez-Páramo, and Norbert Schady. 2003. *Closing the Gap in Education and Technology.* Washington, DC: World Bank.

de Ferranti, David, Guillermo Perry, Daniel Lederman, and William Maloney. 2002. *From Natural Resources to the Knowledge Economy.* Washington, DC: World Bank.

de la Torre, Augusto, Alain Ize, and Sergio Schmukler. 2012. *Financial Development in Latin America and the Caribbean: The Road Ahead.* Washington, DC: World Bank.

de Negri, João Alberto, Ricardo Ruiz, Mauro Lemos, and Fernanda de Negri. 2010. "Fundo Nacional de Desenvolvimento Científico e Tecnológico, sistema nacional de inovação e as empresas do núcleo da indústria no Brasil." Relatório Nº 07. Rio de Janeiro: Finep.

Deeg, Richard. 2005. "Path Dependency, Institutional Complementarity, and Change in National Business Systems." In *Changing Capitalisms?* ed. Glenn Morgan, Richard Whitley, and Eli Moen. New York: Oxford University Press.

Deeg, Richard. 2007. "Complementarity and Institutional Change in Capitalist Systems." *Journal of European Public Policy* 14(4): 611–30.

Deeg, Richard, and Gregory Jackson. 2007. "The State of the Art: Towards a More Dynamic Theory of Capitalist Variety." *Socio-Economic Review* 5: 149–79.

Desai, Mihir, C. Fritz Foley, and James Hines. 2004. "The Costs of Shared Ownership: Evidence from International Joint Ventures." *Journal of Financial Economics* 73(2, August): 323–74.

Di Gropello, Emanuela, ed. 2006. *Meeting the Challenges of Secondary Education in Latin America and East Asia.* Washington, DC: World Bank.

Diniz, Eli. 2011. "Democracy, State, and Industry Continuity and Change Between the Cardoso and Lula Administrations." *Latin American Perspectives* 38(3, May): 59–77.

Doner, Richard, Bryan Ritchie, and Dan Slater. 2005. "Systemic Vulnerability and the Origins of Developmental States: Northeast and Southeast Asia in Comparative Perspective." *International Organization* 59(2, Spring): 327–61.

Dore, Ronald. 2000. *Stock Market Capitalism: Welfare Capitalism. Japan and Germany Versus the Anglo-Saxons.* New York: Oxford University Press.

Ducci, María Angélica. 2001. "Training and Retraining in Latin America." In *Labor Market Policies in Canada and Latin America*, ed. Albert Berry. Boston: Kluwer Academic.

Durand, Francisco. 1996. *Incertidumbre y soledad: reflexiones sobre los grandes empresarios de América Latina.* Lima: Friedrich Ebert.

Duryea, Suzanne, Alejandra Cox Edwards, and Manuelita Ureta. 2003. "Adolescents and Human Capital Formation." In *Critical Decisions at a Critical Age*, ed. Suzanne Duryea, Alejandra Cox Edwards, and Manuelita Ureta. Washington, DC: Inter-American Development Bank.

Duryea, Suzanne, David Lam, and Deborah Levison. 2007. "Effects of Economic Shocks on Children's Employment and Schooling in Brazil." *Journal of Development Economics* 84(1, September): 188–214.

Easterly, William. 2001. *The Elusive Quest for Growth: Economists' Adventures and Misadventures in the Tropics.* Cambridge, MA: MIT Press.

Eberhard, Juan, and Eduardo Engel. 2008. "The Educational Transition and Decreasing Wage Inequality in Chile." Unpublished paper.

ECLAC. 2004. *Foreign Investment in Latin America and the Caribbean.* Santiago: United Nations, Economic Commission for Latin America and the Caribbean.

ECLAC. 2005. *Foreign Investment in Latin America and the Caribbean 2004.* Santiago: United Nations, Economic Commission for Latin America and the Caribbean.

ECLAC. 2006. *Foreign Investment in Latin America and the Caribbean 2005.* Santiago: United Nations, Economic Commission for Latin America and the Caribbean.

ECLAC. 2010. *Foreign Investment in Latin America and the Caribbean 2009.* Santiago: United Nations, Economic Commission for Latin America and the Caribbean.

ECLAC/CEPAL. 2002. *La inversión extranjera en América Latina e el Caribe, 2002.* Santiago: United Nations, Economic Commission for Latin America and the Caribbean.

Egan, Patrick. 2010. "Hard Bargains: The Impact of Multinational Corporations on Economic Reform in Latin America." *Latin American Politics and Society* 52(1, Spring): 1–32.

Egan, Patrick. 2011. "Managing Multinationals: Industrial Policy, State Institutions, and the Quality of Foreign Direct Investment in Brazil." PhD dissertation, University of North Carolina, Chapel Hill.

Elizondo, Carlos. 2011. *Por eso estamos como estamos: la economia política de un crecimiento mediocre.* México, DF: Debates.

Ellul, Andrew, Marco Pagano, and Fabiano Schivardi. 2011. "Family Firms, Shocks, and Employment Security." Presentation at the Hebrew University, Jerusalem.

Engel, Eduardo. 2011. "Malestar Universitario." *La Tercera,* 14 June.

Engerman, Stanley, and Kenneth Sokoloff. 2012. *Economic Development in the Americas Since 1500: Endowments and Institutions.* New York: Cambridge University Press.

Enright, Michael, Antonio Francés, and Edith Saavedra. 1996. *Venezuela, the Challenge of Competitiveness.* New York: St. Martin's.

Esping-Anderson, Gøsta. 1990. *The Three Worlds of Welfare Capitalism.* Princeton, NJ: Princeton University Press.

Estevez-Abe, Margarita, Torben Iversen, and David Soskice. 2001. "Social Protection and the Formation of Skills: A Reinterpretation of the Welfare State." In *Varieties of Capitalism,* ed. Peter Hall and David Soskice. New York: Oxford University Press.

Estrada, Ricardo. 2011. *Profesionistas en vilo: es la universidad una buena inversión?* México, DF: CIDAC.

Etchemendy, Sebastián. 2011. *Models of Economic Liberalization: Business, Workers, and Compensation in Latin America, Spain, and Portugal.* New York: Cambridge University Press.

Etchemendy, Sebastián, and Ruth Berins Collier. 2007. "Down but Not Out: Union Resurgence and Segmented Neocorporatism in Argentina (2003–2007)." *Politics and Society* 35(3): 363–401.

Etchemendy, Sebastian, and Candelaria Garay. 2011. "Argentina: Left Populism in Comparative Perspective, 2003–09." In *The Resurgence of the Latin American Left,* ed. Steven Levitsky and Kenneth Roberts. Baltimore: Johns Hopkins University Press.

Evans, Peter. 1979. *Dependent Development*. Princeton, NJ: Princeton University Press.

Fairfield, Tasha. 2010. "Business Power and Tax Reform: Taxing Income and Profits in Chile and Argentina." *Latin America Politics and Society* 2(2, Summer): 37–71.

Faughnan, Brian, and Elizabeth Zechmeister. 2011. "Vote Buying in the Americas." Americas Barometer Insights Number 57. Vanderbilt, TN: Vanderbilt University.

Feenstra, Robert, and Gary Hamilton. 2006. *Emergent Economies, Divergent Paths: Economic Organization and International Trade in South Korea and Taiwan*. New York: Cambridge University Press.

Feldmann, Magnus. 2007. "The Origins of Varieties of Capitalism: Lessons from Post-Socialist Transition in Estonia and Slovenia." In *Beyond Varieties of Capitalism*, ed. Bob Hancké, Martin Rhodes, and Mark Thatcher. Oxford: Oxford University Press.

Fernandez, Raquel, and Richard Rogerson. 1995. "On the Political Economy of Education Subsidies." *Review of Economic Studies* 62(2, April): 249–62.

Fields, Karl. 1997. "Creating Cooperation and Determining the Distance: Strong States and Business Organization in Korea and Taiwan." In *Business and the State in Developing Countries*, ed. Sylvia Maxfield and Ben Ross Schneider. Ithaca, NY: Cornell University Press.

Finchelstein, Diego. 2004. "El comportamiento empresario durante la década de los noventa: el grupo Macri." *Realidad Económica* 203 (April): 26–49.

Finchelstein, Diego. 2010a. "Corporate Governance in Argentina: Business Groups Adaptation During the Post Market Reforms Period." Unpublished paper.

Finchelstein, Diego. 2010b. "Different States, Different Internationalizations: An Analysis of the Process of Firms' Internationalization in Argentina, Brazil, and Chile." PhD Dissertation. Northwestern University.

Finegold, David, and David Soskice. 1988. "The Failure of Training in Britain: Analysis and Prescription." *Oxford Review of Economic Policy* 4(3, Autumn): 21–53.

Fleury, Afonso, and Maria Tereza Fleury. 2009. "Brazilian Multinationals: Surfing the Waves of Internationalizatioin." In *Emerging Multinations in Emerging Markets*, ed. Ravi Ramamurti and Jitendra Singh. New York: Cambridge University Press.

Fleury, Afonso, and Maria Tereza Fleury. 2011. *Brazilian Multinationals: Competences for Internationalization*. New York: Cambridge University Press.

Fogel, Kathy. 2006. "Oligarchic Family Control, Social Economic Outcomes, and the Quality of Government." *Journal of International Business Studies* 37: 603–22.

Foxley, Alejandro. 2009. *Caminos al desarrollo: lecciones de países afines exitosos (Tomo I)*. Santiago: Uqbar.

Fracchia, Eduardo, Luiz Mesquita, and Juan Quiroga. 2010. "Business Groups in Argentina." In *Oxford Handbook on Business Groups*, ed. Asli Colpan, Takashi Hikino, and James Lincoln. New York: Oxford University Press.

Freitas, Gerson. 2010. "A 'Arabia verde' acorda no canavial." *Carta Capital*, 18 August.

Friel, Daniel. 2011. "Forging a Comparative Institutional Advantage in Argentina: Implications for Theory and Praxis." *Human Relations* 64(4): 553–72.

Gallagher, Kevin, and Roberto Porzecanski. 2010. *The Dragon in the Room: China and the Future of Latin America Industrialization*. Stanford, CA: Stanford University Press.

Gallagher, Kevin, and Lyuba Zarsky. 2007. *The Enclave Economy: Foreign Investment and Sustainable Development in Mexico's Silicon Valley*. Cambridge, MA: MIT Press.

Ganev, Venelin. 2001. "The Dorian Grey Effect: Winners as State Breakers in Postcommunism." *Communist and Post-Communist Studies* 34: 1–25.

Garrido, Celso, and Wilson Peres. 1998. "Las grandes empresas y grupos industriales latinoamericanos en los años noventa." In *Grandes empresas y grupos industriales latinoamericanos*, ed. Wilson Peres. México, DF: Siglo XXI.

Gaspar, Malú. 2011. "Educación: el ejemplo chileno (en serio)." *Que Pasa*, 30 June.

Gasparini, Leonardo, Sebastián Galiani, Guillermo Cruce, and Pablo Acosta. 2011. "Educational Upgrading and Returns to Skills in Latin America: Evidence from a Supply-Demand Framework, 1990–2010." Policy Research Working Paper 5921. Washington, DC: World Bank.

Gates, Leslie. 2010. *Electing Chávez: The Business of Anti-Neoliberal Politics in Venezuela*. Pittsburgh: University of Pittsburgh Press.

Gereffi, Gary, John Humphrey, and Timothy Sturgeon. 2005. "The Governance of Global Value Chains." *Review of International Political Economy* 12(1, February): 78–104.

Gereffi, Gary, and Donald Wyman, eds. 1990. *Manufacturing Miracles*. Princeton, NJ: Princeton University Press.

Gerschenkron, Alexander. 1962. *Economic Backwardness in Historical Perspective*. Cambridge, MA: Belknap.

Gerth, H. H., and C. Wright Mills, eds. 1958. *From Max Weber*. New York: Oxford University Press.

Ghemawat, Pankaj, Michael Rukstad, and Jennifer Illes. 2005. "Arcor: Global Strategy and Local Turbulence." Boston, MA: Harvard Business School.

Goldemberg, José. 2007. "Ethanol for a Sustainable Energy Future." *Science* 315 (9 February): 808–10.

Golder, Matt. 2005. "Democratic Electoral Systems Around the World, 1946–2000." *Electoral Studies* 24(1): 103–21.

Goldstein, Andrea. 2000. "Big Business and the Wealth of South Africa: Policy Issues in the Transition from Apartheid." Working Paper. Paris: OECD Development Centre.

Goldstein, Andrea. 2002. "Embraer: From National Champion to Global Player." *CEPAL Review* 77 (August): 97–115.

Goldstein, Andrea. 2007. *Multinational Companies from Emerging Economies: Composition, Conceptualization and Direction in the Global Economy*. New York: Palgrave Macmillan.

Goldstein, Andrea, and Ben Ross Schneider. 2004. "Big Business in Brazil: States and Markets in the Corporate Reorganization of the 1990s." In *Brazil and Korea*, ed. Edmund Amann and Ha Joon Chang. London: ILAS.

Gonzaga, Gustavo. 2003. "Labor Turnover and Labor Legislation in Brazil." *Economía* 4(1, Fall): 165–222.

González, Maxiliano, Alexander Guzmán, Carlos Pombo, and Maria-Andrea Trujillo. 2011a. "Family Firms and Debt: Risk Aversion Versus Risk of Losing Control." Unpublished paper. Universidad de los Andes, Bogotá, Colombia.

González, Maxiliano, Alexander Guzmán, Carlos Pombo, and Maria-Andrea Trujillo. 2011b. "Family Firms and Financial Performance: The Cost of Growing." Unpublished paper. Universidad de los Andes, Bogotá, Colombia.

Goñi, Edwin, J. Humberto López, and Luis Servén. 2008. "Fiscal Redistribution and Income Inequality in Latin America." World Bank Policy Research Working Paper No. 4487. Washington, DC: World Bank.

Goswami, Omkar. 2003. "India: The Tide Rises Gradually." In *Corporate Governance in Development*, ed. Charles Oman. Paris: OECD and CIPE.

Gottfried, H. 1992. "The Impact of Skill on Union Membership." *Sociological Quarterly* 33: 99–114.

Gourevitch, Peter. 2003. "The Politics of Corporate Governance Regulation." *Yale Law Journal* 112(7, May): 1829–80.

Gourevitch, Peter, and James Shinn. 2005. *Political Power and Corporate Control: The New Global Politics of Corporate Governance*. Princeton, NJ: Princeton University Press.

Granovetter, Mark. 1995. "Coase Revisited: Business Groups in the Modern Economy." *Industrial and Corporate Change* 4(1): 93–130.

Granovetter, Mark. 2005. "Business Groups and Social Organization." In *Handbook of Economic Sociology (Second Edition)*, ed. Neil Smelser and Richard Swedberg. Princeton, NJ: Princeton University Press.

Grindle, Merilee. 2004. *Despite the Odds: The Contentious Politics of Education Reform*. Princeton, NJ: Princeton University Press.

Griner, Steve, and Daniel Zovatto. 2005. "From Norms to Good Practices: A Comparative Regional Analysis of the Funding of Political Parties and Election Campaigns in Latin America." In *Funding of Political Parties and Election Campaigns in the Americas*, ed. Steve Griner and Daniel Zovatto. San José, Costa Rica: Organization of American States/IDEA.

Grosse, Robert. 2007. "The Role of Economic Groups in Latin America." In *Can Latin American Firms Compete?* ed. Robert Grosse and Luis Mesquita. New York: Oxford Univesity Press.

Guillén, Mauro. 2001. *The Limits of Convergence: Globalization and Organizational Change in Argentina, South Korea, and Spain*. Princeton, NJ: Princeton University Press.

Guriev, Sergei, and Andrei Rachinsky. 2005. "The Role of Oligarchs in Russian Capitalism." *Journal of Economic Perspectives* 19(1, Winter): 131–50.

Haagh, Louise. 2002. *Citizenship, Labour Markets, and Democratization: Chile and the Modern Sequence*. New York: Palgrave.

Haagh, Louise. 2004. "The Labour Market and Korea's 1997 Financial Crisis." In *Brazil and Korea*, ed. Edmund Amann and Ha Joon Chang. London: ILAS.

Haagh, Louise. 2011. "Working Life, Well-Being and Welfare Reform: Motivation and Institutions Revisited." *World Development* 39(3, March): 450–73.

Haggard, Stephan. 1990. *Pathways from the Periphery*. Ithaca, NY: Cornell University Press.

Haggard, Stephan, and Robert Kaufman. 2008. *Development, Democracy, and Welfare States: Latin America, East Asia, and Eastern Europe*. Princeton, NJ: Princeton University Press.

Hagopian, Frances, and Scott Mainwaring, eds. 2005. *The Third Wave of Democratization in Latin America*. New York: Cambridge University Press.

Hagopian, Frances, Carlos Gervasoni, and Juan Moraes. 2009. "From Patronage to Program: The Emergence of Party-Oriented Legislators in Brazi." *Comparative Political Studies* 42(3, March): 360–91.

Hall, Peter. 2007. "The Evolution of Varieties of Capitalism in Europe." In *Beyond Varieties of Capitalism*, ed. Bob Hancké, Martin Rhodes, and Mark Thatcher. Oxford: Oxford University Press.

Hall, Peter. 2010. "Historical Institutional in Rationalist and Sociological Perspective." In *Explaining Institutional Change*, ed. James Mahoney and Kathleen Thelen. New York: Cambridge Univesity Press.

Hall, Peter, and Daniel Gingerich. 2009. "Varieties of Capitalism and Institutional Complementarities in the Political Economy: An Empirical Analysis." *British Journal of Political Science* 39(3, July): 449–82.

Hall, Peter, and David Soskice. 2001. "An Introduction to Varieties of Capitalism." In *Varieties of Capitalism*, ed. Peter Hall and David Soskice. New York: Oxford University Press.

Hanani, Alberto. 2006. "Indonesian Business Groups: The Crisis in Progress." In *Business Groups in East Asia*, ed. Sea-Jin Chang. New York: Oxford University Press.

Hancké, Bob. 1998. "Trust or Hierarchy? Changing Relationships Between Large and Small Firms in France." *Small Business Economics* 11(3): 237–52.

Hancké, Bob, Martin Rhodes, and Mark Thatcher, eds. 2007a. *Beyond Varieties of Capitalism: Conflict, Contradiction and Complementarities in the European Economy*. Oxford: Oxford University Press.

Hancké, Bob, Martin Rhodes, and Mark Thatcher. 2007b. "Introduction: Beyond Varieties of Capitalism." In *Beyond Varieties of Capitalism*, ed. Bob Hancké, Martin Rhodes, and Mark Thatcher. Oxford: Oxford University Press.

Hanson, Mark. 2008. *Economic Development, Education and Transnational Corporations*. London: Routledge.

Hanushek, Eric, and Dennis Kimko. 2000. "Schooling, Labor-Force Quality, and the Growth of Nations." *American Economic Review* 90(5, December): 1184–208.

Hassel, Anke. 2007. "What Does Business Want? Labour Market Reforms in CMEs and Its Problems." In *Beyond Varieties of Capitalism*, ed. Bob Hancké, Martin Rhodes, and Mark Thatcher. Oxford: Oxford University Press.

Heckman, James, and Carmen Pagés-Serra. 2000. "The Cost of Job Security Regulation: Evidence from Latin American Labor Markets." *Economia* 1: 109–44.

Heredia, Blanca. 2010. "Mexico's Education Problem: Low Returns to Merit." Working paper, Council on Hemispheric Relations, University of Miami.

Herrera, Ana Maria, and Eduardo Lora. 2005. "Why So Small? Explaining the Size of Firms in Latin America." *The World Economy* 28(7, July): 1005–28.

Hill, Derek. 2000. *Latin America: R&D Spending Jumps in Brazil, Mexico, and Costa Rica*. Washington, DC: National Science Foundation.

Hiratuka, Célio. 2009. "Foreign Direct Investment and Transnational Corporations in Brazil." Paper presented at LASA. Rio de Janeiro.

Hiratuka, Célio, and Fernanda De Negri. 2004. "The Influence of Capital Origin on Brazilian Foreign Trade Patterns." *CEPAL Review* 82 (April): 119–35.

Hirschman, Albert. 1968. "The Political Economy of Import-Substituting Industrialization in Latin America." *The Quarterly Journal of Economics* 82(1): 1–32.

Hirschman, Albert. 1970. *Exit, Voice, and Loyalty: Responses to Decline in Firms, Organizations, and States*. Cambridge, MA: Harvard University Press.

Hirschman, Albert. 1971. *A Bias for Hope: Essays on Development and Latin America*. New Haven, CT: Yale University Press.

Högfeldt, Peter. 2004. "The History and Politics of Corporate Ownership in Sweden." NBER Working Paper 10641. Cambridge, MA: National Bureau of Economic Research.

Holland, Alisha. 2012. "Forbearance: An Electoral Theory of Enforcement." Unpublished paper, Department of Government, Harvard University.

Hollingsworth, J. Rogers, and Robert Boyer. 1997. "Coordination of Economic Actors and Social Systems of Production." In *Contemporary Capitalism*, ed. J. Rogers Hollingsworth and Robert Boyer. Cambridge: Cambridge University Press.

Höpner, Martin. 2005. "What Connects Industrial Relations and Corporate Governance? Explaining Institutional Complementarity." *Socio – Economic Review* 3(2, May): 331–58.

Hoshino, Taeko. 2006. "Estructura de la Propiedad y Mecanismos de Control de las Grandes Empresas Familiares en México." In *Estructura y Dinámica de la Gran Empresa en México*, ed. María de los Ángeles Pozas. México, DF: Colegio de México.

Hoshino, Taeko. 2010. "Business Groups in Mexico." In *Oxford Handbook on Business Groups*, ed. Asli Colpan, Takashi Hikino, and James Lincoln. New York: Oxford University Press.

Huber, Evelyne. 2002a. "Conclusion: Actors, Institutions, and Policies." In *Models of Capitalism*, ed. Evelyne Huber. University Park: Pennsylvania State University Press.

Huber, Evelyne, ed. 2002b. *Models of Capitalism: Lessons for Latin America*. University Park: Pennsylvania State University Press.

Huber, Evelyne, François Nielsen, Jenny Pribble, and John Stephens. 2006. "Politics and Inequality in Latin America and the Caribbean." *American Sociological Review* 71(6, December): 943–63.

Huber, Evelyne, Jennifer Pribble, and John Stephens. 2010. "The Chilean Left in Power: Achievements, Failures, and Omissions." In *Leftist Governments in Latin America*, Kurt Weyland, Raúl Madrid, and Wendy Hunter. New York: Cambridge University Press.

Huber, Evelyne, and John Stephens. 2012. *Democracy and the Left: Social Policy and Inequality in Latin America*. Chicago: University of Chicago Press.

Humphrey, John. 1982. *Capitalist Control and Workers' Struggle in the Brazilian Auto Industry*. Princeton, NJ: Princeton University Press.

Huntington, Samuel. 1968. *Political Order in Changing Societies*. New Haven, CT: Yale University Press.

Hutchcroft, Paul. 1998. *Booty Capitalism: The Politics of Banking in the Philippines*. Ithaca, NY: Cornell University Press.

IDB. 2001. *Competitiveness: The Business of Growth*. Washington, DC: Inter-American Development Bank.

IDB. 2003. *Good Jobs Wanted: Labor Markets in Latin America*. Washington, DC: Inter-American Development Bank and Johns Hopkins University Press.

IDB. Sociometro. n.d. http://www.iadb.org/sociometro/.

IDE. 2004. *Family Business in Developing Countries*. Chiba, Japan: Institute of Developing Economies, JETRO.

IIF. 2004. *Corporate Governance in Brazil: An Investor Perspective*. Task force report. Washington, DC: Institute of International Finance, Inc.

ILO. 2006. *2006 Labour Overview: Latin America and the Caribbean*. Lima: International Labour Organization.

Imbs, Jean, and Romain Wacziarg. 2003. "Stages of Diversification." *American Economic Review* 93(1, March): 63–86.

Iversen, Torben, and David Soskice. 2001. "An Asset Theory of Social Policy Preferences." *American Political Science Review* 95(4, December): 875–93.

Iversen, Torben, and David Soskice. 2006. "Electoral Institutions and the Politics of Coalitions: Why Some Democracies Redistribute More Than Others." *American Political Science Review* 100(2, May): 165–81.

Iversen, Torben, and David Soskice. 2009. "Distribution and Redistribution: The Shadow of the Nineteenth Century." *World Politics* 61(3, July): 438–86.

Izquierdo, Alejandro, Randall Romero, and Ernesto Talvi. 2008. "Booms and Busts in Latin America: The Role of External Factors." Working Paper #631. Washington, DC: Inter-American Development Bank.

Izquierdo, Alejandro, and Ernesto Talvi. 2011. *One Region, Two Speeds? Challenges of the New Global Economic Order for Latin America and the Caribbean*. Washington, DC: Inter-American Development Bank.

Jackson, Gregory, and Richard Deeg. 2008. "From Comparing Capitalisms to the Politics of Institutional Change." *Review of International Political Economy* 15(4): 680–709.

Jenkins, Rhys. 2011. "The 'China Effect' on Commodity Prices and Latin American Export Earnings." *CEPAL Review* 103 (April): 73–87.

Jensen, Nathan. 2003. "Democratic Governance and Multinational Corporations: Political Regimes and Inflows of Foreign Direct Investment." *International Organization* 57(3, August): 587–616.

Johnson, Dale. 1967. "Industry and Industrialists in Chile." PhD Dissertation. Stanford University.

Johnson, Juliet. 1997. "Russia's Emerging Financial-Industrial Groups." *Post-Soviet Affairs* 13(4): 333–65.

Kang, Chul-Kyu. 1997. "Diversification Process and the Ownership Structure of Samsung Chaebol." In *Beyond the Firm*, ed. Takao Shiba and Masahiro Shimotani. New York: Oxford University Press.

Kang, David. 2002. *Crony Capitalism: Corruption and Development in South Korea and the Philippines*. New York: Cambridge University Press.

Karcher, Sebastian. Forthcoming. "Liberalization, Informalization, Segmentation. Business and the Politics of Labor Market Adaptation." Phd Dissertation. Northwestern University.

Karcher, Sebastian, and Ben Ross Schneider. 2012. "Business Politics in Latin America: Investigating Structures, Preferences, and Influence." In *Handbook of Latin American Politics*, ed. Peter Kingstone and Deborah Yashar. New York: Routledge.

Karl, Terry. 1997. *The Paradox of Plenty: Oil Booms and Petro-States*. Berkeley: University of California Press.

Katz, Jorge. 2001. "Structural Reforms and Technological Behaviour: The Sources and Nature of Technological Change in Latin America in the 1990s." *Research Policy* 30: 1–19.

Katzenstein, Peter. 2005. *A World of Regions: Asia and Europe in the American Imperium*. Ithaca, NY: Cornell University Press.

Kaufman, Robert, and Joan Nelson. 2004. "The Politics of Education Sector Reform: Cross-National Comparisons." In *Crucial Needs, Weak Incentives*, ed. Robert Kaufman and Joan Nelson. Baltimore: Johns Hopkins University Press.

Keister, Lisa. 2000. *Chinese Business Groups: The Structure and Impact of Interfirm Relations During Economic Development*. New York: Oxford University Press.

Khanna, Tarun, and Krishna Palepu. 1997. "Why Focused Strategies May Be Wrong for Emerging Markets." *Harvard Business Review* 75(4, July–August): 41–51.

Khanna, Tarun, and Krishna Palepu. 1999. "Policy Shocks, Market Intermediaries, and Corporate Strategy: The Evolution of Business Groups in Chile and India." *Journal of Economics & Management Strategy* 8(2, Summer): 271–310.

Khanna, Tarun, and Krishna Palepu. 2000. "The Future of Business Groups in Emerging Markets: Long Run Evidence from Chile." *Academy of Management Journal* 43(3, June): 268–85.

Khanna, Tarun, and Yishay Yafeh. 2007. "Business Groups in Emerging Markets: Paragons or Parasites?" *Journal of Economic Literature* 45 (June): 331–72.

King, Lawrence. 2007. "Central European Capitalism in Comparative Perspective." In *Beyond Varieties of Capitalism*, ed. Bob Hancké, Martin Rhodes, and Mark Thatcher. Oxford: Oxford University Press.

King, Lawrence, and Iván Szelényi. 2005. "Post-Communist Economic Systems." In *Handbook of Economic Sociology (Second Edition)*, ed. Neil Smelser and Richard Swedberg. Princeton, NJ: Princeton University Press.

Kingstone, Peter. 1999. *Crafting Coalitions for Reform: Business Preferences, Political Institutions, and Neoliberal Reform in Brazil*. University Park: Pennsylvania State University Press.

Kitschelt, Herbert, Peter Lange, Gary Marks, and John Stephens. 1999. "Convergence and Divergence in Advanced Capitalist Democracies." In *Continuity and Change in Contemporary Capitalism*, ed. Herbert Kitschelt, Peter Lange, Gary Marks, and John Stephens. New York: Cambridge University Press.

Knoke, David. 2001. *Changing Organizations: Business Networks in the New Political Economy*. Boulder, CO: Westview.

Kohli, Atul. 2004. *State-Directed Development: Political Power and Industrialization in the Global Periphery*. New York: Cambridge University press.

Kohli, Atul. 2009. "Nationalist Versus Dependent Capitalist Development: Alternate Pathways of Asia and Latin America in a Globalized World." *Studies in Comparative International Development* 40(4): 386–410.

Kong, Tat Yan. 2011. "Pathways to Cooperation: The Transformation of Labour Relations Among Leading South Korean Firms." *Economy and Society* 40(1): 56–83.

Kosack, Stephen. 2008. "Predicting Good Governance: Political Organization and Education Policy Making in Taiwan, Ghana, and Brazil." PhD Dissertation. Yale University.

Kosack, Stephen. 2009. "Realising Education for All: Defining and Using the Political Will to Invest in Primary Education." *Comparative Education* 45(4, November): 495–523.

Kosack, Stephen. 2012. *The Education of Nations*. New York: Oxford University Press.

Kurtz, Marcus. 2004. "The Dilemmas of Democracy in the Open Economy: Lessons from Latin America." *World Politics* 56(2): 262–302.

Kuznetsov, Yevgeny, and Carl Dahlman. 2008. *Mexico's Transition to a Knowledge-Based Economy: Challenges and Opportunities*. Washington, DC: World Bank.

La Porta, Rafael, Florencio López-de-Silanes, and Andrei Shleifer. 1999. "Corporate Ownership Around the World." *Journal of Finance* 54(2, April): 471–517.

Lagos, Ricardo. 1961. *La concentración del poder económico: su teoría, realidad chilena*. Santiago: Editorial del Pacífico.

Lane, Christel. 2003. "Changes in Corporate Governance of German Corporations: Convergence to the Anglo-American Model?" *Competition & Change* 7(2–3, June–September): 79–100.

Lansberg, Ivan, and Edith Perrow. 1991. "Understanding and Working with Leading Family Businesses in Latin America." *Family Business Review* 4(2, Summer): 127–47.

Lazzarini, Sergio. 2011. *Capitalismo de laços: os donos do Brasil e suas conexões*. São Paulo: Elsevier.

Leff, Nathaniel. 1978. "Industrial Organization and Entrepreneurship in the Developing Countries: The Economic Groups." *Economic Development and Cultural Change* 26(4, July): 661–75.

Lefort, Fernando. 2005. "Ownership Structure and Market Valuation of Family Groups in Chile." *Corporate Governance* 5(1): 7–13.

Lefort, Fernando. 2010. "Business Groups in Argentina." In *Oxford Handbook on Business Groups*, ed. Asli Colpan, Takashi Hikino, and James Lincoln. New York: Oxford University Press.

Lefort, Fernando, and Eduardo Walker. 2004. "The Effect of Corporate Governance Practices on Company Market Valuation and Payout Policy in Chile." Unpublished paper, Business School, PUC, Chile.

Leite, Antonio Dias. 2009. *Energy in Brazil: Towards a Renewable Energy Dominated System*. London: Earthscan.

Levine, Daniel, and José Enrique Molina, eds. 2011. *The Quality of Democracy in Latin America*. Boulder, CO: Lynne Rienner.

Levitsky, Steven, and María Victoria Murillo. 2009. "Variation in Institutional Strength." *Annual Review of Political Science* 12: 115–33.

Levitsky, Steven, and Kenneth Roberts, eds. 2011. *The Resurgence of the Latin American Left*. Baltimore: Johns Hopkins University Press.

Lincoln, James, and Michael Gerlach. 2004. *Japan's Network Economy: Structure, Persistence, and Change*. New York: Cambridge University Press.

Lincoln, James, and Masahiro Shimotani. 2010. "Whither the Keiretsu, Japan's Business Networks? How Were They Structured? What Did They Do? Why Are They Gone?" In *Oxford Handbook on Business Groups*, ed. Asli Colpan, Takashi Hikino, and James Lincoln. New York: Oxford University Press.

Lipsey, Robert, and Fredrik Sjöholm. 2005. "The Impact of Inward FDI on Host Countries: Why Such Different Answers?" In *Does Foreign Direct Investment Promote Development?* ed. Theodore Moran, Edward Graham, and Magnus Blomström. Washington, DC: Institute for International Economics.

Locke, Richard. 2013. *Promoting Labor Rights in a Global Economy*. New York: Cambridge University Press.

Longo, Francisco. 2005. "Diagnóstico institucional comparado de sistemas de servicio civil: índices de 21 países." Powerpoint presentation. Washington, DC: Banco Interamericano de Desarrollo.

Lora, Eduardo. 2001. "Structural Reforms in Latin America: What Has Been Reformed and How to Measure It." Working Paper #466. Washington, DC: Inter-American Development Bank.

Lora Eduardo, ed. 2008. *Beyond Facts: Understanding Quality of Life*. Washington, DC: Inter-American Development Bank.

López, Andrés, and Daniela Ramos. 2008. "La industria de software y servicios informáticos Argentina. tendencias, factores de competitividad y clusters." Working paper. Buenos Aires: Centro de Investigaciones para la Transformación.

López-Calva, Luis, and Nora Lustig. 2010. "Explaning the Decline in Inequality in Latin America: Technological Change, Educational Upgrading, and Democracy." In *Declining Inequality in Latin America*, ed. Luis López-Calva and Nora Lustig. Washington, DC: Brookings Institution.

Maddison, Angus. 1983. "A Comparison of Levels of GDP Per Capita in Developed and Developing Countries, 1700–1980." *Journal of Economic History* 43(1, March): 27–41.

Mahoney, James. 2000. "Path Dependence in Historical Sociology." *Theory and Society* 29(4, August).

Mahoney, James. 2010. *Colonialism and Postcolonial Development: Spanish America in Comparative Perspective*. New York: Cambridge University Press.

Mahoney, James, and Kathleen Thelen, eds. 2010. *Explaining Institutional Change: Ambiguity, Agency, and Power*. New York: Cambridge University Press.

Mainwaring, Scott, and Timothy Scully, eds. 2010. *Democratic Governance in Latin America*. Stanford, CA: Stanford University Press.

Maloney, William. 1997. *Labor Market Structure in LDCs*. Working Paper No. 1940. Washington DC: World Bank.

Maman, David. 2002. "The Emergence of Business Groups: Israel and South Korea Compared." *Organization Studies* 23: 737–58.

Manzetti, Luigi. 1999. *Privatization South American Style*. New York: Oxford University Press.

Marchand, Donald, Rebecca Chung, and Katarina Paddack. 2002. "CEMEX: Global Growth Through Superior Information Capabilities." Case study, IMD – International Institute for Management Development.

Marshall, Adriana. 2000. "Labor Market Regulation, Wages and Workers' Behavior – Latin America in the 1990s." Paper presented at the Latin American Studies Association, Miami, FL.

Martin, Cathie Jo, and Kathleen Thelen. 2007. "The State and Coordinated Capitalism: Contributions of the Public Sector to Social Solidarity in Postindustrial Societies." *World Politics* 60 (October): 1–36.

Martinez-Diaz, Leonardo. 2009. *Globalizing in Hard Times: The Politics of Banking-Sector Opening in the Emerging World*. Ithaca, NY: Cornell University Press.

Martínez-Gallardo, Cecilia. 2010. "Inside the Cabinet: The Influence of Ministers in the Policymaking Process." In *How Democracy Works*, ed. Carlos Scartasini, Ernesto Stein, and Mariano Tommasi. Washington, DC: Inter-American Development Bank.

Matsuoka, Sizuo, Jesus Ferro, and Paulo Arruda. 2009. "The Brazilian Experience of Sugarcane Ethanol Industry." *In Vitro Cell.Dev.Biol.* 45: 372–81.

Matte, Eliodoro. 2006. "Por Qué Nokia es Nokia y la Papelera es Papelera." *Capital*. Posted to http://joveneslideresblog.blogspot.com/2006/09/jvenes-lderes-blog-lder-empresarial.html.

Maxfield, Sylvia. 1997. *Gatekeepers of Growth: The International Political Economy of Central Banking in Developing Countries*. Princeton, NJ: Princeton University Press.

McDermott, Gerald. 2007. "The Politics of Institutional Renovation and Economic Upgrading: Recombining the Vines That Bind in Argentina." *Politics and Society* 35(1): 103–44.

McMillan, Margaret, and Dani Rodrik. 2011. "Globalization, Structural Change, and Productivity Growth." Paper prepared for a joint ILO-WTO volume.

Menezes-Filho, Naércio. 2003. "Adolescents in Latin America and the Caribbean: How Do They Decide to Allocate Their Time." In *Critical Decisions at a Critical Age*, ed. Suzanne Duryea, Alejandra Cox Edwards, and Manuelita Ureta. Washington, DC: Inter-American Development Bank.

Menezes-Filho, Naércio, Reynaldo Fernandes, and Paulo Picchetti. 2006. "Rising Human Capital but Constant Inequality: The Education Composition Effect in Brazil." *Revista Brasileira de Economia* 60(4, December): 407–24.

Menezes-Filho, Naércio, and Marc-Andreas Muendler. 2007. "Labor Reallocation in Response to Trade Reform." Unpublished paper, University of California, San Diego.

Menezes-Filho, Naércio, Marc-Andreas Muendler, and Garey Ramey. 2008. "The Structure of Worker Compensation in Brazil, With a Comparison to France and the United States." *Review of Economics and Statistics* 90(2, 2008 May): 324–46.

Miceli, Alexandre di. 2006. "Governança corporativa em empresas de controle familiar: casos de destaque no Brasil." São Paulo: Instituto Brasileiro de Governança Corporativa.

Milgrom, Paul, and John Roberts. 1994. "Complementarities and Systems: Understanding Japanese Economic Organization." *Estudios Economicos* 9(1): 3–42.

Miller, Rory. 2010. "Latin American Business History and Varieties of Capitalism." *Business History Review* 84(4, Winter): 653–57.

Mizala, Alejandra. 2003. "Comment." *Economía* 4(1, Fall): 216–20.

Molina, Oscar, and Martin Rhodes. 2007. "The Political Economy of Adjustment in Mixed Market Economies: A Study of Spain and Italy." In *Beyond Varieties of Capitalism*, ed. Bob Hancké, Martin Rhodes, and Mark Thatcher. Oxford: Oxford University Press.

Moran, Theodore. 1998. *Foreign Direct Investment and Development: The New Policy Agenda for Developing Countries and Economies in Transition*. Washington, DC: Institute for International Economics.

Moran, Theodore, Edward Graham, and Magnus Blomström. 2005. "Introduction and Overview." In *Does Foreign Direct Investment Promote Development?* ed. Theodore Moran, Edward Graham, and Magnus Blomström. Washington, DC: Institute for International Economics.

Morck, Randall, Daniel Wolfenzon, and Bernard Yeung. 2005. "Corporate Governance, Economic Entrenchment, and Growth." *Journal of Economic Literature* 43(3, September): 655–720.

Morgan, Glenn. 2009. "Globalization, Multinationals, and Institutional Diversity." *Economy and Society* 38(4, November): 580–605.

Mosley, Layna. 2010. *Labor Rights and Multinational Production*. New York: Cambridge University Press.

Munck, Gerardo, ed. 2007. *Regimes and Democracy in Latin America: Theories and Methods*. New York: Oxford University Press.

Murillo, M. Victoria. 2001. *Labor Unions, Partisan Coalitions, and Market Reforms in Latin America*. Cambridge: Cambridge University Press.

Murillo, M. Victoria. 2005. "Partisanship Amidst Convergence: The Politics of Labor Reform in Latin America." *Comparative Politics* 37(4, July): 441–58.

Murillo, M. Victoria, and Andrew Schrank. 2005. "With a Little Help from My Friends: Partisan Politics, Transnational Alliances, and Labor Rights in Latin America." *Comparative Political Studies* 38(8, October): 971–99.

Murillo, M. Victoria, and Andrew Schrank. 2010. "Labor Organizations and Their Role in the Era of Political and Economic Reform." In *How Democracy Works*, ed. Carlos Scartasini, Ernesto Stein, and Mariano Tommasi. Washington, DC: Inter-American Development Bank.

Musacchio, Aldo, and Sergio Lazzarini. Forthcoming. *Leviathan Evolving: New Varieties of State Capitalism in Brazil and Beyond*.

Naim, Moisés. 1993. *Paper Tigers and Minotaurs: The Politics of Venezuela's Economic Reforms*. Washington, DC: Carnegie Endowment.

Naím, Moisés, and Antonio Francés. 1995. "The Venezuelan Private Sector: From Courting the State to Courting the Market." In *Lessons of the Venezuelan Experience*, ed. Louis Goodman. Baltimore: Johns Hopkins University Press.

Nölke, Andreas, and Arjan Vliegenthart. 2009. "Enlarging the Varieties of Capitalism: The Emergence of Dependent Market Economies in East Central Europe." *World Politics* 61(4, October): 670–702.

North, Douglass. 1990. *Institutions, Institutional Change and Economic Performance*. New York: Cambridge University Press.

Nunes, Edson. 2012. *Educação superior no Brasil: estudos, debates, controvérsias*. Rio de Janeiro: Garamond.

Nunes, Edson, Enrico Martignoni, and Márcia Carvalho. 2003. *Expansão do ensino superior: restrições, impossibilidades e desafios regionais*. Documento de Trabalho Nº 25. Rio de Janeiro: Observatório Universitário.

Núñez, Javier, and Roberto Gutiérrez. 2004. "Classism, Discrimination and Meritocracy in the Labor Market: The Case of Chile." Documento de Trabajo Nº 208, Departamento de Economía, Universidad de Chile.

OECD. 2005. *Measuring Globalisation: OECD Handbook on Economic Globalisation Indicators*. Paris: Organisation for Economic Co-operation and Development.

OECD. 2008. *Science, Technology, and Industry Outlook*. Paris: Organization for Economic Cooperation and Development.

OECD. 2010a. *Measuring Globalisation: OECD Economic Globalisation Indicators*. Paris: Organisation for Economic Co-operation and Development.

OECD. 2010b. "OECD Statistics Portal," accessed at http://stats.oecd.org/Index.aspx on June 2, 2010.

OECD. 2010c. *PISA 2009 Results: Executive Summary*. Paris: Organisation for Economic Co-operation and Development.

OECD. 2010d. *PISA 2009 Results: What Students Know and Can Do: Student Performance in Reading, Mathematics and Science (Volume I)*. Paris: Organisation for Economic Co-operation and Development.

Oliveira, Marcos de. 2010. "Investimento emergente." *Pesquisa Fapesp* 175 (setembro): 16–20.

Olson, Mancur. 1982. *The Rise and Decline of Nations*. New Haven, CT: Yale University Press.

Österholm, Pär, and Jeromin Zettelmeyer. 2008. "The Effect of External Conditions on Growth in Latin America." IMF Staff Papers, vol. 55, no. 4. Washington, DC: International Monetary Fund.

Ostiguy, Pierre. 1990. *Los capitanes de la industria: grandes empresarios, política y economía en la Argentina de los años 80.* Buenos Aires: Legasa.

Oulton, Nicholas. 1996. "Workforce Skills and Export Competitiveness." In *Acquiring Skills*, ed. Alison Booth and Dennis Snower. New York: Cambridge University Press.

Oxhorn, Philip, and Nancy Postero, eds. 2010. "Living in Actually Existing Democracies." Special issue of the *Latin American Research Review* 45(4): 338–45.

Özel, Isik. 2011. "An Emerging 'Market Economy': The Case of Hybrid Turkish Capitalism." Paper presented at a conference on Global Capitalism. Rio de Janeiro.

Paes de Barros, Ricardo, Carlos Henrique Corseuil, and Miguel Foguel. 2000. "Os incentivos adversos e a focalização dos programas de proteção ao trabalhador no Brasil." *Planejamento e Políticas Públicas* 22 (dezembro): 3–30.

Pagés, Carmen, ed. 2010. *The Age of Productivity: Transforming Economies from the Bottom Up.* Washington, DC: IDB.

Pagés, Carmen, Gaëlle Pierre, and Stefano Scarpetta. 2009. *Job Creation in Latin America and the Caribbean: Recent Trends and Policy Challenges.* Washington, DC: World Bank.

Palma, José Gabriel. 2005. "Four Sources of 'De-Industrialization' and a New Concept of the 'Dutch Disease.'" Unpublished paper.

Palma, José Gabriel. 2009. "Flying Geese and Waddling Ducks: The Different Capabilities of East Asia and Latin America to 'Demand-Adapt' and 'Supply-Upgrade' Their Export Productive Capacity." In *Industrial Policy and Development*, ed. M. Cimoli, Giovani Dosi, and Joseph Stiglitz. New York: Oxford University Press.

Pardinas, Juan. 2010. "Brújula de la incompetencia." *Reforma*, 19 December.

Pauly, Louis, and Simon Reich. 1997. "National Structures and Multinational Corporate Behavior: Enduring Differences in the Age of Globalization." *International Organization* 51(1, Winter): 1–30.

Paus, Eva. 2005. *Foreign Investment, Development, and Globalization: Can Costa Rica Become Ireland?* New York: Palgrave Macmillan.

Paus, Eva. 2011. "Latin America's Middle Income Trap." *Americas Quarterly*, Winter.

Pereira, Carlos, Shane Singh, and Bernardo Mueller. 2011. "Political Institutions, Policymaking, and Policy Stability in Latin America." *Latin America Politics and Society*, 53(1): 58–89.

Pérez, Mamerto, Sergio Schlesinger, and Timothy Wise. 2008. "The Promise and the Perils of Agricultural Trade Liberalization." Washington, DC: Washington Office on Latin America.

Perry, Guillermo, J. Humberto López, William Maloney, Omar Arias, and Luis Servén. 2005. *Virtuous Circles of Poverty Reduction and Growth.* Washington, DC: World Bank.

Perry, Guillermo, Pablo Fajnzylber, William Maloney, Omar Arias, Andrew Mason, and Jaime Saavedra-Chanduvi. 2007. *Informality: Exit and Exclusion.* Washington, DC: World Bank.

Petras, James, and Henry Veltmeyer. 1999. "Latin America at the End of the Millennium." *Monthly Review* 51(3, July–August): 31–52.

Piore, Michael, and Charles Sabel. 1984. *The Second Industrial Divide: Possibilities for Prosperity*. New York: Basic Books.

Piore, Michael, and Andrew Schrank. 2008. "Toward Managed Flexibility: The Revival of Labour Inspection in the Latin World." *International Labour Review* 147(1): 1–23.

Pontusson, Jonas. 2005. "Varieties and Commonalities of Capitalism." In *Varieties of Capitalism, Varieties of Approaches*, ed. David Coates. New York: Palgrave Macmillan.

Portes, Alejandro, Manuel Castells, and Lauren Benton. 1989. "Conclusion: The Policy Implications of Informality." In *The Informal Economy*, ed. Portes, Castells, and Benton. Baltimore: Johns Hopkins University Press.

Prata, José, Nirlando Beirão, and Teiji Tomioka. 1999. *Sergio Motta: O trator em ação*. Geração.

Prieto, Francisco, Sebastián Sáez, and Arti Goswami. 2011. "The Elusive Road to Service Export Diversification: The Case of Chile." In *Exporting Services: A Developing Country Perspective*, ed. Arti Goswami, Aaditya Mattoo, and Sebastian Sáez. Washington, DC: World Bank.

Pumarino, Andrés. 2011. "Chile, Hacia un nuevo sistema de capacitación." *América Economia*, 10 October.

Ramamurti, Ravi, and Jitendra Singh, eds. 2009. *Emerging Multinations in Emerging Markets*. New York: Cambridge.

Reiss, Gerald. 1980. "Development of Brazilian Industrial Enterprise: A Historical Perspective." PhD Dissertation. University of California, Berkeley.

Rettberg, Beatriz Angelika. 2000. "Corporate Organization and the Failure of Collective Action: Colombian Business During the Presidency of Ernesto Samper (1994–1998)." PhD Dissertation. Boston University.

Rivera, Temario. 2003. "The Leading Chinese-Filipino Business Families in Post-Marcos Philippines." In *Ethnic Business*, ed. Jomo K. S. and Brian Folk. London: Routledge-Curzon.

Rodrik, Dani. 2007. *One Economics, Many Recipes: Globalization, Institutions, and Economic Growth*. Princeton, NJ: Princeton University Press.

Rodríguez, Alberto, Carl Dahlman, and Jamil Salmi. 2008. *Knowledge and Innovation for Competitiveness in Brazil*. Washington, DC: World Bank.

Rodríguez, Francisco. 2006. "The Political Economy of Latin American Economic Growth (Appendix C)." In *Sources of Growth in Latin America*, ed. Eduardo Fernández-Arias, Rodolfo Manuellir, and Juan Blyde. Washington, DC: Inter-American Development Bank.

Roe, Mark. 2003. *Political Determinants of Corporate Governance*. Oxford: Oxford University Press.

Roland Berger Consultants. 2008. "Oportunidades e desafios para grandes grupos industriais nacionais." Powerpoint presentation. São Paulo.

Rostow, W. W. 1960. *The Stages of Economic Growth: A Non-Communist Manifesto*. Cambridge: Cambridge University Press.

Rugraff, Eric, Diego Sánchez-Ancochea, and Andy Sumner, eds. 2009a. *Transnational Corporations and Development Policy: Critical Perspectives*. Houndsmills, Basingstoke: Palgrave Macmillan.

Rugraff, Eric, Diego Sánchez-Ancochea, and Andy Sumner. 2009b. "How Have TNCs Changed in the Last 50 Years?" In *Transnational Corporations and Development*

*Policy*, ed. Eric Rugraff, Diego Sánchez-Ancochea, and Andy Sumner. Houndsmills, Basingstoke: Palgrave Macmillan.

Sabel, Charles. 2009. "What Industrial Policy Is Becoming: Taiwan, Ireland, and Finland as Guides to the Future of Industrial Policy." Paper prepared for the Inter-American Development Bank.

Santiso, Javier. 2008. "The Emergence of Latin Multinationals." *CEPAL Review* 95 (August): 7–29.

Sargent, John, and Linda Matthews. 2008. "Capital Intensity, Technology Intensity, and Skill Development in Post China/WTO Maquiladoras." *World Development* 36(4, April): 541–59.

Schmidt, Vivien. 2002. *The Futures of European Capitalism*. New York: Oxford University Press.

Schmidt, Vivien. 2003. "French Capitalism Transformed, Yet Still a Third Variety of Capitalism." *Economy and Society* 32(4, November): 526–54.

Schmitter, Philippe, and Wolfgang Streeck. 1999. "The Organization of Business Interests: Studying the Associative Action of Business in Advanced Industrial Societies." Max Planck Discussion Paper 99/1 [originally distributed in 1981]. Cologne.

Schnabel, Claus, and Joachim Wagner. 2007. "Union Density and Determinants of Union Membership in 18 EU Countries." *Industrial Relations Journal* 38: 5–32.

Schneider, Ben Ross. 1999. "The Desarrollista State in Brazil and Mexico." In *The Developmental State*, ed. Meredith Woo-Cumings. Ithaca, NY: Cornell University Press.

Schneider, Ben Ross. 2002. "Why Is Mexican Business So Organized?" *Latin American Research Review* 37(1): 77–118.

Schneider, Ben Ross. 2004. *Business Politics and the State in 20th Century Latin America*. New York: Cambridge University Press.

Schneider, Ben Ross. 2008. "Economic Liberalization and Corporate Governance: The Resilience of Business Groups in Latin America." *Comparative Politics* 40(4, July): 379–98.

Schneider, Ben Ross. 2009a. "Big Business in Brazil: Leveraging Natural Endowments and State Support for International Expansion." In *Brazil as an Emerging Economic Superpower?* ed. Lael Brainard and Leonardo Martinez-Diaz. Washington, DC: Brookings Institution.

Schneider, Ben Ross. 2009b. "A Comparative Political Economy of Diversified Business Groups, or How States Organize Capitalism." *Review of International Political Economy* 16(2, May): 178–201.

Schneider, Ben Ross. 2010a. "Business Politics and Policymaking in Contemporary Latin America." In *How Democracy Works*, ed. Carlos Scartasini, Ernesto Stein, and Mariano Tommasi. Washington, DC: IDB.

Schneider, Ben Ross. 2010b. "Business Politics in Latin America: Patterns of Fragmentation and Centralization." In *Oxford Handbook of Business and Government*, ed. David Coen, Wyn Grant, and Graham Wilson. Oxford: Oxford University Press.

Schneider, Ben Ross. 2010c. "Diversified Business Groups and the State: Origins, Support, and Decline." In *Oxford Handbook of Business Groups*, ed. Asli Colpan, Takashi Hikino, and James Lincoln. Oxford: Oxford University Press.

Schneider, Ben Ross. 2012. "Contrasting Capitalisms: Latin America in Comparative Perspective." In *Oxford Handbook on Latin American Political Economy*, ed. Javier Santiso and Jeff Dayton-Johnson. New York: Oxford University Press.

Schneider, Ben Ross, and Sebastian Karcher. 2010. "Complementarities and Continuities in the Political Economy of Labor Markets in Latin America." *Socio-Economic Review* 8(4, October): 623–51.

Schneider, Ben Ross, and David Soskice. 2009. "Inequality in Developed Countries and Latin America: Coordinated, Liberal, and Hierarchical Systems." *Economy and Society* 38(1, February): 17–52.

Schneider, Ben Ross, and David Soskice. 2011. "The Low Skill Equilibrium: Latin America in the Global Economy." Unpublished paper.

Schneider, Friedrich. 2005. 'Shadow Economies Around the World: What Do We Really Know." *European Journal of Political Economy* 21(3): 598–642.

Schrank, Andrew. 2005. "Conquering, Comprador, or Competitive: The National Bourgeoisie in the Developing World." *Research in Rural Sociology and Development* 11: 91–120.

Schrank, Andrew. 2009. "Professionalization and Probity in a Patrimonial State: Labor Inspectors in the Dominican Republic." *Latin American Politics and Society* 51(2): 91–115.

Schurman, Rachel. 2001. "Uncertain Gains: Labor in Chile's New Export Sectors." *Latin American Research Review* 36(2): 3–29.

Segovia, Alexander. 2005. "Integración real y grupos de poder económico en América Central: implicaciones para el desarrollo y la democracia de la región." Report to Friedrich Ebert Foundation.

Sehnbruch, Kirsten. 2006. *The Chilean Labor Market: A Key to Understanding Latin American Labor Markets*. New York: Palgrave Macmillan.

Shadlen, Kenneth. 2004. *Democratization Without Representation: The Politics of Small Industry in Mexico*. University Park: Penn State University Press.

Shapiro, Helen. 2003. "Bringing the Firm Back In." In *Development Economics and Structuralist Macroeconomics*, ed. Amitava Dutt and Jaime Ros. Cheltenham, UK: Edward Elgar.

Shleifer, Andrei, and Lawrence Summers. 1988. "Breach of Trust in Hostile Takeovers." In *Corporate Takeovers*, ed. Alan J. Auerbach. Chicago: University of Chicago Press

Siegel, Jordan. 2006. "Is There a Better Commitment Mechanism Than Cross-Listing for Emerging Economy Firms? Evidence from Mexico." Unpublished paper.

Silva, Eduardo. 1996. *The State and Capital in Chile: Business Elites, Technocrats, and Market Economics*. Boulder CO: Westview.

Silva, Eduardo. 1997. "Business Elites, the State, and Economic Change in Chile." In *Business and the State in Developing Countries*, ed. Sylvia Maxfield and Ben Ross Schneider. Ithaca, NY: Cornell University Press.

Silva, Eduardo. 2002. "State-Business Relations in Latin America." In *Emerging Market Democracies*, ed. Laurence Whitehead. Baltimore: Johns Hopkins University Press.

Silva, Eduardo. 2009. *Challenging Neoliberalism in Latin America*. New York: Cambridge University Press.

Silva, Patricio. 2008. *In the Name of Reason: Technocrats and Politics in Chile*. University Park: Pennsylvania State University Press.

Simielli, Lara. 2008. "Civil Society and Public Education in Brazil: A Study on the Coalition of Different Players in the Structuring and Implementation of Public Policies in

Education." Paper presented at the ISTR Eighth International Conference. Barcelona, Spain.

Snower, Dennis. 1994. *The Low-Skill, Bad-Job Trap*. Washington, DC: International Monetary Fund.

Sokoloff, Kenneth, and Stanley Engerman. 2000. "History Lessons: Institutions, Factors Endowments, and Paths of Development in the New World." *Journal of Economic Perspectives* 14(3, Summer): 217–32.

Soskice, David. 1999. "Divergent Production Regimes: Coordinated and Uncoordinated Market Economies in the 1980s and 1990s." In *Continuity and Change in Contemporary Capitalism*, ed. Herbert Kitschelt, Peter Lange, Gary Marks, and John Stephens. New York: Cambridge University Press.

Stallings, Barbara. 2006. *Finance for Development: Latin America in Comparative Perspective*. Washington, DC: Brookings Institution Press.

Stallings, Barbara, and Wilson Peres. 2000. *Growth, Employment, and Equity: The Impact of the Economic Reforms in Latin America and the Caribbean*. Washington, DC: Brookings Institution Press.

Stein, Ernesto, Mariano Tommari, Koldo Echebarría, Eduardo Lora, and Mark Payne. 2005. *The Politics of Policies*. Washington, DC: Inter-American Development Bank.

Steinberg, David. 2010. "The Politics of Exchange Rate Valuation in Developing Countries." PhD Dissertation. Northwestern University.

Steinfeld, Edward. 2010. *Playing our Game: Why China's Economic Rise doesn't Threaten the West*. New York: Oxford University Press.

Stok, Gustavo. 2006. "La era de los negocios K." *América Economia*, June.

Streeck, Wolfgang. 2001. "Introduction: Explorations Into the Origins of Nonliberal Capitalism in Germany and Japan." In *The Origins of Nonliberal Capitalism*, ed. Wolfgang Streeck and Kozo Yamamura. Ithaca: Cornell University Press.

Streeck, Wolfgang. 2005. "Requirements for a Useful Concept of Complementarity." *Socio – Economic Review* 3(2, May): 363–71.

Streeck, Wolfgang. 2009. *Re-Forming Capitalism: Institutional Change in the German Political Economy*. New York: Oxford University Press.

Taylor, Marcus. 2006. *From Pinochet to the 'Third Way:' Neoliberalism and Social Transformation in Chile*. London: Pluto.

Tendler, Judith. 2002. "The Fear of Education." Paper presented at meetings of Banco do Nordeste, Fortaleza.

Thelen, Kathleen. 2001. "Varieties of Labor Politics in the Developed Democracies." In *Varieties of Capitalism*, ed. Peter Hall and David Soskice. New York: Oxford University Press.

Thelen, Kathleen. 2004. *How Institutions Evolve: The Political Economy of Skills in Germany, Britain, the United States, and Japan*. New York: Cambridge University Press.

Tokman, Victor. 2001. "De la informalidad a la modernidad." *Boletín Técnico Interamericano de Formación Profesional* 155: 9–32.

UNCTAD. 2004. *World Investment Directory. Volume IX: Latin America and the Caribbean*. Geneva: United Nations Conference on Trade and Development.

Uzzi, Brian. 1996. "The Sources and Consequences of Embeddedness for the Economic Performance of Organizations." *American Sociological Review* 61(4, August): 674–98.

Valor Econômico. 2005. *Valor 1000: Maiores Empresas*. São Paulo: Valor Econômico.

Vargas, Jaime, and Marina Bassi. 2010. "Hire for Attitude, Train for Skills: Case Study on the Transition from School to Work in Latin America." Inter-American Development Bank. http://www.iadb.org/en/topics/education/hire-for-attitude-train-for-skills,7464.html.

Vega Ruíz, María Luz. 2005. *La reforma laboral en América Latina: 15 años después. un análisis comparado*. Lima: OIT/Oficina regional para América Latina.

Waissbluth, Mario. 2011. "Manifestaciones estudiantiles en chile: una réplica telúrica de la guerra fria." *Foreign Affairs Latinoamérica* 11(4, octubre–diciembre): 32–39.

Ward, John. 2004. *Perpetuating the Family Business: 50 Lessons Learned from Long-Lasting, Successful Families in Business*. New York: Palgrave.

Weiss, Linda. 2010. "The State in the Economy: Neoliberal or Neoactivist?" In *Oxford Handbook of Comparative Institutional Analysis*, ed. Glenn Morgan et al. New York: Oxford University Press.

Weyland, Kurt. 2005. "The Growing Sustainability of Brazil's Low-Quality Democracy." In *The Third Wave of Democratization in Latin America*, ed. Frances Hagopian and Scott Mainwaring. New York: Cambridge University Press.

Weyland, Kurt. 2009. "The Rise of Latin America's Two Lefts: Insights from Rentier State Theory." *Comparative Politics* 41(2, January): 145–64.

Weyland, Kurt, Raúl Madrid, and Wendy Hunter, eds. 2010. *Leftist Governments in Latin America: Successes and Shortcomings*. New York: Cambridge University Press.

Whitley, Richard. 1990. "Eastern Asian Enterprise Structures and the Comparative Analysis of Business Organization." *Organization Studies* 11(1): 47–74.

Whitley, Richard. 1999. *Divergent Capitalisms: The Social Structure and Change of Business Systems*. New York: Oxford University Press.

Williamson, Oliver, and Sidney Winter, eds. 1993. *The Nature of the Firm: Origins, Evolution, and Development*. New York: Oxford University Press.

Wise, Carol. 2003. *Reinventing the State: Economic Strategy and Institutional Change in Peru*. Ann Arbor: University of Michigan Press.

Witt, Michael. 2006. *Changing Japanese Capitalism: Societal Coordination and Institutional Adjustment*. New York: Cambridge University Press.

Wolff, Laurence, and Claudio de Moura Castro. 2003. "Education and Training: The Task Ahead." In *After the Washington Consensus*, John Williamson and Pedro-Pablo Kuczynski, ed. Washington, DC: Institute for International Economics.

Wolff, Laurence, and Claudio de Moura Castro. 2005. "Public or Private Education in Latin America?: Asking the Wrong Question." In *Private Education and Public Policy in Latin America*, ed. Laurence Wolff, Juan Carlos Navarro, and Pablo González. Washington, DC: PREAL.

Woo-Cumings, Meredith, ed. 1999. *The Developmental State*. Ithaca, NY: Cornell University Press.

World Bank. 2004a. *Doing Business in 2004: Understanding Regulation*. Washington, DC: World Bank and Oxford University Press.

World Bank. 2004b. *World Development Report 2005: A Better Investment Climate for Everyone*. Washington, DC: World Bank and Oxford University Press.

World Bank. 2006a. *The Impact of Intel in Costa Rica: Nine Years After the Decision to Invest*. Multilateral Investment Guarantee Agency. Investing in Development Series. Washington, DC.

World Bank. 2006b. *World Development Report 2007: Development and the Next Generation*. Washington, DC: World Bank and Oxford University Press.

World Bank. 2007. *Democratic Governance in Mexico: Beyond State Capture and Social Polarization*. Washington, DC: World Bank.

World Bank. 2011. *Latin America and the Caribbean's Long-Term Growth: Made in China?* Washington, DC: World Bank.

Yadav, Vineeta. 2011. *Political Parties, Business Groups, and Corruption in Developing Countries*. New York: Oxford University Press.

Yamamura, Kozo, and Wolfgang Streeck, eds. 2003. *The End of Diversity? Prospects for German and Japanese Capitalism*. Ithaca: Cornell University Press.

Zeile, William. 1997. "U.S. Intrafirm Trade in Goods." *Survey of Current Business*, February.

Zysman, John. 1983. *Governments, Markets, and Growth: Financial Systems and the Politics of Industrial Change*. Ithaca, NY: Cornell University Press.

# Index

Maria Victoria Murillo, *Political Competition, Partisanship, and Policy Making in Latin American Public Utilities*

Monika Nalepa, *Skeletons in the Closet: Transitional Justice in Post-Communist Europe*

Ton Notermans, *Money, Markets, and the State: Social Democratic Economic Policies since 1918*

Eleonora Pasotti, *Political Branding in Cities: The Decline of Machine Politics in Bogotá, Naples, and Chicago*

Aníbal Pérez-Liñán, *Presidential Impeachment and the New Political Instability in Latin America*

Roger D. Petersen, *Understanding Ethnic Violence: Fear, Hatred, and Resentment in Twentieth-Century Eastern Europe*

Roger D. Petersen, *Western Intervention in the Balkans: The Strategic Use of Emotion in Conflict*

Simona Piattoni, ed., *Clientelism, Interests, and Democratic Representation*

Paul Pierson, *Dismantling the Welfare State? Reagan, Thatcher, and the Politics of Retrenchment*

Marino Regini, *Uncertain Boundaries: The Social and Political Construction of European Economies*

Marc Howard Ross, *Cultural Contestation in Ethnic Conflict*

Lyle Scruggs, *Sustaining Abundance: Environmental Performance in Industrial Democracies*

Jefferey M. Sellers, *Governing from Below: Urban Regions and the Global Economy*

Yossi Shain and Juan Linz, eds., *Interim Governments and Democratic Transitions*

Beverly Silver, *Forces of Labor: Workers' Movements and Globalization since 1870*

Theda Skocpol, *Social Revolutions in the Modern World*

Dan Slater, *Ordering Power: Contentious Politics and Authoritarian Leviathans in Southeast Asia*

Regina Smyth, *Candidate Strategies and Electoral Competition in the Russian Federation: Democracy without Foundation*

Richard Snyder, *Politics after Neoliberalism: Reregulation in Mexico*

David Stark and László Bruszt, *Postsocialist Pathways: Transforming Politics and Property in East Central Europe*

Sven Steinmo, *The Evolution of Modern States: Sweden, Japan, and the United States*

Sven Steinmo, Kathleen Thelen, and Frank Longstreth, eds., *Structuring Politics: Historical Institutionalism in Comparative Analysis*

Susan C. Stokes, *Mandates and Democracy: Neoliberalism by Surprise in Latin America*